T0330132

ANALYSING THE HISTORY OF BRITISH SOCIAL WELFARE

Compassion, Coercion and Beyond

Jonathan Parker

First published in Great Britain in 2023 by

Policy Press, an imprint of
Bristol University Press
University of Bristol
1–9 Old Park Hill
Bristol
BS2 8BB
UK
t: +44 (0)117 374 6645
e: bup-info@bristol.ac.uk

Details of international sales and distribution partners are available at
policy.bristoluniversitypress.co.uk

British Library Cataloguing in Publication Data
A catalogue record for this book is available from the British Library

ISBN 978-1-4473-6369-9 hardcover
ISBN 978-1-4473-6371-2 ePub
ISBN 978-1-4473-6372-9 ePdf

The right of Jonathan Parker to be identified as author of this work has been asserted by him in
accordance with the Copyright, Designs and Patents Act 1988.

Cover design: Nicky Borowiec
Front cover image: Adobe Stock/Archivist
Bristol University Press and Policy Press use environmentally responsible
print partners.
Printed in Great Britain by CPI Group (UK) Ltd, Croydon, CR0 4YY

Contents

List of tables

List of abbreviations

BCE	Before the Common Era (marking the Western, Judæo-Christian dating system)
BIEN	Basic Income Earth Network
BMA	British Medical Association
CCETSW	Central Council for the Education and Training of Social Workers
COS	Charity Organisation Society
CQSW	Certificate of Qualification in Social Work
DipSW	Diploma in Social Work
DWP	Department for Work and Pensions
ESA	Employment and Support Allowance
EU	European Union
GDP	Gross Domestic Product
GSCC	General Social Care Council
HB	Housing Benefit
LSE	London School of Economics
NHS	National Health Service
NSPCC	National Society for the Prevention of Cruelty to Children
OBR	Office for Budget Responsibility
PIP	Personal Independence Payments
SAP	Single Assessment Process
TOPSS	Training Organisation for Personal Social Services
UBI	Universal Basic Income
UC	Universal Credit
UKIP	United Kingdom Independence Party
WBG	Women's Budget Group
WBI	World Basic Income

About the author

Jonathan Parker is Professor of Society & Social Welfare at Bournemouth University, Honorary Visiting Professor at the University of Stavanger, Norway and Doctoral programme team member at Università Cattolica del Sacro Cuore, Milan. He was Chair of the Association of Teachers in Social Work Education until 2005, Vice Chair of the Joint University Council for Social Work Education from 2005 to 2010, and is a Fellow of the Academy of Social Sciences. He has published widely on disadvantage, marginalisation and violence, Southeast Asia, social work and welfare education internationally. He is author of the best-selling book *Social Work Practice* (SAGE, 2021) and series editor for the highly successful *Transforming Social Work Practice* series (SAGE).

Acknowledgements

There are always many people to acknowledge in a project such as this book, and I start with both a grateful thanks to everyone who has helped and inspired my task and a plea for forgiveness from those I do not mention by name. All my past students taking my *Histories of Social Welfare* module over the years, far too numerous to mention, have given untold assistance to my thinking, argument and focus. You all have been the inspiration for this book. Also, my colleagues at the various universities I have worked and collaborated with have shaped and honed my thinking, which has latterly been expertly guided by the anonymous reviewers for the proposal and the typescript. I thank you all and pick out for especial mention my friends and colleagues Tadakazu Kumagai of Kawasaki Medical University in Japan, Azlinda Azman of Universiti Sains Malaysia, and Magnus Frampton of the University of Vechta in Germany. Our long discussions, eased by good food and, often, good wine, have been so valuable intellectually and personally.

Of course, a book can never come into being without the skilled offices of the publishing team and my heartfelt gratitude must go to everyone at Policy Press, especially commissioning editor Laura Vickers-Rendall, and editorial assistants Zoe Forbes and Jay Allan, whose timely, apposite and clear advice have kept me on track – even during the oblique fogs of 'long-COVID', our contemporary 'long Lankin'!

Writing a book is a protracted affair, one that demands sequestration by the task, and I must, therefore, highlight the thanks due to my family whose forbearance, food and drink has made the undertaking smoother and much more pleasurable. My thanks, as always, must go to my incredible wife and fellow academic, Sara. There is no better person with whom to share this journey!

Concepts, continuities and critique

Throughout the long, complex and sometimes convoluted histories of social welfare in Britain, it is possible to identify various continuities and interconnections alongside seemingly unconnected transformations in policies, practices and assumptions. Imputing causal links between historical policies, practices and perspectives is difficult and remains, for the most part, tentative, as does searching for the catalysts that led to innovative developments, if, indeed, there are any. However, when we consider the contexts and practices of British social welfare as a whole, we can begin to discern common features that erect a scaffolding for understanding some of the underlying assumptions and overt beliefs held about social welfare among policy makers and the general public, alongside those practising in welfare settings. It is central to negotiating current policy and practice, and to future welfare developments, to have an awareness of this architecture so that nuances, complexities and entrenched beliefs are illuminated and subject to disquisition. It addresses questions about why social welfare policies should follow certain paths and why practices may complement or challenge these directions. The interconnections, continuing and seemingly disconnected themes include:

- *The twin drivers of economy and compassion as a means of suppressing potential violent conflict and social disturbance which are manifest throughout the history of social welfare.* The balance has been achieved through limited assistance through outdoor relief, less eligibility through the Poor Laws, and various shifts in the development and continual reformation of the welfare state.
- *Elements of both care and control which permeate the creation and development of formalised social welfare systems.* Care and control link directly to economic interests and compassion in providing a workforce healthy enough to be economically viable and one that is behaviourally compliant and morally in tune with the vested interests of those providing and controlling welfare.
- *Those with vested interests who are often able to set the terms of social organisation and hierarchy through underlying belief systems and political ideologies, affecting the will and agency of others.* These assumed and unspoken systems of behaviour and belief influence what is considered appropriate or acceptable in respect of social welfare and its receipt, creating a closed system of control.
- *The discourses underpinning social life have created binary distinctions, which have, and may now be designed to, produce stigma, control and hegemonic normativity*

in the system through the replication of tropes of moral fecklessness and shirking of self-responsibility. This is clear within the 1834 reform of the Poor Law and reproduced in contemporary media and political statements concerning benefit claimants.

- *Increasing administrative control which characterises the formal development of social welfare.* The bureaucratic regulation of people by, for example, class, gender, age, ethnicity and health status, acts as a function of a regulated society serving certain groups by its reproduction. Arguments concerning centralised versus local control are replayed in attempts to rein in a Leviathan–like beast.
- *Concern for administrative control which has led to a propensity towards centralisation and standardisation, convergence in service provision and assumed simplification of welfare systems,* alongside unanticipated and unintended consequences associated with these tendencies, including the assumed homogenisation of needs as a means of addressing inequalities in treatment.
- *(Un)official recognition of poor practices in welfare provision which is evident at various stages in welfare's history.* For instance, in the late 18th century the Elizabethan Poor Law became associated with creating dependency and failing to address poverty; the Poor Law Guardians of the amended Act were cast as inept and, in some cases, taking advantage of the system, and recently the Department for Work and Pensions (DWP) has attracted criticism for continuing the stigma associated with welfare receipt and treating people without respect (Baumberg, 2016).
- A tension that runs throughout the history of social welfare and pits care and compassion against control and coercion, which categorises people as deserving and undeserving, and is located in debates about *universality versus differential eligibility or the means-testing of benefits.*

These continuities and departures are explored throughout this book to examine some of the reasons why social welfare in Britain is reproduced in the ways it is, and what driving forces underpin welfare policies and practice. We do so without direct causal imputation, but seek to expose some of the underlying dynamic and psychosocial links. It has long been recognised that the opposing elements of compassion for fellow humans, and coercion to contribute and produce economically, form key elements within the development of welfare policy and practice throughout history (Piven and Cloward, 1971, 1993; Wacquant, 2009; Finkel, 2019). Hidden assumptions and underlying, unspoken beliefs about social welfare will be uncovered in a diverse range of examples of social welfare development. In doing so, the book will draw on Foucault's approach to discourse and Bourdieu's notions of *habitus*, those enduring and embodied dispositions which structure the ways in which people 'see' or experience the social world, fields and capital. Within this theoretical context, social welfare will be conceptualised, in psychosocial terms, as an ambivalent activity and policy domain. It is embedded within the fabric of British society and in some ways it is championed by those in power and the general public, while, at the same time, those in receipt of benefits are prone to demonisation, and, by association, those providing and promoting welfare may also be so stigmatised. This ambivalence is embodied in the dispositions of citizens and analysing it will illuminate why welfare policy and practice has sometimes developed in the ways it has and why recipients of welfare services are often portrayed in the ways they are in popular media and thought, by politicians, professionals and the general public. Towards the end of the book, I use social work to exemplify this ambivalence after considering some of the discourses at work in various aspects of welfare history.

The Office for Budget Responsibility (OBR) (2022) estimated, that, in 2016–2017, the welfare state budget amounted to 25 per cent of Gross Domestic Product (GDP), about £484 billion. Forty-two per cent of this figure was spent on pensions, which are generally well supported throughout society, while media, populist politicians and many of the general public continued to rail against the skivers, scroungers and 'bogus' claimants, often including refugees and migrants, sick and disabled people, and single parents. Yet, on the other hand, concern for the National Health Service (NHS) and fixing what is perceived as a broken social care system attracts almost universal support, as seen during the COVID-19 pandemic (Bambra et al, 2021). More limited, but nonetheless powerful, support remains for such policies as maintaining the triple lock on state pensions, which raised considerable debate when its removal was debated to pay for social and health care (Jeffries, 2021). This ambivalence highlights the need to understand our enduring relationship with welfare and to address potentially dangerous misconceptions when seeking to develop reform or implement social welfare policy and practice. The OBR welfare trends report of 2021 discusses increased welfare spending and reduced GDP as a consequence of COVID-19 and the introduction of the Coronavirus Job Retention Scheme and the Self-Employed Income Support Scheme (HMRC, 2021). Again, these were popular initiatives as they supported a population considered to be 'deserving'.

The oppositional forces in social welfare (of good and bad recipients or deserving and undeserving ones) are set within a context of psychosocial ambivalence. Social welfare is something which is both loved and feared, which helps explain the complexities arising within the diverse histories of welfare development, implementation and reform.

Conceptualising social welfare

Social policy concerns those areas of public life that have a bearing on the ways in which we live and the problems of living with which people contend as individual and social beings. Social policies can have restrictive and coercive elements as well as assistive and empowering ones (Blakemore and Warwick-Booth, 2013; Lansley, 2022). For instance, education policy makes aspects of education compulsory, drawing on the force of the law to ensure compliance, but it can also enhance the life chances of people, bringing them out of poverty and expanding their opportunities and possible futures (Brewer et al, 2021). Alongside these two contrasting elements, education policies create the conditions in which some of the assumptions of right and wrong behaviours become embedded in society. Also we must remember that policy makers and those who implement the policies stem from this context. Social policies are functional and seek to regulate and ration access to benefits and entitlements, to attain certain goals and to maintain social norms. Increasingly, there is a more global aspect to social policies as countries emulate the practices in others, to gain political favour and access to economic opportunities with others (Hill and Irving, 2020). There is, to draw on organisational sociology, a tendency towards global isomorphic convergence (DiMaggio and Powell, 1983). Policies mimic those of 'successful' or 'developed' societies, are increasingly driven by statute, agreement or convention, and become normalised, accepted and unquestioned. This tendency may have positive and negative consequences. Social policies frequently concern social welfare and it is important to provide a general understanding of what this term means.

What is welfare?

Public or social welfare is important to individual citizens and to society. It concerns what the state and public sector provides, how it does so and for whom it is provided, but social welfare also concerns the provision and regulation of not-for-profit non-state sector and private organisations. Greve (2008, p 50) states: 'Welfare is the highest possible access to economic resources, a high level of well-being, including the happiness of the citizens, a guaranteed minimum income to avoid living in poverty, and, finally, having the capabilities to ensure the individual a good life.'

The roots of the English word 'welfare' connect with the German *Wohlfahrt*, meaning journeying or travelling well. The etymological roots of the noun 'welfare' are middle English, joining the adverb 'well' and the verb 'fare' (middle English is of course Germanic in its roots as well as Latinate) and its meaning is twofold: first, relating to well-being, happiness, health or prosperity (Garrett, 2018); and second, a more technical meaning which has evolved to refer to state support for people in society (see Spicker et al, 2007). Garrett (2018) recognises that the meanings of words change over time but also shape practices through assumed connotations which become second nature (Foucault, 1972; Bourdieu, 1994). Both elements of this malleable concept will be used in this book as they intersect the formal and informal, the compassionate and the coercive.

Jordan (2008) considers the development of welfare as almost synonymous with well-being during the 20th century in which a materialist and economic approach took centre stage often, in the earlier part of the century, drawing on Marxist approaches to economics (Pareto, 1909; Pigou, 1920) and influencing political approaches to welfare. Towards the end of the 20th century, however, fundamental liberal principles of free choice in satisfying one's desires was once again embraced politically. This has resulted in ambivalent attitudes towards social welfare. For instance, during the rise of the New Right in the latter half of the 20th century, and more recently during the austerity of the second decade of the 21st century, spending on public welfare was, paradoxically, largely maintained while those claiming benefits have been increasingly demonised and the retrenchment of benefits has become a core mantra of governments (Pierson, 1994; Garrett, 2018). Individualism as a social 'good' in itself began to replace the focus on collective interdependency, which, in public welfare terms, encouraged the use of contracts to maximise public utility and preferences in services rather than to provide services directly (see Dwyer, 2004; Greve, 2019). However, this shift did not, in Jordan's view, increase overall well-being and life satisfaction, rather it led to public services and mission statements disconnected from real life and seemingly more intent on function and systems-maintenance. The depersonalisation of contemporary social and political life finds its epitome in the rise of financial and employment insecurities, or precarities, associated with marketised economies which raise their own questions about social welfare (Standing, 2016). Greve (2019) recognises that quality of life, well-being and happiness may well be affected by welfare levels, given their association with equality or inequality. In the 21st century a cynical position developed in which 'we do not think that there is any plausible correspondence between welfare, as measured in the statistics published by governments and firms, and the way we experience the quality of our lives' (Jordan, 2008, p 247). This situation can only be addressed by refocusing on social value by building cultures of mutuality, respect and belonging.

In similar vein, Dwyer (2004) links welfare with the complex and contested concept of citizenship which traverses a pathway through individual rights and liberties and communitarian commitments and obligations. Drawing on Marshall's (1949/1992) citizenship elements of civil, political and social rights and Faulks's (1998) legal, philosophical and socio-political definitions, Dwyer focuses on social citizenship as a relationship between individual and state that conveys membership, belonging and a claim to state-organised welfare services. In this way individual and, indeed, corporate welfare are intimately connection with the organisation and function of the state.

5

Gregory (2018) focuses on rights and responsibilities and well-being and happiness; the capacity to live a good life. This conceptualisation emerged from the 'Third Way' espoused by New Labour as they juggled compassion with the New Right's legacy-manacles of the market. Gregory employs Fitzpatrick's (2001) components of welfare, which, alongside happiness, also include income security, preferences, needs, desert and relative comparisons to others. It includes, therefore, a moral element that requires deciding between people and ranking the order of their deservingness.

Changes in the use of language and practices associated with welfare are reflected in increased surveillance and behavioural compulsion. The term social security, which has been the language of the welfare state, has been replaced with welfare reform and an attendant negativity attached to the latter playing on the implication that 'reform' is necessary because the system must be flawed and those who use it must also be implicated within these imperfections. Indeed, a common-sense understanding has developed which associates those claiming benefits with being morally suspect, undeserving or workshy. This shift has resulted in the maintenance of power relations, which Garrett (2018) views as evocative of Gramscian hegemony, aided by the media portrayals of welfare recipients whose demonisation allows for the development and implementation of draconian, conditional welfare policies. Following on from a language-based analysis, Greve (2015) suggests that how we understand welfare depends on the way we approach it, and he develops a four-perspective model looking at the macro-level (state, market) or the micro-level (civil society) combined with either objective or subjective indicators and measures. These factors tend to combine. For instance, if we count the number of people at risk of poverty we are using an objective approach but if we add perceptions of being poor we include a subjective dimension. Whichever approach is in the ascendancy tends to influence welfare policies and practice in that context.

Sealey (2015, p 7) focuses on a subjective approach covering basic human needs that are central to welfare and human well-being from 'pre-birth to beyond the grave'. 'Need' itself is, of course, an elusive and contested concept (Dean, 2020). Concepts of well-being are increasingly included in approaches to the study and practice of welfare, especially since public health has moved from the health service to become the responsibility of local government once again (Department of Health, 2012). Well-being is also a concept that is hard to define and can include subjective perceptions of one's own well-being and more objective measures. Two particular approaches to well-being are identified: the hedonic and the eudaimonic approaches. The hedonic approach focuses on pleasure and minimising difficult, painful or problematic experiences, while the eudaimonic is concerned with existential meaning and the self-realisation of individuals. Both are used in social welfare discussion (see Ryan and Deci, 2001).

There are also many ways to understand the connections between well-being and welfare. Greve's (2015) approach includes economics and well-being which includes markets and choice but also social cohesion and capital (Bourdieu and Wacquant, 1992; Putnam, 2000), recognising that many social indicators are needed to provide a rounded understanding of such concepts. For Greve, the delivery of welfare by state social policy has three core approaches: *need* – means-tested; *merit* – social insurance, conditionality; and, *equality* – guaranteed unconditional income and universal services, each of which is seen in the various iterations of state welfare developed within European nations especially (Esping-Andersen, 1990; Aspalter, 2021a, 2021b).

These are hotly contested political approaches and we need to understand where these have come from. Gregory (2018) situates the pursuit of welfare and well-being in the structural context of the welfare state, and links with rights, capabilities and citizenship responsibilities. Social rights and rights to welfare are socially constructed and distributional in respect of resources to meet accepted and agreed needs (Dean, 2002). Dwyer (2004) indicates that wants and preferences are important when determining what constitutes a need. Defining need is complex; note Dean's (2020) glossary categorising 40 types of need. A need can be felt or subjective, defined by experts, or comparative and depending on socio-political context can be understood in broad terms, which is likely to lead to universalist welfare provision, or narrowly defined leading to residual and discretionary welfare. In Britain, we have seen movement from a more universalist approach promoted at the nascence of the British welfare state, back to a residual one over the latter half of the 20th century and into the 21st century. Context and culture are important when studying social welfare. Greve (2019) encourages us to consider wealth, public spending on welfare, poverty levels and happiness when considering welfare effectiveness. This, again, represents a philosophical position in respect of welfare and we must remember that neutrality in the study of welfare is not possible and that the terms under consideration are often disputed and require definition.

Examining welfare policies and provision helps us to understand states, politics and the ways in which compassion and socio-behavioural regulation is understood, developed and organised, what is valued and how individuals across a range of social divisions – age, health status, disability status, gender, ethnicity, religion, class and so forth – are viewed within a particular 'society'. The relevance of the study of social policy is highlighted by Sealey (2015) in key points, which affect us personally as individuals in our everyday lives. However, there are many approaches to studying social welfare history (Brundage, 2002). Early works tended to be politically motivated surveys about the administration of relief policy such as George Nicholls' 1854/1898 work, *A History of the English Poor*

Law (Nicholls, 2016), which advocated deterrence; or Sidney and Beatrice Webb's three-volume 1927–1929 *English Poor Law History*, polemically advocating on behalf of the poor. Marxist approaches are evident in which the Poor Laws are set within the socio-economic development of capitalism, such as Karl Polanyi's (1944) *The Great Transformation*, and E.P. Thompson's (1963) *The Making of the English Working Class*. More recently, we have seen critiques of the welfare state tracing its development back to the Poor Laws as progression from them or revolutionary shift (Barnett, 1986). There are also economic approaches, political historical approaches focusing on the post-war welfare state, notably Esping-Andersen (1990). From a post-structuralist perspective, Foucauldian approaches, which see the workhouse (or indeed any state or public institution such as schools or hospitals) as a 'carceral archipelago ... designed to produce submission and conformity', have come to the fore (Foucault, 1991, p 297). Foucault also considered a carceral continuum in which the processes and institutions can be described. For instance, a disabled person who receives a diagnosis of his or her disability may become subject to (imprisoned within) a process of care that requires acquiescence to its spoken and unspoken rules and attendance at certain institutional settings and engagement in prescribed behaviours in order to receive the care and benefits allotted to that particular disability. This critique can be applied to other forms of welfare, from libertarian perspectives on state welfare to benevolent care and concern for others, or approaches from critical theory. What must be remembered is the historical context and philosophical context in which forms of welfare are developed, applied or critiqued.

Discourses and power

Foucault's *Discipline and Punish* (1991) provides a theoretical substrate that helps us understand the power relations inherent in changing and developing welfare practice and social policies. Power in these terms moves beyond the Marxist analysis of power as resting within certain institutions and is seen rather as a strategy operating within social relations. These technologies of power concern *decentring the subject*, which means that the individual is not the centre of meaning or focus, rejecting Sartre's existentialism which asserts that individuals have the power to resist forms of domination. Rather, Foucault's conception suggests that 'the subject is a social construction, produced through social discourses (language, thought, symbolic representations) which position subjects in a field of power relations and within particular sets of practices' (Layder, 2003, p 117). Technologies of power allow the impact of history and social-structural factors to shape subjectivities and create multiple reasons for actions. There are some similarities to Bourdieu's idea of 'field' which we introduce later.

One of the most important elements of Foucault's approach rests in his concept of discourses which relate to all that is thought, written or said about a thing – in our case social welfare – its recipients and those who organise or deliver it. Discourses are no longer envisaged as 'groups of signs (signifying elements referring to contents or representations) but as practices that systematically form the objects of which they speak' (Foucault, 1972, p 49). Those people with specific knowledge of something assume control over those not possessing that knowledge. So, for example, lawyers, doctors, magistrates, social security workers, social workers and politicians have knowledge which allows them to exert power over those who come to them for a service. This power is demonstrated and legitimated through the practices of those delivering welfare services.

This leads to 'truth claims' which are made through intimate knowledge of a particular area. Those involved must accept the power relations inherent in such a relationship. Professional discourses highlight the power to control others; some of these are not codified but remain 'common-sense'. For instance, we can identify some of the labels made of people who claim benefits here to see the ways in which discourses operate. Think of the common tropes of 'skivers and strivers' and 'hard working families' and 'decent people'. In Chapter 3 we explore these discourses and practices further.

Foucault (1991) identifies historical shifts in the different forms of power: sovereign power, disciplinary power and bio-power (see also Foucault, 1984). The latter suggests the 'capillary' nature of modern forms of power – how ideology spreads, almost osmotically, throughout the whole social system at many different levels (Layder, 2003).

In the Middle Ages it was the sovereign or monarch who embodied unlimited or absolute power over subjects. Poverty and dissent, which were often interconnected, represented a potential threat to sovereignty by either metaphorically challenging the beneficence of the sovereign or by those in poverty actively and politically challenging that sovereign authority, both evidenced in Gerrard Winstanley's 'diggers' during the reign of Charles I. Therefore, poverty and dissent had to be punished in public and spectacular ways, thus reaffirming sovereign power. For instance, the punishment of beggars and vagabonds was not considered a gratuitous act but a ritual enactment of power and social balance. This power was not continuously exercised but intermittent and prohibitive, attempting to regulate and preserve power. Even expressing support for those in poverty could raise fears as the humanist Juan Luis Vives wrote concerning his *De Subventione Pauperum* in 1525: 'By word of mouth I would explain the titles and the arguments of my books to you, the best of my friends without a doubt; but I dare not entrust them to a letter, lest they laugh at me, if it fell into other hands.'

The replacement of absolute monarchy and the subsequent turn towards parliamentary power and governance saw a change in the ways in which the strategies of power operated. In the 17th and 18th centuries, in Foucault's schema, surveillance, whether continuous or intermittent but certain in the mind of the observed, rather than specific physical punishments replaced absolute, sovereign power. Control through the threat of physical coercion, such as whippings and beatings, was gradually replaced by a pervasive and impersonal external surveillance that began to permeate the intrapsychic self. This led to self-discipline through behavioural and cognitive alignment to assumed and expected norms of being and behaving and through fear of being seen and exposed to others. This took place through developing welfare technologies such as the workhouse, the Poor Law overseers, hospitals and asylums, factories and schools. It was also enacted by non-state actors promoting the moral discourses associated with social control and development such as the Charity Organisation Society, the Police Court Missionaries, the Temperance Movement and the Settlement Movement. Focus shifted onto individuals and the control of their own behaviour, recognising the observational power of others.

In this way, constant surveillance led to subjective regulation. In the early 19th century, Jeremy Bentham's panopticon prison became a reality. It became impossible to avoid the gaze of others, and this surveillance was internalised, ensuring that constrained or observed behaviour became automatic rather than the result of external and ritualised coercion that was consciously applied.

Disciplinary control, in this Foucauldian sense, allowed for the pacification and control of large bodies of people. They experienced a pressure to conform to normative expectations of behaviour within the domain of surveillance. Indeed, the purpose of surveillance, in this sense, is to achieve 'normalisation'. Current systems of behavioural conditionality and reporting on social welfare practices extend this means of control; the technologies of power have increased. Webster and Robins (1993) indicate bureaucracy and computers extend disciplinary control into the virtual as well as the actual lives of an individual's behaviours – surveillance and internalised regulatory power not only through the disciplines but also through mundanities of everyday life. By making benefits such as Universal Credit 'digital by default' surveillance is normalised and behavioural normativity is promoted.

The concept of bio-power focuses on the body but targets populations rather than individuals (Foucault, 1981). Governmental control of populations has been important for those holding political office. For instance, being able to predict and account for birth and death rates is necessary when preparing for future economic growth, warfare and pensions viability. However, it is also recognised to be difficult. From the 18th century, therefore, a focus grew on regulating 'normal' forms of sexuality, sexual expression and intimate partnerships. Discourses constructed in society involved moral and religious strategies designed to create a sustainable social order. Professional and disciplinary groups contribute to new technologies of power that carry into everyday lives, normalising and making deviant according to what is deemed permissible or acceptable and what is not. For instance, the bastardy laws of the 19th century entrenched patriarchal and misogynistic assumptions of women's responsibility for conception and children, while in the 21st century similarly unpalatable assumptions are reflected in joint payments under Universal Credit, which are usually made to the male partner in a heterosexual couple (Parker and Veasey, 2021) (see Chapter 6).

While bio-power affects populations, power is ever-present in the social body as a whole and operates within society as continuous, dispersed and localised; thus affecting individuals. Foucault conceptualised this wider spread of power as a system of capillaries interconnecting society through power relations in which everyone takes part. Power and knowledge are linked in society through discursive power which is present in practices as well as texts and can be 'read'. So, the earlier 20th-century attachment of stigma to unmarried mothers was also 'read' in their children, highlighting the child's deviance, as well as the mother's, from expected normative ways of being, of being 'illegitimate'.

Disciplinary and bio-power, and its capillaric reach, can be used in multiple ways: to care and to control; to manage risks and to monitor and control populations. In terms of social welfare, the classification and evaluative categorisation of social activity and social division, such as employment, health status, social class, forces citizens to behave in social, culturally normative and common-sense ways.

Currently surveillance generates social control practices – community sentencing, indeterminate sentences for mentally ill people, the ubiquity of closed-circuit television. Discipline is dispersed and new forms of deviance are subjected to surveillance and control – litter, cigarettes, alcohol use, drug and alcohol abuse, and alleged benefit fraud. The gaze began through increased legislation and social policy development which exerted a punitive control on society and those vulnerable within it. Surveillance gaze is asymmetrical and is designed to promote self-surveillance in regulating an individual's own behaviour. It is designed to foster obedience as we all become the judge of normality and propriety in others and ourselves.

Habitus, capital, fields and practices

The concept of everyday practices is important in formulating notions concerning social actions and relations. Practices are constitutive of their subject as Foucault opined in his notion of discourses. Thus social welfare at a policy and practice level may be deemed to construct it as well as being constructed by it.

The beginnings of a concern with everyday practices, as a specific constitutive structure, lie with Bourdieu (1977). He attempts to explain how the external world is internalised by individuals and how this is reflected back on the world, similar to Berger and Luckmann's (1966) social constructionism in which the external world is internalised and interpreted by our experiences and expectations of it. The resulting structures are constitutive of a particular type of environment, and produce what Bourdieu terms *habitus*. *Habitus* represent 'systems of durable, transposable dispositions' (Bourdieu, 1977, p 72), which orchestrate and structure practices, or what we do behaviourally, at an everyday level; actions are guided by how we think. While individual social actors are producers and reproducers of meaning, their actions and words are often the product of unconscious assumptions and the internalisation of external social relations.

One of the effects of the *habitus* is the production of a 'common-sense' world endowed with objectivity which is secured by a consensus view of the meaning of certain everyday practices or *doxa* (Bourdieu, 1996), and the normative becomes an assumed objective reality on which the foundations of social systems can be built. So, we might consider that social welfare as an objective social category represents a *structuring structure* which is one that helps to create what it is and how it is understood. However, it is also a subjective social category that is a *structured structure* which is one created by the objective social category it also represents. In this sense the objective social category helps to order actions and representations in individual entities which in turn reflect back and reproduce the objective social category. So, welfare policy and practice acts as a means of creating a view of what it, itself, comprises, where social needs lie and what we must do in order to address them. Following from this, some of the ways in which social welfare is construed are played out within populist society and may reflect back some of the expected practices. In this way there is a connection with earlier labelling theory in which deviance acts as a self-fulfilling prophecy (Lemert, 1967).

Practices may result in a group *habitus* of expectations associated with particular social entities: 'As an acquired system of generative schemes objectively adjusted to the particular conditions in which it is constituted, the habitus engenders all the thoughts, all the perceptions and all the actions consistent with those conditions, and no others' (Bourdieu, 1977, p 95). Thus, a system of tacitly assumed norms underpin social welfare policy, practice and popular media representations that continually reinforce and reproduce the schema that mould social welfare initiatives and reforms. This is aided by those discussions that constitute normative thinking about welfare and claimants through welfare practice (Foucault, 1972).

It is important, also, not to ignore the academic and researcher's involvement in the (re)construction of the concepts and practices studied which militate against or increase the associated disadvantage with working and researching in this area. Smith's (1987) feminist sociological analysis sees practices in a broadly similar way to Bourdieu, as an ongoing, co-ordering of activities that bring the world into being. She adds the important point, however, that the researcher is also part of the world in which these practices take place, and that knowledge gained or created becomes part of that world. The researcher contributes to the production and reproduction of social entities by her/his involvement and study. The exchange between researcher and researched is constitutive of whatever social entities and processes it is articulated to. While Bourdieu's theory of practice accounts for the reproduction of social entities, it does not always seem to account for the possibilities of change and challenge to existing orders (Morgan, 1999).

Everyday practices

Morgan (1996, 1999) provides an articulation of practices in which he introduces difference and diversity as core to understanding. Using the term 'family', he challenges the uncritical usage of the term as potentially rigidifying and normalising, and we may perhaps recognise the same problems in respect of terms such as social welfare especially in respect of the assumptions made about people in receipt of benefits. Seeing the term as a verb rather than noun helps us to understand how we might respond to it in society because we understand something of its generation and reproduction.

Similarly to *habitus*, practices draw upon common-sense, everyday understandings and how these are used reflexively to structure that world. Bernades (1997) adds that they also demarcate from practices not assumed or considered to be part of that site of practice. Practices are concerned with cognitive constructions but also with the significance for those parties involved. They are 'a way of looking at, and describing, practices which might also be described in a variety of other ways' (Morgan, 1996, p 199). Practices can, therefore, be described by others involved in an observational or descriptive role.

There are three sets of agencies involved in constructing practices (Morgan, 1999). First, the social actors involved in the social entity themselves make links between activities and general notions of the practice. These linkages, activities and notions are constantly negotiated and redefined by individual experience and reflection. Second, more abstract agencies are involved, which may include welfare professionals and policy makers. These practices may build a cultural resource which provides meaning for individuals. Reflexive monitoring of one's own routine practices against some standard of normality becomes reproductive of those standards as a

Foucauldian disciplinary practice. The final agency involved is the observer. Morgan suggests that observers are often ignored in discussions of social construction. This is central to discussions of the ways in which welfare professionals are understood.

For Morgan (1999), there is a sense of interplay between the different perspectives of the social actor, the individual whose actions are being described and the perspectives of the observer. In this sense, practices relate to the active rather than passive or static. There is a sense of 'doing' which both constitutes and derives from notions of social welfare provision and receipt, policy and practice. These actions take place in the mundane, everyday arena, and can often be seen in routine or repeated actions that constitute part of the everyday taken-for-granted worlds. Practices flow into other practices that are similar. They have both a societal and historical dimension as well as one concerned with individual social actors.

Bourdieu (1998) illuminates competing hegemonic constructs as *fields* of activities and practice regulated by their own disciplinary and bureaucratic rationales, these being the 'fields' of capital, social, cultural and symbolic domains. The policy constructs and practices of social welfare operate within a *habitus* of competing fields. The discourses and practices that continually (re)construct and (re)produce social welfare policies and practice are seen in both detractors and supporters, in those who champion the rights of individual citizens and those who demonise others as claimants, and in policy makers who wish to control and regulate a dangerous other and those who wish to enable, promote and support humans in need. There is a clear split between supporters of social welfare and opponents but also ambivalence across society when discussing social welfare. It is to this that we now turn.

Ambivalence and social welfare

Psychoanalytic concepts have an established history in social and health service delivery but can also be of use in interpreting wider public reactions and responses to social welfare policy and practice. In this book we use elements of Freud's psychoanalytic theory – specifically ambivalence – as a mode of social analysis. This draws on previous work concerning the ambivalent relationship the British public have with social work, which may be construed as the personal social services arm of the welfare system (Parker, 2020).

Freud attempted to explain how the mind affected behaviour. He suggested the mind had a conscious element, comprising those things we are aware of, and a subconscious aspect that contains thoughts and feelings we can access if we wish, alongside an unconscious part made up of repressed feeling and thoughts. This view of the mind is closely linked to our personality, which, for Freud, also comprises three elements: (1) the largely subconscious *id* containing our basic drives such as libido and aggression and which is guided by the pleasure principle; (2) the *superego* which is mainly conscious and seeks to inhibit the *id* in response to external authorities and expectations; (3) the *ego* which mediates between the *id*, the *superego* and the external world through the deployment of mental defence mechanisms. Imbalances in resolving internal negotiations between these elements can lead to neuroses in individuals and we can see similar processes at work in wider society.

The concept of ambivalence in Freudian psychoanalytic terms represents a conflict in individuals between a continuing instinct and an internalised external prohibition of acting on that instinct (Freud, 1962). As a psychical fixation it is not easily resolved as there is a constant wish to perform an act that is also, at the same time, detested. The positive and negative components of this emotional attitude 'are simultaneously in evidence and inseparable, and … they constitute a non-dialectical opposition which the subject, saying "yes" and "no" at the same time, is incapable of transcending' (Laplanche and Pontalis, 1973, cited in Steinmetz, 2006, pp 452–453). Abraham (1927/1988) extended this thinking through a sadistic fantasy associated with urinary and digestive functions that moved from pre-ambivalence to post-ambivalent integrity. His four-stage development of ambivalence was designed to apply to individuals, but it offers a way of approaching social welfare as a social practice. Abraham's model moves through a four-stage violent developmental journey related to consumption, digestion and expulsion:

1. *Late oral stage* – seeking total incorporation of the object (cannibalistic phase) – in our social analysis this may represent those times when governments seek to incorporate social welfare systems into mainstream social and political functions, ending with welfare state construction.
2. *Anal-sadistic stage* – seeking expulsion and destruction of the object, or blaming, punishing and redefining social security and welfare as 'leftist', as supporters of the 'feckless', and as anti-self-responsibility, making welfare residual at best and seeking to impose austerity to deter claimants.
3. *Late anal-sadistic stage* – seeking conservation and dominance of social welfare policy and practice – the subsequent reform and control of social welfare to control public spending while also providing basic welfare.
4. *Genital phase* of love towards a complete object (post-ambivalence) – a stage which has not yet been reached in respect of social welfare.

In such a view, social welfare in British society represents a social neurosis in which assumed social constructions of 'good' and 'bad' in social welfare policy and its beneficiaries are in conflict to different degrees at different points in history. Building on Abraham's extension of ambivalence, Freud sets ambivalence in the Oedipal complex as a reaction formation or displacement. The Oedipal complex represents a rite of passage in which the 'son' seeks to displace his 'father' in terms of authority (in the original myth by killing him) – the positive forces of social welfare being replaced by anger and blame for migration, benefit fraud, dependency and other myths. Rosenzweig (1938), on the other hand, considers that the ambivalence rests with the stimulating object rather than the responding subject (suggesting social welfare finds itself in a complex liminal position as part of society but at the same time also seeking to change that society), and the latter, the general public, may experience ambi-tendencies resulting from earlier repressed experiences with ambivalent objects which leads to conflict.

Ambivalence can lead to displacement (*Verschiebung*) as a social defence mechanism by which society directs negative emotions aroused by perceived transgressions of normative social order on to social welfare policies, benefit recipients or social workers or social work as less threatening entities, with the latter maybe acting as a societal scapegoat. The aim is to shift feelings on to this less threatening object (Freud, 1937) and thereby to resolve internal conflicts. Any transgression of the social norms can elicit such displacement reactions, which, over time, lead to the diminution of the transformative potential of social welfare policies through increased control and regulation of it. A different response is required for social welfare to grow positively.

Taking the argument a little further, in Rosenzweig's (1938) analysis we may identify three ways in which ambivalence operates in social welfare. First, as an integral part of government machinery, it operates as a *stimulating object* for the general public who have faced ambivalence in public institutions and governments as well as in interpersonal relationships. Second, however, social welfare policy and practice also represents an *ambivalent object* that stimulates the general public who express hatred and loathing, while at the same time desiring the care and support offered by the welfare system when they or their families are in need. Third, we can see that social welfare acts as a stimulating object for government who want to control a despised and costly object, which supports those who are stigmatised and demonised in society, while also wanting to ensure people are treated with concern and helped, especially if this gains votes.

Overview of the book

While the major theoretical positions taken in this book have been delineated here, individual chapters seek to elucidate the complex histories of social welfare by drawing also on other cognate perspectives.

In Chapter 2 we present an overview of key historical changes in human social welfare from early bio-archaeological records, the development of organised religious charity, political beginnings and British Poor Law, comparative developments in other countries in Europe and around the world to the development of the British welfare state set in an international context. We consider the fall of the consensus and neoliberal, marketised challenges to collective approaches to compassion and social welfare. The chapter delineates how the concept of social welfare is being employed, considering formal (governmental) and informal (philanthropy, charity/third sector, familial) approaches to care, support and welfare. It is in this chapter that we see some of the continuities and recycling of welfare discourses and practices.

Chapter 3 considers the development and perpetuation of binary distinctions between deserving and undeserving, skivers and strivers, and other moral-judgemental views that reflect normative positions and popular approaches to social welfare. These reflect some of the underlying discourses, *habitus* and ambivalences in which welfare is cast. We consider Lévi-Strauss' position on binary distinctions and offer a critique of the normative positioning and power play that stems from it and reinforces popular assumptions.

Chapter 4 examines the contribution of philanthropy and philanthropists to social welfare. It is not only the Cadburys' concern for their workers that links chocolate and welfare, but includes Elizabeth Fry's campaign for prison reform, especially for women in prison; and also Seebohm Rowntree's concerns and the development, alongside Charles Booth, of the social survey sociology as a political tool to highlight the plight of people in poverty. When we consider flowers we extend the philanthropic reach to consider the development of spaces, worker well-being and the development of garden cities. This chapter examines the centrality of religion-inspired and humanistic philanthropy in the development of welfare approaches to the twin goals of economy and compassion. Theoretically, the balance of these seemingly antithetical bedfellows shows again ambivalence and hidden aspects, or discourses, shown only when one digs under the everyday notions of philanthropic action and how those acting philanthropically are viewed.

In Chapter 5 we explore our ambivalent attitude towards welfare, further considering the contribution of war and conflict in addressing welfare demands for those left behind or bereaved, whose living spaces are ransacked, crops and livelihoods destroyed, and for those returning disabled, injured or simply demobbed and jobless. The burden of care has often been borne by women who were more likely to have needy dependents and to lack independent means. Alongside the needs created by misfortune and difficult times, developments in care and welfare have taken place. We have known that invention takes off at times of national need, necessity being the 'mother of invention'. This chapter examines war, warfare and its place in demanding and creating the conditions for the reform of welfare in Britain.

Chapter 6 considers the impact of welfare on women throughout history and into the present. In terms of sex differences, women have held a central place in welfare in terms of their provider role, as catalysts for change, but they also experience welfare through patriarchal givens and normative expectations (Oakley, 2019). Thus, there is a gendered ambivalence in welfare. The welfare state, however, building on previous practices, has continued to organise welfare around assumptions or discourses of family and breadwinners, usually presuming the latter is male (Pascall, 2012). This ambiguous and somewhat contradictory positioning of women is explored in the context of gender-power relations and feminist approaches to formal and informal welfare practices and philosophies. Welfare institutions act as gender-structuring systems which are also structured by gender, reflecting Bourdieu's (1977) concept of *habitus*.

Chapter 7 explores the socio-political rationale for austerity measures and analyses this in terms of power relations and the, often, socially and politically mandated ritual sacrifice of the poor. Durkheim's concept of 'piacularism', as a collective social rite of mourning, and Giraud's concept of mimetic violence and the scapegoat are introduced as conceptual metaphors for some of the ways in which social policies are enacted and 'sacrifice' those considered poor, vulnerable and marginalised while loading them with social 'sin' that requires punishment and, in contemporary society, demands and legitimises the stigmatisation and punishment of those in poverty. Sacrificial practices reflect everyday, embedded discourse illuminating understandings of welfare, which may be positive or negative.

Chapter 8 considers the ongoing need to reduce administration and bureaucracy resulting in Duncan Smith's 'Dynamic benefits' and, subsequently, the rollout of Universal Credit (Centre for Social Justice, 2009). This is explored alongside historical demands for a Universal Basic Income. Twin aims have permeated formal policy directions: the need to simplify the systems of benefit and to examine novel ways of ensuring either a more equal or a more equitable distribution of income. While not the only rationale for reform, the simplification agenda remains important. Welfare simplification has an economic rationale in attempting to reduce administrative cost and to ensure that welfare is directed to those who most need it. This leads to consideration of calls for further reform from both right- and left-wing commentators in terms of a Universal Basic Income. Discourses from the right and left are played out in debates relating to the everyday working of tax-benefit systems.

Chapter 9 examines the clearly ambivalent features of formalised welfare through the development of social work as an accepted function of capitalist societies but also as a potential social irritant. The history of social work and its diverse beginnings within the system and promoting its sustainability and in radical political and community movements is considered (Bamford and Bilton, 2020; Burt, 2020; Jones, 2020). Personal social services straddle state welfare functions and personal needs and demands for change.

As such, attitudes towards them are ambivalent and can be used to offset failings in governmental support.

Following examination of social work as a two-edged sword, the final chapter debates where welfare might go if, indeed, it survives as a formal citizen entitlement post-Brexit, following the global pandemic and the rippling effects of the war in Ukraine. Rather than suggest likely ways for the development of welfare (Hantrais, 2019, 2020; Pierson, 2021; Spicker, 2022), this chapter looks at a variety of possible futures, drawing upon Merton's theory of unintended consequences and Urry's (2016) anticipation of multiple futures. It concludes by bringing together the debates developed throughout the book. The question of whether or not we want a state welfare system, a marketised, individual responsibility system, a 'Third Way', an anarchic system of compassion or something else is deliberated. This draws on psychosocial understandings of the regulatory selves we are and the compassionate selves we may be.

2

A brief history of British social welfare

Social welfare, concern for the well-being of others, permeates human history. It says much about what we are as a species and how we organise our social ecologies. It helps us learn how people construct the world, design, develop and implement its systems that assists us in responding to changing situations, and, from knowledge of the past, to address future social needs. We present, here, an overview of key shifts in human compassion and social welfare from early archaeological records, the development of organised religious charity, state-organisation and politicisation of welfare in the Poor Laws, the development of the welfare state, the demise of the assumed welfare 'consensus', and the growth of neoliberal and marketised approaches. The focus is thematic and chronological, identifying some of the discourses, ambivalences and continuities that permeate these histories and the functions they provide.

Care and welfare before human recorded histories

Pinker (1979/2021) posited, with a nod to ambivalence, that social welfare is embedded in our social transactions and loyalties, representing both egoism and altruism, or functional, self-interested approaches as well compassion. He challenged conventional ideas that welfare began with social policy interventions, latterly delivered through welfare states. Similarly, Finkel (2019) argued that compassion represents a core feature of human societies through the ages. As we noted in Chapter 1, social policy concerns the different ways in which human interaction is codified and embedded into the social fabric. Once this happens, various political discourses frame and shape the workings of social welfare and attach differing values and responsibilities to giving and receiving it. However, the archaeological record, our window into societies before the written word, indicates that people who were sick, disabled or in need were looked after in societies in which hunger, drought and danger were everyday challenges. For instance, Cassidy et al (2020) report identifying a young, still breastfeeding male infant from Poulnabrone in Ireland with a clear trisomy of chromosome 21, which they believe is the earliest example of a case of Down's syndrome. While the child died at around six months, he was buried in a large Neolithic burial mound that indicates privilege and which suggests, despite his disability and however this was recognised at that time, he was valued. Similarly, Tilley and Nystrom

(2018) report the care of a young Peruvian boy from the late Nasca period about 700 CE who had tuberculosis and lower body immobility.

These examples might be considered to be strange given the demands of looking after people. However, it suggests two things: compassion for the other is embedded in societies, and that life's vicissitudes may create cohesion for all members of a society, as Pinker (1979/2021) suggested. Australian archaeologist, Lorna Tilley (2012, 2015), states that babies are usually cared for in all societies so the burial of the Down's syndrome child in Ireland should not be a surprise. Tilley offers clear evidence of intensive and prolonged caregiving when describing a range of remains including Man Bac Burial 9 in northern Vietnam. This was a man born with Klippel-Feil syndrome who became quadriplegic from adolescence until his death as an adult. She concludes that these people required the care of others to survive and that caring for others represents a defining characteristic of what it means to be human. Archaeology provides a wealth of evidence for living with disabilities, diseases and trauma in prehistoric times (Trinkaus and Zimmerman, 1982; Frayer et al, 1987; Canci et al, 1996). Tilley developed a four-stage bio-archaeological methodology for researching caregiving and care receipt. In stage 1, serious pathology is identified in the remains of an individual and placed in as much context as possible. At stage 2, the likely impacts of the pathology on that individual and their needs for the support of others is considered (Tilley and Oxenham, 2011). Stage 3 estimates what types of care were likely to have been provided, how many people this may have involved and for how long it would be needed. Some deduction can be made of care practices such as the staunching of blood, keeping people clean, free from pressure sores, hydrated and nourished and also the extra work necessary to ensure this in a hunter-gatherer society. The fourth stage seeks to make sense of the processes of care in the context of that society.

We should not be surprised that compassion forms part of the historical foundations for social welfare. MacLean's (1990) concept of the 'triune brain' brought an evolutionary psychology perspective to our understanding of care and compassion. While his concepts of brain development have been rejected it is interesting to note his ideas moving from instinct and autonomic response, a limbic system of emotional connection, care seeking and giving, to a higher order adaptive function in thinking and behaviour (Deacon, 1990; Northcutt, 2002). His ideas have been used to demonstrate why we develop systems of care as survival techniques for the social collective rather than the individual (Heard and Lake, 1997). While less complex social systems may function by altruism, survival through adaptation perhaps creates the conditions for egoistic compassion to grow. As societies develop internal complexity and complete external transactions, more formalised state-supported welfare becomes important and often embedded in belief systems.

Prehistory gives us an insight into some of the emotional-political elements of the human condition and, as such, is important in identifying potential archetypal drivers of care. Compassion for our fellow human beings, especially when they are experiencing misfortunes and vulnerabilities, provides a foundation from which local 'welfare' protection grew. These were practices and dispositions of compassion and functional regulation necessary for the survival of society as Kropotkin argued in 1902 when championing the concept of mutual aid.

Early roots of welfare: religion and charity

The beginnings of codification and more formal welfare systems reach far back into history but interlink with philanthropy, charity and serving fellow human beings, concepts intimately linked with compassion (Vallely, 2020). These are embedded within the philosophies and theologies of the world religions (Faherty, 2006). Help for the poor and needy was demanded in early Judaism, the teachings of Jesus and early Christian church, Hindu and Buddhist hospital care, Islamic charity from 650 CE, and Roman Catholic canon law. Faherty (2006) charts the first three centuries of Christianity and asks us to reimagine social welfare as an integral part of what it is to be human (Pinker 1979/2021; Finkel, 2019). He identifies the Greek, Roman and Jewish heritage underpinning alms-giving, charity and concern for the poor, vulnerable and disadvantaged, illuminating gendered practices such as ministering to the sick and to children (female), and grave-digging and organising burials (male). This aspect of the early church is almost unquestioned and somewhat hidden within church history, although Chadwick (1993) considers the egalitarian and charitable aspects of the early church to represent one of its defining radical features in the ancient world. Berg-Weger (2016) outlines varied aspects of formal help from the first evidence of legal codification prescribing welfare in the Code of Hammurabi 1750 BCE, in which subjects must help others in times of need. The obligation to support others was also required in non-theistic philosophies in ancient Greek states, Confucian philosophy and in Cicero's Rome (Pinker, 1979/2021; Payne, 2005). These actions say much about religious and philosophical perceptions of humanity but also concern the legitimation and systematic regulation of social life (Vantsos and Kiroudi, 2007).

The historical association of charity, welfare and Islam is exemplified by Ottoman public kitchens or 'imaret, run from the 14th to the 19th centuries, necessarily associated with political power (Singer, 2005). Imperial giving reinforced support for the Sultanate and offset potential rebellion or threats to his power, perhaps something that lies at the heart of state welfare in giving enough to prevent political trouble but not enough to ensure a fundamental shift in power relations in society.

Welfare and charitable giving is complex and cannot be reduced to a single purpose or system of belief. However, religious charity in the Abrahamic religions to some extent influenced the development of welfare legislation which formalised the care and control of vulnerable groups, notably those in poverty.

The English Poor Law

Alongside religious charity, the long history of legislation concerning the treatment of people in poverty continually (re)constructs views of those people receiving alms or support. Addressing needs, and distinguishing between those 'deserving' help and nuisances, represented manorial and ecclesiastical duties and created unquestioned moral and behavioural categories. The binary distinctions within the legislation that link to 'deserving and undeserving' welfare recipients, retribution/blame and alms-giving, presage our contemporary system of welfare conditionality.

Systematic legislative approaches to vagrancy and the dispossessed go back to the time following the Black Death (Charlesworth, 2010a). In 1388, Richard II instituted parochial responsibilities towards the poor, reinforced later by Henry VII. In 1389, Richard detailed the role of Justices of the Peace in regulating wages and fixing prices. It was in Tudor times, however, that the Poor Laws were refined (Slack, 1990), resulting finally in the comprehensive formalised Poor Law of Elizabeth I in 1601.

The early days of the Elizabethan Poor Law seemed advanced and far-reaching in terms of the management of and support for the population of Britain (Thane, 2000; Fraser, 2017). The experience of it was, however, mixed and often harsh (Kelly and Ó Gráda, 2011). The Poor Law was the first comprehensive, mandatory system of publicly funded poor relief, creating an enduring parochial administrative framework for its management, collection by taxation of the unpopular poor rate, financial relief and setting to work of the poor. Administration rested in the hands of churchwardens and overseers of the poor who were named annually by local magistrates, who themselves were usually farmers and middle-ranking householders.

Determining parish responsibility for people in poverty and need was fraught and the poor were often shunted to different parishes to reduce the financial burden on individual parishes. Women took the settlement of their husbands, children their parents, which added complexity. The Act of Settlement 1662 attempted to resolve this by allowing the return of paupers to their 'rightful' parish, that with responsibility for that person. This could be done on the order of two magistrates, where the person was resident less than 40 days and was not renting a property worth at least £10 a year (Slack, 1990). The settlement code was changed in 1692 to allow apprenticeships, hiring of people for a year, paying of poor rates and so forth. However, a certificate of irremovability was allowed in 1697, which provided details of the parish responsibility. The Settlement Act regulated and monitored labour migration but did little to reduce litigation between parishes. Parish applications for removal were not simply rubber-stamped. People's backgrounds, character and circumstances were scrutinised carefully by magistrates before a decision was made, presaging welfare investigation and assessments that rely on moral as well as administrative eligibility criteria. It is interesting to note that, in recent years, local authorities have provided funds for one-way tickets to homeless/rough sleepers to return to their places of origin, mirroring this parochial view of welfare provision (Communities and Local Government, 2006).

The 1601 Act laid the foundations of localised state welfare, a proto-civil-society (Charlesworth, 2010b). Family responsibility for paupers and vulnerable family members was expected, but rate-payer-supported workhouses and poorhouses developed in the 17th century. The able-bodied poor were to be set to work rather than housed, stemming from a belief that able-bodied paupers were often workshy, but it was often difficult to make this work. In the late 17th century, Matthew Hale and Josiah Child examined workhouses in Holland and advocated unions of parishes that could harness the 'able-bodied workshy' and turn a profit. The workfare idea has arisen in recent times in the US, and through New Right thinking in the UK, albeit supported by Labour politician Frank Field, and has been moulded into benefit conditionality and sanctions since (Mead, 1997).

Workfare for children was promoted, while casual giving was banned, and physical punishment (whipping, branding and putting in stocks) was common. However, there was a more compassionate alms-giving from the parishes to those deemed impotent by Poor Law legislation. Alms-giving was administered through overseers and justices of the peace; the beginnings of social welfare regulation. Attitudes towards the poor hardened in the 18th century and deterrence came to be advocated, which meant enforced entry to the workhouse or being contracted to a private institution was often the only way to ensure parochial assistance remained. This was allowed by the Workhouse Test 1723 Act, which presaged the New Poor Law of 1834, and the 'workhouse test' in which there was no need to inquire into the character or situation of the poor. Despite hardening attitudes the effects were modest. The 1723 Act allowed the farming out of settled paupers to private contractors to undertake work or to be contained or looked after – akin to local authority gangmasters' approaches in the contemporary era. The process was that labour was hired out to those who needed it and the income was used to supplement poor relief (see Dickens' *Oliver Twist*, 1837–1839/1994). Where farming out did not take place the responsibility lay with the overseers who were extremely busy assessing needs and rates and collecting the poor rates, determining applicants' settlement, possibly securing a removal order and engaging in lengthy court proceedings. Outdoor relief, the payment of a supplement to inadequate wages, was often cheaper than keeping a person, and family, in a workhouse. This concerned payment to individuals to keep them from starvation when they had no income or to top up inadequate wages. Most relief was paid to the aged, the infirm and children. Outdoor relief rather than workhouse was usually offered and this was unlikely to be enough to maintain those people. Maintenance orders from families were common.

Jonas Hanway, a philanthropist, brought to parliament's attention the unsanitary conditions of the London workhouses which led to the deaths of about 50 per cent of infants before the age of two years. This led to Hanway's Act 1762, which allowed for the boarding out of infants in the suburbs or countryside. Brundage (2002) suggests that Poor Law reform and philanthropy overlapped here with an emphasis on a healthy workforce that provided useful hands, such as Thomas Coram's Foundling Hospital and Hanway's Marine Society. But in the 19th century fear of a 'surplus population' grew, care was costly and exacted a toll on parish purses.

The formalisation of welfare systems grew during the 17th century. In 1647 and 1649 the Corporation of the Poor, in London, erected workhouses and created an administration system to manage the legislation and people who fell within its remit. This was extended to Bristol and 14 other towns in Acts of William III between 1696 and 1712. Between 1748 and 1785 there were many local acts that allowed the incorporation of parishes to work together to provide poor relief.

The mid-18th century saw a wish to broaden the administration of poor relief from the local parochial system. The 1723 Act facilitated the union of parishes but few took the opportunity. Those that did, such as the East Anglia union, were considered to be sufficient in operation and generally humane (Slack, 1990). Indeed, some Poor Law reformers and critics dubbed them 'pauper palaces'. Unions removed the administration and control from the parochial overseer moving to a system of elected and salaried persons. In this process we can see the beginnings of the 'professionalisation' of welfare policy and practice.

In the so-called Gilbert's Act 1782, local parish approaches to the poor were further 'professionalised', acting as a precursor to the ways in which we act towards the poor, needy, unemployed, sick and disabled people in our society today. There was also a political-legal concern to reduce, simplify and consolidate legislation, which could be seen in the 1714 Act. This was echoed in New Labour's desire for joined up and consolidated thinking from 1997 to 2010, the Conservative/Liberal Democrat Coalition's desire to reduce the 'burdens' of multiple bureaucracy from 2010 to 2015, and taken further by the Conservative government from 2015 in the rollout of Universal Credit (UC). In the closing years of the American Revolutionary War in

1782, Thomas Gilbert, MP for Lichfield, presented his bill to parliament. There was concern for the soldiers and sailors returning home, and calls to reform the Poor Law so that unions of parishes could be formed and to build and oversee workhouses for the impotent, aged and children, leaving the responsibility for finding work for able-bodied men with the overseers. Gilbert's Act took time to develop but by the time the New Poor Law was passed, 924 parishes had combined into 67 Gilbert Act unions in the East, South-East and Midlands. These varied in efficiency and reputation (Slack, 1990). The rest of England remained parochial. Gilbert also gained a requirement for the overseers to submit Poor Law expenditure for 1783–1785, providing the first national database of relief statistics. Presaging a standardised and professional welfare and benefit system initiated within the welfare state, Gilbert proposed a national system of poor relief but did not succeed in getting this through parliament. The unequal system of raising poor rates in each parish remained where parishes with few landowners could discourage resident labourers or even demolish dwellings to reduce the rate, although the latter was rare.

Changing social and political mores created unanticipated consequences throughout society. The enclosure movement, decline of cottage industries and industrialisation had an effect on pauperism throughout the country, albeit with different effects across different geographical regions (Thompson, 1963; Griffin, 2018). These changes happened at a time of rapid population growth. In the 1790s, bad weather and bad harvests, political upheaval in France following the revolution and war with England being declared in 1793 exacerbated problems with expenditure on poor relief; costs soared. The prime minister, William Pitt, attempted to further Gilbert's approach for the centralisation of poor relief. While the Act failed, a system of allowances-in-aid-of-wages was introduced. Setting the scale of these allowances was complex and took into account the cost of living needs. The most famous system was the Speenhamland sliding scale of poor relief, which we consider later. A minimum wage bill was defeated.

Towards reform

By the time of the Battle of Waterloo in 1815, Britain was at the midway point of a major social upheaval. Industrialisation continued to grow; mills, mines and manufacture were developing; cotton, wool and heavy industries were increasing. The industrialisation/urbanisation thesis, which suggests that industrialisation changed the concept and use of space, exerted a tremendous impact on the social psychology of people involved (Thompson, 1963; Griffin, 2018).

Agrarian as well as urban life changed. Enclosure consolidated fields, common and wasteland, and agriculture became a more efficient and market-driven business. The majority of the land, however, was owned by a small number of wealthy landowners and labourers were increasingly dispossessed of smallholdings and rights as farm workers.

In the 1820s, the social reformer, William Cobbett, rode through the countryside of Britain documenting the poverty and injustice he observed (1830/2001). Cobbett was an interesting politician and radical, being from farming stock, serving in the military and exposing abuse and unfairness in the army in a way similar to many whistle-blowers today. He was a Tory politician but left after becoming more radical in terms of social reform, even being imprisoned and then later forced to flee to America when the government repressed dissent following the Napoleonic wars. He catalogued the degrading life and injustice experienced by farm labourers and influenced later thinkers such as Marx. While both old and new landed gentry were wealthy, the labouring classes experienced rising corn prices, rents alongside wages that were not sufficient to live by and complaints against poor relief supplements. Cobbett contrasted this with the payment of war pensions, saying:

> [N]ot a word of complaint is heard about these five millions and a quarter (for war pensions), while the country rings, fairly resounds, with the outcry about the six millions that are given to the labourers in the shape of poor-rates, but which, in fact, go, for the grater part, to pay what ought to be called wages. (Cobbett, 1830/2001, Winchester, Sunday morning, 29 September 1822, np)

He continued ten years later on a rural ride in the north of England:

> [T]he rest of the Malthusian crew, are constantly at work preaching, content to the hungry and naked. To be sure, they themselves, however, are not content to be hungry and naked … they tell the working-people that the working-folks, especially in the North, used to have no bread, except such as was made of oats and of barley. That was better than potatoes, even the 'nice mealy ones;' especially when carried cold to the field in a bag … these vagabond authors, who thus write and publish for the purpose of persuading the working-people to be quiet … take care not to tell the people, that these oatcakes and this barley-bread were always associated with great lumps of flesh-meat; they forget to tell them this, or rather these half-mad, perverse, and perverting literary imposters suppress the facts, for reasons that are far too manifest to need stating. (Cobbett, 1830/2001, Newcastle upon Tyne, 23 September 1832, np)

The use of stigma has functional benefits for property owners, governments and those controlling or regulating systems. Moral arguments enabled those with power to hold on to it by stigmatising those who do not. This technique of power allowed the maintenance of power imbalances, the development of an ineffective system of welfare, and promoted moral arguments against poor relief and those receiving it.

Poor relief supplemented the wages of labourers. While it is argued that it may have pauperised and demoralised farm labourers over time it did alleviate starvation. It helped the large farmers, landowners and rich. The clearest example of poor relief as a contested system of wage supplements is seen in the Speenhamland system. This introduced a tabular system which made it easy to work out the amount of dole for families as the cost of living index changed. (This system was replicated in the 2000s through Tax Credits, UC and in-work conditionality [Veasey and Parker, 2021].)

At the peak of the poor relief in 1818, £8 million was paid out – a remarkable sum although this subsequently declined (Webster, 2015). One effect of this system was to reduce the need for farmers to pay a living wage and forced parish rate payers to supplement farmers' wage bills by paying parish relief, which was resented all around, and became the focus of reformers who wanted the cessation of allowances. A report in the *Reading Mercury* on 11 May 1795 offers a glimpse into the thinking behind the scheme:

At a General Meeting of the justices of this County, together with several discreet persons assembled by public advertisement, on Wednesday the 6th day of May, 1795, at the Pelican Inn in Speenhamland (in pursuance of an order of the last Court of General Quarter Sessiods) for the purpose of rating Husbandry Wages, by the day or week, if then approved of, [names of those present]. ...

Resolved unanimously,

That the poor state of the Poor does not require further assistance than has been generally given them.

Resolved,

That it is not expedient for the Magistrates to grant that assistance by regulating the Wages of Day Labourers, according to the directions of the Statutes of the 5th Elizabeth and 1st James: But the Magistrates very earnestly recommend to the Farmers and others throughout the county, to increase the pay of their Labourers in proportion to the present price of provisions; and agreeable thereto, the Magistrates now present, have unanimously resolved that they will, in their several divisions, make the following calculations and allowances for relief of all poor and industrious men and their families, who to the satisfaction of the justices of their Parish, shall endeavour (as far as they can) for their own support and maintenance.

That is to say,

When the Gallon Loaf of Second Flour, Weighing 8lb. 11ozs. shall cost 1s.

Then every poor and industrious man shall have for his own support 3s. weekly, either produced by his own or his family's labour, or an allowance from the poor rates, and for the support of his wife and every other of his family, Is. 6d.

When the Gallon Loaf shall cost 1s. 4d.

Then every poor and industrious man shall have 4s. weekly for his own, and 1s. and 10d. for the support of every other of his family.

And so in proportion, as the price of bread rise or falls (that is to say) 3d. to the man, and 1d. to every other of the family, on every 1d. which the loaf rise above 1s.

By order of the Meeting.

W. BUDD, Deputy Clerk of the Peace.

In 1830, the Poor Law was still built around the architecture of the 1601 Elizabethan Poor Law, and was in dire need of reform. It had become a tangle of inconsistent regulations that left people trapped in poverty and assisted the wealthy landowners rather than those in poverty. Parochial responsibility was no longer adequate to administer growing need and an increasingly complex system of meeting it.

Poor Law (Amendment) Act 1834

Sealey (2015) relates the context underpinning calls for Poor Law reform to war, industrialisation and urbanisation changing the political and social landscape in the latter part of the 18th and early part of the 19th centuries. He points to the significance that changes in population structures over the 19th century had for social life and welfare problems. In 1801 the population of England and Wales was around ten million, and just under one-third lived in urban areas, whereas by 1901 the population had risen to over 35 million people, of whom four-fifths were living in urban conurbations. This rapid population rise and shift over the century led to increased poverty, unemployment, squalor and disease, and an increased need for welfare, or poor relief. Thus social geography, and the changing use of space, was also important in subsequent demands for reform.

The degrading conditions of the poor alongside increasing uprisings against injustice and in favour of reform were key to the growing campaign for changes in the Poor Law. In 1819 in Peterloo, Manchester, the army charged demonstrators, leaving between 10 and 20 dead and over 600 injured (Metropolitan and Central Committee, 1820). In 1830 starving field labourers from Southern counties in England rioted in favour of a half-a-crown a day wage – the outcome led to hangings and transportation as a reaction to the uprising (Hobsbawm and Rudé, 2001).

The Old Poor Laws were complex and costly. Throughout the 18th and early 19th centuries many intellectuals wanted reform. The economist Adam Smith (1776/1982) recognised the importance of the Poor Laws and argued against the Settlement Act as, in effect, preventing economic migration which he considered part of the free market. Smith promoted self-interest as the best way to meet welfare needs. Later economic writers challenged his views. Edmund Burke suggested poor relief should be abandoned altogether as a moral evil and Sir Frederic Morton Eden indicated that poor rates seemed inversely related to wages, and thus prevented people earning sufficient to manage for themselves (Eden, 1797). David Ricardo (1817) argued that there was a finite supply of money in the economy and that money paid from the Poor Laws was part of that finite whole and thus reduced what could be paid in wages, which, therefore, reduced earnings and increased poverty for those in work. (This thinking later influenced the New Right and monetarists such as Milton Friedman and Margaret Thatcher.)

Perhaps the most infamous commentator was the Rev Thomas Malthus who, in 1798, suggested that if 'the poor' are simply given more food they would increase in number exponentially and that disease and poverty provided a natural check on the population (Malthus, 1798/2015). He believed the Poor Laws were harmful as they automatically increased pressure on populations. This kind of thinking permeated much popular philosophical thinking of the day, suggesting that the increasing Poor Law expenditure resulted from over-generous benefits that encouraged people to remain in poverty (Sealey, 2015). These views of welfare dependency still permeate popular thought today. If you pick any tabloid/red top newspaper you will be able to see articles that suggest that people in poverty are there because it pays to be so (Baumberg et al, 2012; Lugo-Ocando and Harkins, 2015). Malthus stated: 'To remedy the frequent distresses of the common people, the poor laws of England have been instituted; but it is to be feared, that though they may have alleviated a little the intensity of individual misfortune, they have spread the general evil over a much larger surface' (Malthus, 1798/2015). Criticism also came from political philosophy. William Godwin (1793/1985) contended that people were concerned for their own welfare rather than the general welfare of others, which meant that government administration would work for the ends of those in power rather than for the general welfare of people. He argued against, therefore, political interference through Poor Laws.

Jeremy Bentham (1789/2007) was influenced by Malthus' thought but differed significantly in his conclusions. He proposed a 'felicific calculus' which meant that maximising happiness and minimising misery became central calculations in the development of policy. His basic premise was that people are motivated by the desire to seek pleasure and avoid pain. At first, Bentham was much opposed to state interference in social and economic life but then turned to legislative and welfare reform. Bentham proposed that centralisation of poor relief was important, indicating it was a public responsibility. He believed that poverty and starvation produced political revolution and turbulence and that there should be no discrimination between the 'deserving' and 'undeserving' poor. He proposed building workhouses based on his idea of a panopticon – a huge polygonal structure designed on a radial principle in which the supervisor could sit at the hub unseen by the inmates but be able to observe and survey inmates in rooms on the outer periphery. Inmates would recognise they may be being watched and alter their behaviours accordingly.

Two key figures in the overhaul of the system were Nassau Senior and his protégé Edwin Chadwick, who was influenced by Benthamite utilitarianism. They brought political economy into the world of Poor Law reform. Senior and Chadwick headed a commission in 1832, which reported in 1834 and from which came the Poor Law Amendment Act in the same year. There are connections here with the welfare reform measures of the Coalition government of 2010–2015, austerity measures and welfare residuality continued by the 2015 Conservative government, especially in the continuing use of such stigmatising concepts as 'deserving' and 'undeserving' and moral fecklessness which have permeated welfare debates throughout history.

The report set out the arguments that the Poor Laws were too generous and militated against self-help, that over-generous benefits contributed to rapid population growth, and that Poor Law payments restricted wages as the following evidence from the report demonstrates:

> [O]ne third of our labourers do not work at all ... the rising population learn nothing, the others are forgetting what they knew. ... Relying upon parish support, they are indifferent ... are less industrious. The system of allowance is most mischievous and ruinous, and till it is abandoned, the spirit of industry can never be revived. (House of Commons, 1834, p 39)

The cushioning effect of the Poor Laws curtailed the free market by restricting wages to a certain level. The commission considered how best to deal with the able-bodied poor, making a sharp distinction between them and the aged, sick, orphaned and mentally ill. Outdoor relief was to be abandoned for able-bodied people and their families except for medical relief and the apprenticeship of children although there was to be a transition of two years in which relief in kind was to gradually replace financial relief.

The New Poor Law increased the systematic bureaucratisation of welfare and further entrenched the backdrop for contemporary systems and, paradoxically, increased expenditure. The amended legislation sought to establish efficient local administrative units, supervise the work of locally elected guardians, prescribe the qualifications of local officials and make regulations for the general administration of relief. The principle of 'less eligibility', in which workhouse conditions should be made less preferable than those of the lowest paid labourer, permeated the policy and practice. This was to be achieved by separating different classes of pauper, prohibiting outdoor relief (relief outside the workhouse) and abolishing 'rate-in-aid' (grants to supplement low wages). Englander (1998) suggested that the workhouse concept was developed as a 'punishment' of the poor for their moral fecklessness; it was intended to discourage moral deficiencies and illuminated some of the persisting discourses of people in need and poverty. This is fictionalised well in Dickens' description of Mr Bumble in *Oliver Twist* (Dickens, 1837–1839/1994). The unemployed were paid less than those in work to encourage them to work. This deterrent assumed that poor and unemployed people were in some way to blame for their situation and could work if they so wished. In the workhouse food provided was to be adequate but dull and families were to be split up. The intention again was deterrent. This continued the moral crusade of discrimination enshrined within the Old Poor Laws, which were themselves based on the principles of 'deserving' and 'undeserving' and distributed through a form of means-testing. The idea was to discourage applications so they were only used in times of dire need. This in turn stemmed from the belief that it was individual failings that led them into poverty rather than any external structural causes (Sealey, 2015).

Section 62 of the Poor Law (Amendment) Act allowed parishes to raise money for the emigration of poor people to the colonies and address surplus population concerns and rising poor rates. Howells (2003) argues, however, that assisted emigration was not simply 'shovelling out paupers' as suggested by Charles Buller MP. Examining the policies of rural Bedfordshire, Northamptonshire and Norfolk, he found that rich and poor interacted to gain mutual benefit by focusing on the idea of a better life abroad. Officially, 20,015 people were assisted over 25 years but many more were assisted without the Act and many more voluntarily emigrated, although hostility to the practice was widespread. It could not be enforced but did act as a push and is immortalised in Ford Madox Brown's 1855 painting, *The Last of England*.

The administration of relief was tightened and restricted, and responsibility for its oversight was transferred from the parishes to an elected board of Poor Law Guardians who worked under the general instructions of the Poor Law Commissioners in Somerset House. (Elected local bodies and centralised control became a much emulated model of public administration and one which continues to ebb and flow.)

The New Poor Law promoted uniformity in the treatment of separate classes of paupers, such as disabled/ill and able-bodied, but diversity in treatment between classes. The commissioners did not fully enforce the principles and asylum, orphanage and poorhouse were often mixed. Where outdoor relief was abolished it was often the case for all poor people and not just the able-bodied. In doing so it encouraged an approach based on stigma and assumption, treating all paupers as being so because of their own actions, inactions or integral moral fault.

Local government changed as a result of the Poor Law. Landed gentry no longer held all the power through the Justices of the Peace. Elected guardians did include the justices *ex officio* but responsibilities were shared and all had to submit to the three powerful Poor Law Commissioners. However, the parishes still held separate responsibility for meeting the costs of relieving their own poor despite the centralisation of control. The Poor Law Commission was replaced by the Poor Law Board in 1847 under a minister responsible to parliament. The essential functions, however, did not change until 1871 when it was merged with the new Local Government Board.

The Act did check some of the demoralisation and pauperisation that had grown under the old system, although costs remained a problem. The Poor Law Reform Act 1834 held sway in England with some social insurance reforms, additional social regulatory legislation and changes in the way that people were seen and treated until Beveridge's reforms in the 1940s. Changes made in 1930 began to shift elements of the Poor Law and to introduce social services akin to those initiated by Beveridge. Responsibility was passed to local government from the Poor Law Guardians. However, the feared and hated Poor Laws still resonated with some people and throughout the 20th century it was not uncommon to find hospitals built alongside Old Poor Law workhouses and for older people to live in dread of hospital, poverty and incapacity as a result.

20th-century changes in welfare: towards the welfare state and beyond

At the end of the 19th century and beginning of the 20th, a range of factors coalesced, creating the right conditions for welfare and social policy reform and the development of the welfare state in 1948. These resulted from the passage of time, social and political changes and, as with the reform of the Poor Law in the previous century, increased industrialisation and urbanisation, and fear of social conflict. However, the drive towards reform began much earlier and, perhaps somewhat paradoxically, with the architect of the New Poor Law, Edwin Chadwick, and his subsequent discovery of the impact of environmental and structural factors in the cause and maintenance of poverty.

In 1838, Chadwick turned his attentions to health, setting up a board of doctors to investigate the causes of death and destitution: first in London, then throughout the country. In 1842 he published his *General Report on the Sanitary Condition of the Labouring Population of Great Britain* in which he revised his impression that moral fecklessness led to poverty and dependence on the Poor Law. He identified that disease, increased industrialisation, population growth and urbanisation, overcrowding and pollution were causing poverty and degradation and he began to advocate a more proactive benefit system and centralised public health measures. It is interesting to note that his change of heart has had little effect on subsequent pejorative views of people in need (Sealey, 2015).

Chadwick's report led to the setting up of a commission of inquiry into town life, which reported in 1846, and legislation in 1848 concerning the gross inadequacy of water supplies, drainage and refuse disposal. A Central Board of Health was set up along the same lines as the Poor Law Commissioners – under local boards. It was abolished in 1858 but, after a further outbreak of cholera in 1865–1866, local authorities were obliged to employ sanitary inspectors. A further commission in 1869 led to a statement of basic conditions necessary for civilised life in terms of income and living standards. Sanitary inspectors were assimilated into the local government board in 1871, the Ministry of Health in 1919 and continued within environmental health/public health legislation, oscillating between health and local government ever since.

The reformist social legislation of the 19th century grew from a deeper recognition of the importance of social structures and the centrality of reforming figures from the anti-Poor Law campaigners such as Richard Oastler, Rev Joseph Rayner Stephens, the Chartists, and later Charles Booth and Seebohm Rowntree. It provided a backdrop to the early 20th-century attempts at social reform of the Liberal government, interrupted by the First World War, and ultimately provided the context for William Beveridge's work and the beginnings of the welfare state after the Second World War. Reform and advance in welfare is a dialectical affair the results of which cannot always be anticipated.

The conditions for welfare reform

Industrialisation constructed a new and terrible society, a Leviathan that consumed the rural population, digesting them in the gastric fluids of new urban spaces and excreting social problems, which, while not new in themselves, provided diagnostic evidence of some of the ills created by such monumental changes. Of course, such a dystopic view of the industrial revolution is somewhat one-sided, making invisible the political, economic and social benefits that Britain accrued as a result of these changes (Griffin, 2018). However, it reflects the human cost paid to achieve such transformations. Throughout the 19th century reformers made small cuts into the skin of this Leviathan – prison reform, child labour acts and educational reform – which added to social policy and welfare development.

Prison inspectors were appointed by the Gaols Act 1835; prison officers became salaried and appointed employees by 1877. The Prison Act of 1878 closed some of the more abusive prisons, adopting some of the reforms of the 18th-century reformer John Howard (who gives his name to the Howard League for prison reform), and following Elizabeth Fry's reforms for women. In 1894–1895 Gladstone's Committee on Prisons indicated that criminality took hold of people between the mid-teens and mid-20s, which led to the setting up of Borstals in an attempt to divert young people from offending. Factory reform grew from Peel's 19th-century committee of investigation into child labour, which offered protections to labourers, especially children. Alongside these protections education became compulsory and free towards the end of the 19th century under the Elementary Education Act 1870, the Education Act 1880 and the Fee Grant Act 1891. Agitation in industrialised cities, the development of trade unions and the formation of the Labour Party in 1900 added weight to the drive towards reform and state provision, as did recognition of the poor physical health of soldiers in the Boer War (1899–1902) (Mitton, 2012).

William Beveridge is the figure most associated with 20th-century reforms leading to the British welfare state in 1948, having had a significant impact on earlier Liberal social and health reforms. While he was a friend of the socialist reformers, Sidney and Beatrice Webb, he was himself not associated with any political party. In 1905, aged 26, he worked as a lead writer on the *Morning Post* which led him into contact with Winston Churchill. In 1908 he took a post as a civil servant in the Board of Trade in which he played a significant part in creating a network of labour exchanges and formulating the liberal social insurance scheme drawing on Bismarck's social insurance scheme in Germany.

Bismarckian-style welfare reform developed until the First World War. Schoolchildren were given medical checks and school meals were introduced apart from the Poor Law. A means-tested old age pension was developed for people over 70 years of age, marking another change from the Poor Law. The 1911 National Insurance Act covered interruptions in earnings through sickness or unemployment. Panel doctors were introduced as part of a national system that also brought in maternity benefits and sick pay. These reforms faced great opposition but gradually many realised they had not gone far enough (Mitton, 2012).

After leaving the civil service in 1919, Beveridge entered academic life as director of the London School of Economics (LSE) where he met future Prime Minister Clement Attlee and Hugh Dalton when they were lecturers there. In 1937 he became Master of University College, Oxford where he employed Harold Wilson as a research assistant. His friendship with the economist John Maynard Keynes and relationship to R.H. Tawney were also instrumental in his future development of the architecture of the welfare state.

Between the wars the Labour Party grew in strength. In 1918 some women were given the vote, with full suffrage in 1928. Health and pensions were uppermost in the mind of government. Chamberlain's government introduced the Widows, Orphans and Old Age Contributory Pensions Act in 1925, which granted widow's benefit and pensions at 65 years. However, the still-hated Poor Law was in operation, even when statutory control passed to local authorities in 1930. This provided the backdrop to the further development of the welfare state post-Beveridge.

In June 1941, Arthur Greenwood, Minister without Portfolio in the Coalition government, invited Beveridge to chair a committee to tidy the mess around sickness and unemployment benefits. He came to see the role, according to Sullivan (1996), as a way of changing British social policy. Beveridge did not feel constrained by the terms of reference given and, outraging other civil servants, extended the work of the committee to consider social insurance as a whole. He recommended bringing together existing insurance schemes, believing intervention was necessary in many areas such as creating a national health service, developing systematic approaches to family allowance and unemployment benefit. Beveridge recommended moving away from means-testing, recognising that the stigma associated with it could prevent people taking up their entitlements.

The report, *Social Insurance and Allied Services*, was published in 1942 to a great reception. This report argued for the creation of a post-war welfare state as a way of overcoming social evils and unifying society. His ideas advanced on those of Otto von Bismarck, the 19th-century German chancellor and architect of German unification, who had developed social security benefits which were adopted by the Liberal government reforms of the early 20th century.

The report was underscored by three guiding principles:

1. fundamental changes were necessary;
2. social insurance formed the basis of contributory social policies that attacked the five giants – Want, Disease, Ignorance, Squalor and Idleness; and
3. social security linked the individual and the state but did not stifle personal initiative or voluntary service.

There appeared to be a consensus of agreement and universalism became an agreed paradigm with even the Labour Party and Churchill in concert over the development of collectivist welfare policies following wartime experiences (Douglas and Philpott, 1998). The proposed reforms were based on continued antipathy to the New Poor Law. Beveridge suggested that people prefer contributory benefits rather than charity and being categorised as deserving or undeserving. The depression of the 1930s confirmed some of the inadequacies of the Poor Law in meeting social security needs (Payne, 2005).

Education policy had been debated before the war but a clear state system was created by Butler's 1944 Education Act. Creation of the Emergency Hospital Service (EHS) opened the eyes of doctors and others to poverty and inequities in provision. The National Health Service (NHS) gained wide support as an idea in the war. Discussion had begun prior to the war and was seen as a potential expansion of the health insurance scheme. In 1941, perhaps because of the EHS, this policy direction morphed into a comprehensive national health service against the British Medical Association (BMA) concerns.

The economic practicalities and costs were hotly debated. But in 1944, the White Paper on Social Security emerged from the report, was accepted by Churchill, and led to the creation of the welfare state in 1948. The intention was to set welfare benefits at a level that enabled families to survive through the provision of grants such as family allowances, marriage grants, maternity grants and death grants. It was focused on families rather than individuals and patriarchal by design. In respect of social security, the contributory principle (insurance) had advantages as it was universal for those who contributed and their families and not an unearned handout. The National Insurance Bill 1946 suggested payment by stamp; however, it was not possible to be fully self-financing because the immediate introduction of the full pension demanded two-thirds of the expenditure following the implementation of the National Insurance Act 1948.

While contributory benefits implied an integral connection with employment, there was also provision for those who had not paid in through the National Assistance Act 1948. This allowed a degree of universality of provision as claimed, although this aspect remained means-tested.

Birth and growth of the welfare state

War had ravaged the economic fabric of Britain but following the Labour Party's election in July 1945 people expected immediate economic and social change and full implementation of Beveridge's reforms. Lend-lease borrowing from the US and Canada increased to £2.8 billion by June 1945 and exports had decreased; industrial capacity was down because of labour shortages. It was not until 31 December 2006 that the final repayment was made (BBC, 2006). However, the nascent welfare state benefited from a peace dividend resulting from less expenditure on defence and continued high taxes.

The birth of the NHS was more difficult because of power relations between various interest groups and there being no consensus on health needs. In order to get the BMA on board, who opposed the creation of the NHS, Bevan allowed general practitioners (GPs) to retain capitation fees rather than be salaried, giving some concessions that allowed private practice to continue. On 5 July 1948 the NHS was established under the Ministry of Health, combining three elements – hospital, family-oriented and local authority services.

Until 1951, housing was part of the Ministry of Health. There was political agreement on the need for housing but most builders were in the forces and the country's finances were in difficulty. Also, the focus was on local authority rather than private builders which led to political contest. Local authority quality specifications were higher than pre-war ones and much building was delayed until the Conservatives came back to power in 1951.

Impact of the welfare state

Analysis suggests that the changes were conservative and geared towards reinforcing social stability and paternalism rather than radical change (Rowntree and Lavers, 1951; Fraser, 2017). There remained, however, a number of right-wing objections to it (Sullivan, 1996; Fraser, 2017; Timmins, 2017). Social equality was considered to be against the natural order, restricting initiative and threatening freedom of choice. Taxation was high and therefore limited choice of how to dispose of income, and Barnett (1986, 1995) suggested that investment in welfare rather than industry led to the end of Britain as a significant player in the world economy. Others suggest that the welfare state created the conditions in which industry could flourish and see it as an institution of late capitalism.

Paradoxically, during the early years of the welfare state it was the Conservative Party who developed and financed it (Fraser, 2017). After the Labour Party's election defeat in 1951, the Conservatives had 13 years in power between 1951 and 1964. Over this time, the value of pensions increased and housing was built more quickly than before, while the Robbins report of 1963 expanded higher education (Page, 2011). Having said this, there were perturbations in political consensus. Iain MacLeod and Enoch Powell argued that welfare should be provided only on the basis of need (Macleod and Powell, 1952). They proposed a return to the means tests and principle of 'less eligibility' of the Poor Law. These economic and ideological arguments reflected a gradual growth in market ideology. Welfare was, however, ameliorative and seen to create opportunity rather than equality.

The key intellectuals advising on the British welfare state, unsurprisingly however, came from centre-left political backgrounds. Richard Titmuss, a social administration academic, argued that the laws of supply and demand could not operate in the health service and that there was no real freedom of choice because medicine was technical and turning doctors into entrepreneurs would break public trust. Anthony Crosland took a centrist view and while arguing for the mitigation of inequality he was not necessarily egalitarian, rather, he argued for a mixed economy that considered each person's different potential. T.H. Marshall had no formal Labour Party political ties but represented a social democratic approach. He analysed the role and function of the welfare state in promoting citizenship in the contemporary world. In the 1960s, Peter Townsend's 'rediscovery of poverty' added a new critique of the welfare state which warranted analysis from different political perspectives.

Similar approaches to social welfare and support were developing throughout Europe at this time; partly in a response to the war and seeking 'better times'. Welfare was necessary for restructuring, redevelopment and stability (Payne, 2005). Nordic countries set up the most comprehensive systems of welfare while Southern European states, especially Spain and Portugal, were slowed from creating welfare state initiatives by the Catholic church who thought this took away from individual and religious responsibility. Esping-Andersen (1990) is most closely associated with the critique of the welfare state in Europe. Others have later considered welfare state development in Asia (Aspalter, 2021b).

Until the consensus formally broke down in the 1970s, the welfare state was seen as a means of redressing economic power imbalances by giving equal social rights to all, which was seen as a mark of a civilised society. However, in 1969, Frank Field, the Child Poverty Action Group director, suggested that poverty had increased under Labour between 1964 and 1969, although, in fact, the figures were said to have been misinterpreted (Sullivan, 1996), and Abel-Smith and Townsend's (1965) 'rediscovery' of poverty raised questions about the efficacy of the welfare state. The Labour government at the time was promoting better economic performance and welfare improvements but was wrong-footed by a financial crisis.

Fiscal pressures rose after the first oil crisis of 1973 and increased welfare expenditure could not be sustained, especially in the light of demographic changes which entailed rising health needs, costs and pensions. These difficulties plagued the 1974–1979 Labour government. However, they did increase the value of pensions and benefits for long-term unemployed people and introduced the State Earnings Related Pension Scheme in 1975, which took the best 20 years of a person's earnings as a marker for pensions, mainly helping women and those who had breaks in their careers. Disability benefits were also introduced. In terms of housing, council house rents were frozen and there was greater protection for women experiencing domestic violence and homeless people. The scrapping of direct grants schools and the phasing out of pay beds in the NHS led, paradoxically, to a growth in private education and private medicine (Page, 2014). Poor economic performance throughout the period challenged the Keynesian economics that promoted public spending for economic growth. The first left-of-centre governments challenged by these changes, however, had no appetite to change or reduce public spending any further. Callaghan's government was the first Labour administration to respond to pressures arising from the quadrupling of oil prices (Fraser, 2017). By the end of the 1970s the need to take action was clear as a result of stagflation – high unemployment and high inflation. Rising unemployment, widespread strikes in public services and the 'winter of discontent' led to Thatcher's election in 1979 (Page, 2014).

Margaret Thatcher in the UK and Ronald Reagan in the US set a new course retreating from government involvement in state provision, suggesting that the welfare state was a cause of poor economic performance not a victim of it and that high taxes simply discouraged investment (Pierson, 1994). Fraser (2017) summarised contemporary criticism of the welfare state. Right-wing arguments were economic and moral. Disproportionate resource costs from a strong commitment to welfare undermined the economic performance of Britain. Welfare benefits reduced incentives to find work with some people better off on benefits than working. The over-generous welfare state, like the Poor Law before it, had demoralised people and created an underclass dependent on it, and increased benefit fraud. Press stories of abuse led to political criticism across the parties. The massive bureaucracy needed to administer and deliver the welfare state was unsustainable. While left-wing activists suggested the welfare state was not flexible enough to respond to changing patterns of social behaviour, such as the increase in divorce, single-parent families, the role of women and so on. Beveridge's uniform society no longer held sway (Pascall, 2012).

Rolling back the frontiers of the state: the New Right and welfare

Margaret Thatcher's coruscating criticism of the welfare state stated:

Welfare benefits, distributed with little or no consideration of their effects on behaviour encouraged illegitimacy, facilitating the breakdown of families, and replaced incentives favouring work and self-reliance with perverse encouragement for idleness and cheating. The final illusion – that state intervention would promote social harmony or solidarity or in Tory language, 'one nation' – collapsed in the 'winter of discontent' when the dead went unburied, critically ill patients were turned away from hospitals by pickets and the prevailing mood was one of snarling envy and motiveless hostility. To cure the British disease with socialism was like trying to cure leukaemia with leeches. … They had given up on socialism – the 30-year experiment had plainly failed and were ready to try something else. That sea change was our mandate. (Thatcher, 1993, p 8)

Thatcher saw her role as 'rolling back the frontiers of the state', reducing public expenditure, conquering inflation, reducing personal taxation, restoring incentives and addressing the perceived evils of the welfare state. She broke with Keynesian social democracy and pursued a monetarist ideology, promoted earlier by Milton Friedman and Friedrich Hayek, which championed individualism, entrepreneurialism and enterprise rather than state bureaucracy and provision.

Fiscal restraint was a painful necessity for some, but Margaret Thatcher saw retrenchment as an end in itself (Pierson, 1994). It was a social good that would assist in cutting inefficiencies and reducing the burden of high taxation. However, public welfare policies remained popular. The welfare state contributed to post-war society in economic and political terms, and offset market failures and prevented under-investment in the workforce by business. Despite the tough rhetoric of government, the reform process was slow and only gathered pace after Thatcher's third election victory in 1987 when unemployment was used as an economic tool to contain inflation.

In her first administration, Thatcher made important and symbolic changes. The 1980 budget reduced social security benefits and brought in other income reductions for poorer families. The 1982 Social Security and Housing Benefit Act removed earnings-related supplements to unemployment and sickness benefit; pensions were increased in line with prices rather than earnings. (In 1981 pensions were 23 per cent of average earnings but 15 per cent in 1995.) At the same time there were cuts in personal taxation and council homes were offered for sale to tenants. Unemployment rose from 3 per cent in 1974 to 12 per cent in the winter of 1982–1983, peaking at over three million, similar to in the depression of the 1930s.

These changes were a precursor to a more fundamental review of state welfare in the second administration carried out by Norman Fowler in 1984, who claimed he wanted to get back to Beveridge. The review was published in four Green Papers in 1986 and finally led to the 1986 Social Security Act. The Act aimed to simplify and rationalise a complex system of means-tested benefits. Such simplification appears thematically similar to the development of UC in the 21st century and to that undertaken with reform of the Old Poor Law. Family Income Supplement was replaced by

Family Credit, Income Support replaced Supplementary Benefit and the Social Fund changed from a grant to a loan. Fowler reduced guarantees and encouraged private pension schemes, which led to gross mis-selling of pensions and public resistance to saving for retirement. The ramifications of this are still being worked through (Pemberton, 2018). Fowler's review simplified administration and reduced the number of claimants, making some benefits easier to claim for young families and children. It did not reduce poverty but reduced social expenditure a little.

Thatcher's third administration, from 1987, was more radical, and included the privatisation of utilities, the introduction of the Poll Tax, the break up of state bureaucracies and privatisation in the public services. The 1988 Education Reform Act came about as a long-term consequence of a debate started in the 1970s. A ten-subject National Curriculum was introduced, including a range of tests at different ages. Local authority control over education was loosened, schools were allowed to opt out and polytechnics were removed from local authority control. This long process was sustained in the subsequent Major government with the creation of Ofsted and the introduction of education league tables.

The control over housing was weakened; tenants and districts could opt out and become part of Housing Action Trusts. The main provider of social housing became the Housing Associations rather than local authorities. The Griffiths report into community care needs, however, recommended that local authorities were ultimately responsible for care but should become enablers rather than providers (Griffiths, 1988). Community care heralded a mixed economy and partnership.

Thatcher was wary about tampering with the NHS because of the public affection for it and its universal application. There were concerns about waiting lists and the unequal geographical distribution of care. It was the largest corporate employer and yet, in her eyes, characterised by a producer culture and the inefficiencies of state bureaucracies. In 1983, Griffiths suggested improvements in management systems based on the private sector. The many vested interests, especially the BMA, just as with the introduction of the NHS almost 40 years earlier, resisted reform, leading the health secretary of the day, Nigel Lawson (1992, p 613), to state: 'The National Health Service is the closest the English have to religion, with those who practise in it regarding themselves as a priesthood. This made it extraordinarily difficult to reform.' Lawson's reforms tried to introduce consumer pressure to improve performance. The BMA again resisted. Kenneth Clarke carried through the reforms, accusing the BMA of always 'feeling for their wallets' when reform was discussed, not dissimilar to Bevan when creating the NHS in the 1940s.

The 1989 White Paper *Working for Patients* allowed Thatcher to claim the NHS is 'safe with us'. It reaffirmed commitment to it while introducing an internal market and purchaser/provider split. It was thought that competition could improve the service. Well-functioning hospitals would become independent as self-governing trusts, GPs would become fund-holders and purchasers. Funding was to follow the patients. Reform was difficult but the White Paper resulted in the NHS and Community Care Act 1990, with the reforms in the NHS coming in 1991 and those in community care being fully implemented in 1993. To the surprise of opposition politicians, 300 GP fund-holders came forward and 57 trusts were ready to begin, which led to dramatic changes in power relations in the NHS. The belief in strategic and operational management created many more managers, however, administration costs increased from 5 per cent to 12 per cent – 10,000 managers in 1986 and 26,000 in 1995.

By the time the reforms became operational John Major's government was in power. He continued the reforms by increasing consumerism through the Citizen's Charter 1991 and the NHS variant the Patient's Charter. These were reinforced by the White Paper *The Health of the Nation* (1991), which set targets for improvements in health standards and rates of disease reduction. The reforms led to concern for the outputs of the welfare state rather than financial inputs. Other changes in education, local authorities and community care led to performance indicators and league tables being introduced.

John Major won the 1992 election at a time when unemployment was growing again, public expenditure and the budget deficit were increasing. A new period of public expenditure retrenchment was necessary. Chief Secretary to the Treasury, Michael Portillo, targeted welfare dependency in a wide-ranging review of social security. There were 5.6 million people claiming Income Support in 1993, more than five times those claiming National Assistance in 1948. Benefit fraud and young single mothers became the target of the media, aiding the government's endeavours to reduce costs. Unemployment insurance was renamed Job Seeker's Allowance, which was means-tested after six months and dependent on the search for a job.

Retrenchment was limited, however (Pierson, 1994). Income inequality rose but the overall social expenditure maintained its share of Gross Domestic Product (GDP) and the components of the welfare state remained despite service and benefit cuts and tightened eligibility criteria. Housing programmes and unemployment insurance were constrained, state pensions were reformed. Systemic retrenchment did not happen. Thatcher's institutional reform aimed at undermining the welfare state was not effective. Pierson suggests this was because the past political context structures current operations and creates a resistance to wholesale reform. However, by 1997 the welfare state was more market-based, pluralistic and less state-controlled. The universalism of Beveridge was in retreat; the welfare state was a residual safety net, but it had survived. New Labour extended rather than reversed these reforms.

Communitarianism and the social contract: New Labour and welfare

After 18 years of Conservative government, New Labour was elected under Tony Blair's premiership in 1997. Blair built on market-led welfare reforms with a New Public Management approach of 'what works', partnership with the private sector, increased regulation of the public sector and 'empowerment' of those using services and welfare. Blair adopted a 'Third Way' between right-wing traditional pro-market approaches and left-wing traditional public ownership. Clause Four of the Labour Party constitution, which called for 'common ownership of the means of production, distribution and exchange', was repealed while private finance initiatives grew and the state was shrunk.

Citizenship under New Labour was increasingly predicated on an economic model in which the construction of active citizenship is associated with economic viability in terms of societal contribution. In Foucauldian terms, individuals making up societies are expected and expect to police themselves, to be responsible for their own actions and thoughts and, therefore, economic security and welfare (DiMaggio and Powell, 1983; Foucault, 1991). This requisite change is significant in distinguishing citizenship claims. Some of the background to this can be traced through Giddens' (1994, 1998) 'Third Way' taken from the applied sociology of Etzioni and communitarianism (Etzioni, 2003). The Third Way, which lay between old notions of collectivism and the individualised and global self, exerted great influence on Blair's New Labour project, stating that social problems cannot be left to either the market or the state alone but should be engaged with by a civil society that involves voluntary organisations and local communities in a mixed economy of provision that democratises the state and decentralises its power. Equality remained important for the cultivation of human potential, but opportunities for inclusion replaced redistribution, stemming from Putnam's (2000) work on social capital, itself drawn from Bourdieusian thought, and Sen's (1999) and Nussbaum's (2011) promotion of capabilities and capacity.

Greater self-reliance, as promoted by Margaret Thatcher, was endorsed by New Labour as important for the future of welfare, and people needed to be facilitated to take charge of their welfare. This involved a shift from the old welfare state model to a social investment state (Lister, 2004), that again began under the previous government. New Labour introduced a 'modernising' government seen almost immediately in social policy with Frank Dobson's 1998 White Paper *Modernising Social Services* detailing social care policy for the government. In respect of the NHS, Blair's government claimed removal of the internal market structures but increased and promoted patient choice and competition between providers and kept most of the internal market elements. Decreasing unemployment allowed for increases in health and education spending, the latter being crucial in social investment. Welfare reform was, however, a central part of the government including an element of compulsion and incentive.

The introduction of a National Minimum Wage in 1999 was designed to make work pay. Non-contributory Tax Credits were needed to supplement the National Minimum Wage and expenditure rose from £1 billion in 1999–2000 to £28 billion in 2010–2011. Other non-contributory benefits included Pension Credit and Winter Fuel Allowance and illustrated a shift from Beveridge, from universality to welfare policy based on the principle of tackling social exclusion. However, the Labour government also promoted devolution and decentralising to turn back some of the centralising tendencies of the previous Conservative administrations.

Welfare reform: the crash, the Coalition and the Conservatives

A global financial crash in 2008 led to decreased GDP, increased expenditure and actions on behalf of government to bolster the banks. At the same time a change in prime minister, from Tony Blair to Gordon Brown, seemed to exacerbate a mood for change. In 2010 the newly elected Coalition government quickly instituted austerity measures that included cuts and reform in welfare expenditure except for the NHS. As in the reform of the Old Poor Law in 1834, they argued that welfare expenditure takes too much of government expenditure, is too generous and leads to welfare dependency and that it is too extensive (Sealey, 2015). Reform and simplification of welfare benefits became the solution by removing Child Benefit for those earning over a certain income, setting a cap on benefits and moving towards greater conditionality through the Employment Support Allowance which built on the 1995 Jobseekers Act – a norm in contemporary politics (Pierson, 1994; Lansley, 2022).

Following a report by the Centre for Social Justice, 'Dynamic benefits' (2009), reform through a simplified system of UC found its way into statute in the Welfare Reform Act of 2012. The process of introducing it into welfare payments was slow and fraught with delays, while recipients faced increased hardships (Baumberg, 2016). In 2015, then Chancellor of the Exchequer, George Osborne, announced a £5 billion cut to UC in an attempt to further reduce expenditure.

The Brexit referendum vote in June 2016 was held in the context of austerity, with the European Union used as a scapegoat for the resulting hardships. Social welfare continued to be restricted, unemployment issues were blamed on migrant workers but not resolved although some unemployment fell, the NHS's spiralling costs were not offset by the vote for withdrawal and the crisis in employing social care staff grew. The election of Prime Minister Boris Johnson's government in December 2019 announced there would be no more austerity. The election coincided with the beginnings of the COVID-19 pandemic, which exacted a tremendous economic cost including a £20 a week uplift for those on UC, whose number rose significantly during that period (Patrick et al, 2022a). The uplift was withdrawn in October 2021, creating further hardships, although the taper was amended to allow claimants to keep more of their earnings. These changes in regulations reinforced the emphasis on employment (or being open to it) as a conditional prerequisite for desert. The long-awaited policy concerning health and social care provided little for social care and a melting pot for welfare policy and reform has been stirred for the decade and beyond (Pierson, 2021; Spicker, 2022).

Social welfare is at a crucial point in its development in Britain. Major demographic, political and global health care concerns abound. Society and the population are increasingly divided socially, politically and economically. The pathways social welfare may take are varied, but recognising our historical ambivalence towards it, towards those in need of it, and the repetitions in policy, practice and philosophy over the centuries may help us recognise, and policy makers negotiate, humane ways of delivering compassion and state responsibility for fellow human beings. The rest of the book explores and analyses specific examples of the complexities of social welfare in historical and contemporary times.

3

Philosophical binaries and normative judgements

In 2014, the prime minister at the time, David Cameron, set out a characterising claim for his government in a speech to the Relationships Alliance. He stated that the government was 'on the side of hard-working families in Britain' (Gov.UK, 2014). The claim created a clear division between people in need that he found acceptable and those that were not, thereby problematising those who were outside of families, out of work or might be construed as somehow workshy. While it raised, and continues to raise, many questions, the term 'hard-working families' has not been explained. This chapter examines the development and perpetuation of binary distinctions of such concepts as 'deserving and undeserving', 'skivers and strivers', and other judgemental views such as 'bogus claimants' or 'broken Britain'. Such binaries and pejorative terms reflect the normative positions adopted within popular approaches to social welfare. Moreover, these contemporary understandings, which are tacitly accepted as givens, are explored within their historical contexts and continuities across time are examined as a means of illuminating the ambivalent social psychology inherent in our relationship with social welfare policy, practice and with those who receive it. They are political weapons that create and reinforce opposition.

The chapter outlines Lévi-Strauss' position on binary distinctions, or more forcefully oppositions, and offers a critique of the normative positioning and power play that stem from these. The distinctions will be shown to underpin and influence the discourses and *habitus* of citizens. The critique will problematise binary thinking and the history of social welfare policies promoting and relying on such for their acceptance in wider society. Our period of analysis stems from the Elizabethan Poor Laws to contemporary times and, alongside the Poor Laws, considers gender relations, the amendments made to the Poor Law and 19th-century developments, the introduction of the welfare state and contemporary oppositional perspectives. Experiences of welfare practices in the Old Poor Laws (King, 2019; Jones and King, 2020); Dickens' association with the workhouse (Richardson, 2012); Mayhew's personal accounts of the Poor Law (Amendment) Act (Mayhew, 2005); Jack London's accounts of the East End of London at the turn of the 20th century (London, 1903); Hubble et al's (2019) examination of lives around the time of the introduction of the British welfare state; and O'Hara's (2020) consideration of the toxic language employed to describe and shame people in receipt of welfare evidence the ways in which they act to create discourses of undeservingness, reinforcing policy direction throughout history, from Edwin Chadwick to Lawrence Mead (1997) and Charles Murray (1990).

Binary opposition and distinction: developing normativity in social welfare

Binaries have been identified as a feature of linguistics that concern sense-making and understanding. This is explored in many areas such as ethnic meaning-making through the use of lexical antonyms such as black and white or developed and undeveloped (Batkalova, 2018). They do not just have linguistic application, however, and apply also to meaning-making in social life. They act as demarcations between what is valued and what is 'other' and to be disparaged. For instance, in simple terms the distinction between someone who receives welfare benefits and someone who does not seems, superficially, to be merely a socio-economic category. Linguistically, however, these distinctions may suggest deeper meanings and reflect underlying assumptions about the social value of protagonists in each category – the worthy and the unworthy. Using examples from their work with Indigenous groups in Malaysia, Ashencaen Crabtree et al (2018) and Parker et al (2019) identify the ways in which such oppositional binaries act to diminish those considered in need and underdeveloped by those who have the power to set the terms of the argument. This highlights important assumptive positions in which a negative aspect of the binary opposition is considered to convey less right or power to those defined by the binary, while increased power is accorded to the positive side. This power play underpins the tacit assumptions at work in attitudes towards social welfare.

The anthropologist Claude Lévi-Strauss developed a theory of binary opposites that help develop plot lines in a narrative by creating contrast. While neutral, these contrasts have often been imbued with values and can create stereotypes that perpetuate negative thinking about certain groups and so link with our excursus in social welfare. They also link with our understanding of discourse informing the practices of the included towards the excluded (Foucault, 1972), and *habitus* as employed by Bourdieu that underpin the perceptions people have of self and others in various social positions (see Chapter 1). We need first to consider Lévi-Strauss' structural anthropology and the concept of binary oppositions as a mode of analysis that we can use to understand the ambivalent views taken of social welfare.

The background to Lévi-Strauss' structural anthropology is diverse, being influenced by Durkheim's and Mauss' structural functionalist sociology, by the structural linguistics of de Saussure, Jakobson and Troubetzkoy, and by psychoanalytic and later Gestalt concepts (Clarke, 1978; Jeanpierre, 2010;

Wheater, 2017). Using the social activity of gift-giving, Lévi-Strauss (1958, 1973) describes a universal duality of binary oppositions that structure the social and cultural world – in this case, the giver and the receiver, which immediately lends itself to considering the power relations between those providing alms, charity or social welfare and those in need and receipt of the same. Gift-giving raises questions of entitlement, political and power play as seen in the anthropologies of Mauss (1967) and Malinowski (1984).

Binary oppositions are antagonistic pairs of abstract constructs that create social meaning (Erikson and Murphy, 2017). However, binary oppositions also operate in relation to one another at an unconscious level, rather like social discourses, and an unconscious meta-structure emerges through the relational pairing of opposites. Indeed, the binary oppositional concepts can only be understood in relation to one another. Take, for instance, the political use of the phrase 'hard-working families', employed by different political parties to describe those people who represent the focus of their attention and used in the introduction to this chapter. Marsh (2015) explores the use of this language as the hub of the Conservative Party's 2015 election campaign. Immediately, single people without families and those people out of work, including children, students, pensioners, and some sick and disabled people become stigmatised, marginalised and potentially 'othered' as opposites to the expected norm (O'Hara, 2020; Baumberg Geiger et al, 2021). This occurs in the mindset of citizens although the exact meaning of the phrase 'hard-working families' remains unclear. It only enjoys meaning with the listener when its opposites are identified.

In developing his cultural and structural anthropology, Lévi-Strauss indicated that the methods of analysis were to identify the binary distinctions underpinning social action and, thereby, giving meaning to that society or culture through practices in relation to those oppositions (Lévi-Strauss, 1973). This is recognised as problematic and difficult (Lizardo, 2010). Indeed, Derrida (1976) believed that because binary oppositions play with and refer to one another there can be no substantive meaning underlying the processes of distinction and therefore deeper deconstruction is necessary. However, if the relational processes between the binary oppositions are to be understood, Lévi-Strauss (1971) suggested they needed to be seen in relation to the whole system – the whole being greater than the sum of the parts, in Gestalt terms. If we consider this in respect of attitudes towards social welfare, we can see that concepts of the deserving and undeserving poor will act in relation to one another, and play off one another according to socio-historical and cultural settings, but need to be seen within the context of the overall social welfare policy system and, indeed, beyond as a reflection of societal mores. So, those in receipt of welfare services, and those delivering them, are associated with the broader meanings made of people who are seen as not quite part of or contributing to 'right' society or those not in receipt of benefits. Thus, welfare becomes a functional, ambivalent activity that is required for society to function and for civil and human compassion to be expressed but looked down on as it relates to people accorded a lesser worth in that society.

The relationship between binary oppositions is key to understanding what meanings are being expressed, and these relationships are mediated by social action as Erikson and Murphy (2017, p 86) indicate: 'In structuralism, binary oppositions are part of an integrated system of logically connected categories of meaning that structure social activity and the way that activity is conceptualized.' Thus, again, the social welfare system can be understood and described by the binary oppositions that structure its context. However, binary oppositions may also be much more nuanced than a simple or single distinction as, for example, indicated by studies of narratives of those with addictions or substance use problems (Moore et al, 2017). Herdin (2012) explains that typologies are often used to explain cultural differences, especially the individualism versus collectivism construct – one that is quite central to social policy debates. While these are Western concepts and limited in explanatory power they can form a useful part of more nuanced discussions and work well within the British context. Moore et al (2017) suggest that a binary opposition between those people with substance use problems and 'positive' attitudes towards health and well-being are much more complex than simple binary distinctions allow. Challenging ingrained ideas associated with 'good' and 'bad' oppositions and 'healthy' versus 'sick' lifestyles allow us to consider other ways of understanding and working with people with addictions, which is itself a contested term, or problematic substance use, another term imbued with moral judgement. This simple critique of language demonstrates the complex nuances of welfare work that should move beyond or dig deeper than binary relationships, but which often become enmeshed within them, creating the conditions in which prejudices and ambivalences can develop.

In respect of migration, Sparke (2018) argues that the concept of welcome complicates the binary distinction between citizenship and refugee in contemporary welfare, creating a liminal space in which the negativities of rejection of the other are contested. Kingori and Gerrets (2019) also see this in problematising the real/fake binary in respect of health practices, recognising that there is often an in-between or liminal messiness that must explore alternative narratives and critique the underlying discourses.

Earlier, we identified the important role of religious teaching in the development and provision of welfare and poverty relief. Taking just the Abrahamic religions – Judaism, Christianity and Islam – we see distinctions in wealth, that recognise binary oppositions between the rich and the poor, being acknowledged, but injunctions to help and support those in need as the following verses show:

There will always be some Israelites who are poor and in need, and so I command you to be generous to them. (Deuteronomy 15:1)

You will always have poor people with you, and any time you want to, you can help them. (Mark 14:7)

The true believers, both men and women, are friends to each other. They enjoin what is just and forbid what is evil; they attend to their prayers and pay the alms-tax and obey Allah and His Apostle (pbuh). (Holy Quran 9.71)

Thus, the religious approach to binary oppositions between rich and poor assumes a moral perspective that acts in favour of those who have rather than those who have not. That is to say, the poor are not necessarily demonised but play a central role in the moral enterprise of religious acts of doing good. Rather than rich and poor acting in primary relation to one another it is the charitable act or not that assumes the focus, although, of course, this is mediated by relationship. However, it is the poor who represent a function for the rich, or at least the 'non-poor', and in this those in poverty are constructed as 'Other' and remain second class. The non-poor in this case represent normative society or the religious, thus ensuring the deviance of the poor and poverty remains. At a social level, this creates significant meaning for the construction of social welfare as an ambivalent entity, both wanted and not wanted.

The history of social welfare and our attitudes to people in poverty and need, however, has been peppered with stark binary distinctions and evaluations of moral worth (Tihelková, 2015). Romano (2015, p 67) argues that 'the resurgence of a moralising drift in the welfare state and the new social representation of those undeservingly living on welfare – the Shirker – present all the elements of the past stereotypes of the undeserving poor'. Romano's stereotypes include being parasitic, criminally minded, fraudulent and substance-abusing, among others. These morally driven and infused binary oppositions allow differential treatment of groups who are outside normative social mores by developing internalised discourses of the poor and the demonised 'other' that become internalised. Jensen and Tyler's (2015) concept of 'benefit broods' echoes this derogatory politicised discourse. These stereotypes are also shown in O'Hara's (2020) excavation of the ingrained narrative of poverty that persists in focusing on the deficits of individuals and detracts attention from structural causes of welfare need. Quoting actor Jameela Jamal, O'Hara says:

In order to twist the narrative around all poor people, they'll find a picture of one young man smoking weed in a council flat and they'll use that image as the poster child for all poor people. I think there's a deliberate twisting of the story of poor people in order for the media to help the government justify not helping them: to make it seem like they don't want to help themselves. (O'Hara, 2020, p 175)

Thus Lévi-Strauss' work identified the social plot lines and characterisations of the poor, but we need, also, Foucault's understanding of discourse and practice and Derrida's emphasis on deconstruction to inform how these distinctions became embedded in social policy, practice and thought. We must also problematise the simple binary distinction and untangle its many nuances according to the complex diversities enjoined by those experiencing need or developing those policies that account for need in society. We will consider the distinctions and normative discourses underpinning the ways in which welfare is formed, enacted and considered through a series of historical times, events and welfare enactments. The core areas considered relate to the Tudor, Elizabethan and 'Old' Poor Laws, distinguishing between vagabonds and the impotent poor and how the 1834 Poor Law (Amendment) Act continued and added emphasis to the categories of deserving and undeserving, which were themselves reinforced by some of the key thinkers of the period. The initial developments of systematised welfare through the work of the Charity Organisation Society and Hospital Almoners, among others, continued the deserving/ undeserving binary while the concept of universalism under Beveridge ostensibly changed tack, although the hidden binaries of the non-eligible and the feckless remained. We shall conclude by exploring contemporary distinctions and pejorative media discourses.

Vagabonds, beggars and the impotent poor

Throughout British history there has been persistent discrimination between the deserving and underserving poor (Seabrook, 2013; Tihelková, 2015). In the Tudor and Elizabethan Poor Laws, the deserving poor were categorised as those unable to work, such as children, the sick and the old, whereas the undeserving were pejoratively described as rogues, vagabonds and beggars. We can see this in the legislation of the time.

From 1531 to the passing of the 1601 Elizabethan Poor Law there were seven pieces of legislation concerning the punishment of vagabonds, beggars or rogues – all of whom were considered to be 'underserving' and feckless. There were also seven pieces of legislation concerned with the relief of those poor or impotent individuals considered 'deserving' of help. Three of these Acts included both groups in their title and one focused on workfare, although many contained provision for those considered poor through no fault of their own (see Table 3.1) (Slack, 1990).

Table 3.1: Legislation for managing poverty, 1531–1598

Legislation for the undeserving poor	Legislation for the deserving poor	Combined legislation
Concerning Punishment of Beggars and Vagabonds, 1531	For the Provision and Relief of the Poor, 1552	For the Punishment of Vagabonds and Relief of the Poor and Impotent Persons, 1547
For Punishment of Beggars and Vagabonds, 1536	For the Relief of the Poor, 1555	For the Punishment of Vagabonds and Relief of the Poor and Impotent, 1572
Touching the Punishment of Vagabonds and Other Idle Persons, 1550	For the Relief of the Poor, 1563	For Setting of the Poor on Work, and for the Avoiding of Idleness, 1576
For the Punishment of Rogues, Vagabonds and Sturdy Beggars, 1598	For the Relief of the Poor, 1598	

Those considered poor by choice, the able-bodied but impoverished and/ or unemployed, were criminalised and attracted whippings, being returned to their places of birth, forced into labour, burned through the ear or gaoled (Seabrook, 2013). The impotent poor, on the other hand, were registered as such, beginning a process of social administration and regulation, demarcation and surveillance – bureaucratic distinction – that has continued over time. The latter were supported by taxes collected by overseers in each parish (Slack, 1990).

This moral distinction was construed in the 1601 Poor Law, as recognised in its reputation for harshness. However, the latter analysis has been questioned. The Poor Law of 1697 included provision for badging paupers – a clear example of repressive practices in respect of poor, needy and vulnerable people. However, its enforcement is open to question and, as Hindle (2004) notes, even Sydney and Beatrice Webb were unsure of its wide and consistent application. The Elizabethan Poor Laws are still seen by many as a beacon of benevolent welfare practice in the historical context in which they came into force (Thane, 2000).

Despite such revisionist histories, however, it is not difficult to see how even the impotent poor, those considered to be deserving of help, became demonised in similar ways to those deemed to be undeserving, creating a discourse that to be in need of welfare and poor relief was wrong. Being poor for whatever reason rendered that individual morally culpable and, therefore, to be avoided even if a compassionate approach to poor relief is, overtly, adopted. Given that poor relief relied on the collection of taxes or rates from others in the parish, it engendered anger and disdain towards the poor. There was no consideration of socio-political factors causing poverty; being poor was an individual failing.

Throughout the 17th and 18th centuries, and in response to various economic and political shifts, the 'poor' became increasingly identified as immoral and a burden on the public purse (Seabrook, 2013). The discourse of the 'idle poor' was used to characterise those in poverty who relied on dole or poor relief (Romano, 2015), as exemplified by Frederick Morton Eden's descriptions of the poor, such as:

> J.R. aged 17. His parents having neglected putting him to a trade, or bringing him up to a regular course of industry, he has contracted many loose and disorderly habits. Twice he has been put out to service, but was always turned off for ill behaviour. Decent people will not employ him; and he can neither be persuaded, nor forced, either to go to sea, or to enlist for a soldier. (1797, p 695)

This became embedded in public criticism of the Poor Laws for the next two centuries as calls for fundamental reform grew. While not necessarily based on binary oppositions, the tropes demarcating those in receipt of poor relief and those who were not formed distinct groupings, with the former attracting considerable opprobrium for their assumed voluntary idleness, pauperism and dangerousness to society. These views became entrenched in society and daily practices when considering such situations, whether actions were led by compassion or punishment.

Towards the end of the 17th century questions concerning the management of the poor were increasingly identified with discussion about trade and economics. Josiah Child, governor of the English East India Company, advocated the development of a national or at least provincial system of poor relief, which would allow people to be set to work in whatever region or parish they found themselves and thus paying for their relief (Child, 1690). Just over a decade later, in 1702, the economic strain on the country became even more pronounced when Queen Anne declared war on France. Not only was war intimately connected with poor relief and welfare on economic grounds, as we see in Chapter 5, but also in respect of fear of revolution and dangerousness arising from want.

As part of continuing deliberations concerning poor relief, which as Slack (1990) points out also included discussion of the collection of the parish rate as well as the national economy, increasing debate of institutional approaches to addressing the need for poor relief became evident. The Tory Member of Parliament, Sir Humphrey Mackworth, presented a bill to parliament that proposed the establishment of public workhouses dedicated to manufacture in every parish so as to reduce the costs of poor relief (Mackworth, 1704). The writer Daniel Defoe opposed this in his pamphlet *Giving Alms no Charity* (Defoe, 1704) on the grounds that this would stifle internal trade and that public workhouses would lead to an increase in the numbers of the poor because each region had developed its own divisions of labour to support local economies.

Defoe was a proponent of natural law in poor relief, something taken up in the following century by the Rev Thomas Malthus. He suggested that the generosity of the Poor Law undermined incentives to find work and he suggested there was plenty of work around if people were to look for it (Persky, 1997; Hayashi, 2010). Defoe identified four key maxims in his pamphlet:

1. There is in England more labour than hands to perform it, and consequently a want of people, not of employment.
2. No man in England, of sound limbs and senses, can be poor meerly for want of work.
3. All our work-houses, corporations and charities for employing the poor, and setting them to work, as now they are employ'd, or any Acts of Parliament to empower overseers of parishes, or parishes themselves, to employ the poor, except as shall be hereafter excepted, are, and will be publick nusances, mischiefs to the nation which serve to the ruin of families, and the encrease of the poor.
4. That 'tis a regulation of the poor that is wanted in England, not a setting them to work. (Defoe, 1704, np)

Defoe's thinking resonated with those seeking greater regulation and control of people alongside blame for a predicament believed to be personally inflicted and outside of governmental control. It also showed the ways in which underlying binaries create meanings that become accepted as self-evident. Poverty was a moral issue and voluntary idleness, as poverty was considered to be, was something that the individuals concerned needed to address in their lives. The economic aspect of poverty, and its association with ability, employment or searching for it as a prerequisite for deserved assistance, was embedded in the political and policy psyche. That such an understanding necessarily rendered those not earning, searching for work and so forth as non-people or dependent was not considered. Legislation continued to demonstrate oppositional thinking about the poor.

Deserving and undeserving Victorians

The crucible of 19th-century amendments to and implementation of the Poor Law shows the focus of the moral economy of poverty as demonising the poor and needy in society. It is more complex than a simple binary opposition will allow, however. The development of social action, political economy and sociological thinking also developed alongside notions of moral culpability as can be seen in the literature of Charles Dickens, Benjamin

Disraeli, Harriet Martineau and Jack London, and in the rising importance of the social surveys and poverty maps from Jeremy Bentham to Henry Mayhew, Charles Booth and Seebohm Rowntree.

There is a wealth of literature concerning the tropes of deservingness and undeservingness and shame associated with poverty (Sen, 1983). Piven and Cloward's (1993) work identified the political uses of the Poor Law in terms of regulating the populace, reducing discontent and ensuring that vested interests remained unchallenged. The concepts of deservingness and undeservingness were important in dividing the needy, creating a subdued and grateful class alongside a punished element considered, because of asocial actions or characteristics, to be morally feckless. The families of the latter were also deemed to be defective. The development of such binary thinking ensured the continuation and functioning of society, and while political action grew, the discourses of moral deservingness became ingrained in the minds of all. Thus it became easy to develop legislation, policy and practices that discriminated against those in need or receipt of poor relief. It would have been strange if it had not because the immediacy of blame and opprobrium allowed the more fortunate to justify and value their privileged positions but also to fear its loss.

The Poor Law (Amendment) Act 1834 was built on the principle of 'less eligibility', making a stark division between those who needed Poor Law support and those who did not. The moral opprobrium accorded to claimants resulted in harsh treatment as a means of controlling those considered to be responsible for their own misfortune. As Englander (1998, p 12) states: 'The assumption behind the redefined poor law principles was that poverty was a voluntary and therefore reversible condition. The pauper was not so much the victim as the perpetrator of his own distress. Poverty, the commissioners insisted, arose from "fraud, indolence or improvidence".' Regardless of the distinction between the able-bodied poor and the infirm, sick, older people and orphans in the Royal Commission and in the amended Poor Laws, treatment was often similar, leading to the assumed homogenisation of Poor Law claimants.

In Chapter 7, we show how these assumptions allowed for the sacrificing of the poor, needy and vulnerable to maintain moral righteousness and set oneself apart from the undeserving. However, the discourse and mindset created by the concept of less eligibility led to those receiving Poor Law assistance being considered and treated as different, other and morally culpable for their situation. No acknowledgement was made of the socio-economic, structural and political reasons for poverty; rather it was the result of individual fault. These perspectives have continued to dominate discussion and serve to excuse governments from addressing expensive structural problems relating to social justice, which in turn reinforces the ambivalence with which the general public approach social welfare and its recipients. Fear of the Poor

Law, or rather requiring its assistance, remained throughout the 19th century and into the 20th century, even after the boards of guardians ceased to exist in 1930 (Brundage, 2002). This powerful *habitus* acted as a means of structuring the changes wrought as former guardians often moved to public assistance committees and those of county and county boroughs, bringing their perspectives and dispositions to their new roles: 'relief applicants were still scrutinized closely according to the hated household means test. An inquisition into all the resources of family members and lodgers to determine eligibility and amount of relief, the means test represented to the poor the continuation of the poor law' (Brundage, 2002, p 152).

It was not just in state-funded poor relief that these attitudes held sway. The assessment criteria of the Charity Organisation Society and the underpinnings of the Settlement Movement were firmly entrenched in a moral sensibility of self-responsibility and hard work as being inimical characteristics of the deserving poor. Later political calls for changes in legislation continued to emphasise paid labour as a moral goal and as a way for individuals to escape poverty, something that continues to underpin welfare initiatives today, as seen in the taper in Universal Credit.

Despite these ingrained dispositions the appetite for changes in practice was rife, aided by the increased role played by the state in providing social security and pensions from the early 20th century, the rise of the Labour Party, the depression and finally the Second World War.

Universalism?

A shift from the oppositional discourses constructed through the Poor Laws appears evident in the public clamour for their dissolution and for greater equality, given people's experiences of quality of provision during the war and Beveridge's 1942 report on social insurance, which, on the surface, promoted universal entitlement at the point of need, was widely welcomed. Of course, being based on social insurance, that universality was limited to those in paid employment and their dependents, and, as a result, was gendered in its structure, favouring the 'male breadwinner'. When we consider the development of British social welfare in particular we look to Christianity's influence on charity and welfare, although all the Abrahamic religions reveal gendered approaches. These will be dealt with in more detail in Chapter 6. However, it is important to note the continuation of underlying patriarchal assumptions pertaining to gender roles that influence the development of welfare, and thereby the distinct treatment of males and females as welfare claimants and recipients, and their differential eligibility. This permeated Charles Murray's 'underclass' thesis and was taken up by British politicians on the right and left of the political spectrum (Murray, 1990, 2013; Jones, 2012).

In Beveridge's reforms, the need remained for a means-tested element of assistance to account for those who were not eligible for help in other ways. However, the welfare state resulting from his report changed the established *habitus*, based on binary and pejorative distinctions, to a discourse of citizen entitlement (see Marshall, 1949/1992). Universal entitlements represent a different discourse based on equality of experience, opportunity and state benefit. The discrimination between rich and poor is removed and entitlement is based on aspects of belonging and being part of something. The fact that universality under the welfare state was partial does not detract from it as an underpinning concept or discourse that has continued to inform discussion and policy formation (see Chapter 8).

During the post-war welfare consensus the pejorative stereotypes associated with 'underserving' welfare claimants were lessened, perhaps based on the more equal experiences of people during the war years (Harris, 2004; Fraser, 2017). However, as the fragile consensus on the welfare state began to wane, the concept of the 'scrounger' and 'fraudster' reappeared during the oil crisis and later financial crisis in Britain in the 1970s. These financial pressures led to austerity measures being demanded by James Callaghan's Labour government in 1976 as a prerequisite to securing a loan from the International Monetary Fund (Romano, 2015). The continuing crisis led to the rise and eventual election of Margaret Thatcher with her monetarist New Right thinking drawing on the economic analyses of Milton Friedman in the US and Austrian–British Friedrich Hayek. Marketised approaches to public policy and economics, characterised by inequalities, have continued through New Labour to the present day. The return to pejorative binaries has been attractive as a means of justifying retrenchment on state involvement in welfare provision, harsher treatment and as a means of diverting attention from state responsibilities towards those in need. Once again individuals become responsible for their own situations and self-responsibility replaces collective concern.

Populist discourses in the contemporary world

Allied with the economic downturn following the 2008 fiscal crisis, and associated with the shift from welfare to workfare that had taken place some years earlier (Bambra and Smith, 2010), the stigmatisation of the unemployed 'other' or benefit claimant as 'shirker' grew (Romano, 2015; Tihelková, 2015). The distinction here concerned those who 'chose' not to work and were economically irresponsible and now included those who were on long-term sick (Bambra and Smith, 2010; Romano, 2015). Bambra and Smith explore how the change from Incapacity Benefit to Employment Support Allowance demonstrates a change from welfare support to economic viability and employment and could be used to demonise another group of welfare recipients. The rise of John Stuart Mill's concept of *homo economicus*, in his 1836 definition of political economy, has been established through the ubiquity of pejorative binaries relating to welfare claimants, alongside the discourses or dispositions associated with them (Veasey and Parker, 2021). Indeed, economic activity in society is a central discursive element integral to ways in which people are seen and Mill (1836, in Robson, 1965, p 321) clearly attests to the ambivalences of wealth, leisure and poverty, saying that political economy 'makes entire abstraction of every other human passion or motive; except those which may be regarded as perpetually agonising to the desire of wealth, namely, aversion to labour, and desire of the present enjoyment of costly indulgences'.

Such ambivalence exposes binary distinctions between deserving and undeserving as the products of a disquiet mind which requires a scapegoat to assuage its guilt (see Chapter 7). Garthwaite (2011) charts the use of terms such as 'shirker' and 'scrounger' to describe people who were ill or disabled and claiming benefits. This takes the discourse further and reflects a change from compassion towards those often considered 'deserving' to blame, and, as we saw in the New Poor Law, homogenising all who are in receipt of welfare benefits.

Although the press has had historical influence, the shift in the modern age has been driven, to a large extent, by the British media who have the power to shape discourses and debates through the portrayal of poverty, welfare and the recipient (Baumberg et al, 2012; Lugo-Ocando and Harkins, 2015). Media is ubiquitous and accessible across many different platforms. Chauhan and Foster (2014) recognised the discourses of poverty developing in newsprint media in their study of representations of domestic and non-UK poverty, seeing internal, domestic poverty as relating to vulnerable groups and their characteristics rather than socio-economic causes and non-UK representations as concerning socio-economic inefficiencies, both of which serve to distance readers from the 'other in poverty'. This analysis serves to entrench readers' reactions and allow distance and negative images to surface while removing responsibility to fully address social issues from governments because poverty, vulnerability and need are seen as individual rather than societal failures.

Tihelková (2015) uses frame theories to explain the rise of undeservingness discourses in the right-wing British press. Claimants are referred to as feckless, anti-social and living in a something-for-nothing culture whereas the more progressive press tend to refute the labels of undeservingness and consider structural explanations of poverty. One unfortunate consequence is that the type of media position read by people is likely to be the one they most agree with and, therefore, debate does not take place and readers are not exposed to alternative views. The binary distinction between the deserving and undeserving has been fairly persistent but has made a forceful comeback since the 2008 financial crisis and the introduction of austerity measures by David Cameron's Coalition government in 2010. It draws upon a critical distinction between individual perspectives of failure, portrayed in the press by episodic events describing moral fecklessness and self-responsibility for one's situation, and structural, thematic approaches that challenge these tropes. 'Hard-working families' are pitted against 'shirkers' in a moral cock-pit that allows division to grow and for the so-called feckless to be demonised (Hudson et al, 2017). This, in turn, allows government to apportion blame, to deflect attention from structural causes that are expensive to address and to focus on the rights or moral entitlements of those who agree with their analysis.

The continuity of the political exploitation of these binary oppositions was seen in Sims-Schouten et al's (2019) study comparing a sample of children in Children's Society care between 1881 and 1918 and a contemporary sample of children. They found that the binary distinction between deserving and undeserving was evident in both groups and was used to justify not being able to meet needs. Children who had complex needs, mental health problems and behavioural issues attracted labels of blame, responsibility for their own predicament and therefore were undeserving. Tarrant (2021) noted similar distinctions between 'good' and 'bad' fathers that she believes underpin the ambivalent expectations of men in society and as fathers. She draws attention to the moral political discourses concerning 'absent' fathers and 'involved' fathers. The ambivalence is heightened when considering Griffin's (2020) historical portrayal of the good 'breadwinner' figure. As Tarrant highlights, the breadwinner must often be absent, yet the good 'involved' father's earning capacity may be reduced as a result of that involvement in his family. In low-income, single-mother families fathers are denigrated as causing the social problems experienced by that family and by others in society.

Such analyses are not confined to Britain alone, however, as can be seen by the *Faulheitsdebatte* (laziness debate) in Germany. According to Oschmiansky et al (2001), the tropes of idleness, being workshy and lazy are used at times of election to garner support. These right-wing positions are assumed to attract popular backing because those in receipt of welfare benefit and support are still considered to be individual responsible for their predicament and to represent a drain on the 'hard earned' monies of those in employment or with means (Parker and Frampton, 2020).

Similar to Tihelková's (2015) use of frame theories, welfare reform in Denmark has been analysed to demonstrate that the political use of the media framing of welfare recipients as 'underserving' assists politicians in making the reduction of benefits more acceptable (Slothus, 2007; Esmark and Schoop, 2017; and, in the United States, by Reid, 2013). Whereas young refugees in Sweden appear to be cast into a developing discourse in which the young people create narratives of their own deservingness as hard-working, responsible and diligent as the deservingness/undeservingness trope, also recognised in Britain (Sales, 2002), has moved to one of 'threat' and danger (Wernesjö, 2020). Using vignettes, Kootstra (2016) compared a sample of 5,000 British respondents and 4,000 from the Netherlands to examine the impact of ethnicity and migration status on people's concept of deservingness, finding that recent migration, failure to look for work or a short work history was related to negative attitudes towards welfare benefit claimants. Similar negativity was found in Corrigan's (2009) study of social citizenship in Britain and Ireland and confirmed by Devereux and Power (2019).

Conclusions

An analysis using Lévi-Strauss' concept of binary distinctions identifies a relational pairing of deserving and undeserving people. In turn, this creates social discourse structures that describe and define a society in which the hated and demonised 'other' carries the sins of that society – moral fecklessness, being workshy, taking from the deserving and so on. The benefit claimant can, therefore, be sacrificed as a result (see Chapter 7). Social discourses of the poor and their deserving/undeserving statuses are constructed through relations between oppositional binaries which construct underpinning assumptions that become part of popular common-sense and deflect attention from structural issues, returning, instead, to individual causes and blame. The welfare practices that result separate the worthy and unworthy and apportion discriminate treatment that assume moral worth.

The 2019 Conservative Party manifesto continued to construct such distinctions, albeit through omission: 'We will help people and families throughout their lives by bringing down the cost of living and making sure that work always pays' (p 7).

The focus on work, in the manifesto, including the idea that benefits build 'a clearer pathway from welfare into work' (p 17), excludes those who cannot work or do not work for whatever reasons and in doing so construct a system of valued and de-valued citizens. Acceptance of this in the common psyche allows governments of all political hues to create a problem focus and to deflect attention from more complex and nuanced understandings. Somewhat ambivalently, this mindset may have allowed the 'better off' in society to provide charity and to build personal salvation through their works – an agonistic rather than antagonistic consequence!

4

Chocolate, flowers and social welfare reform

Social welfare's complex rationales and development has been intertwined with state, religious and voluntary effort throughout its history, as introduced in Chapter 2. This chapter builds on that multifaceted base and examines the centrality of religion-inspired and humanistic philanthropy and voluntarism in the development of social welfare and its continuation within contemporary policy and practices. These broad drivers represent a means of addressing the twin goals of economic productivity and human compassion; integral parts of a complex and twisted double helix in the historical development of social welfare in Britain that developed alongside social administration, policy and state provision. Voluntarism is associated with both collaboration and collective actions as well as a means of regulation and moral control across social strata. Our excursus shows that the goals of welfare are not always singular in purpose nor are they always clear. They are messy and complex, exposing some of the ambivalence associated with human support and social welfare.

In the context of Elizabethan Poor Law and Poor Law reform in the 19th century, we will consider the work of some key philanthropic characters in the development of social welfare including the chocolatiers the Frys in Bristol, Cadburys in Birmingham and the Rowntrees in York, and those businesses involved in the development of garden cities, such as James Reckitt in Hull and the Lever brothers at Port Sunlight on the Wirral in Cheshire. The context will also acknowledge the changing political landscape of the 19th century in which calls for factory and labour reform, health improvements, education and increased enfranchisement began to grow in strength as the agrarian landscape morphed into industrial conurbations and social need correspondingly increased. Alongside these changes, charitable bodies concerned for the moral welfare of individuals, often religiously inspired, methodical and formal in outlook, also secured traction in the panoply of welfare provision, the most renowned of these for the development of the personal social services being the Charitable Organisation Society founded in 1869. Towards the end of the 19th and early 20th centuries, and inextricably connected with concomitant socio-political change, came the beginnings of systematic and applied sociology taking shape through the survey work of Seebohm Rowntree and Charles Booth. The development of surveys as a means of understanding and/or seeking change started much earlier with calls for national administrative surveys to monitor need and expenditure by MP Thomas Gilbert at the end of the 18th century in the so-called Gilbert Act of 1782, and enacted in Glasgow in the early 19th century through the work of Thomas Chalmers in assessing need, encouraging self-help and referring people on for further assistance (Woodroofe, 1962; Payne, 2005; Prochaska, 2006). The chapter will also highlight the, sometimes uncomfortable, connections between economy and welfare, especially where the chocolate trade was built on the sugar cane and cocoa industry serviced originally by slaves. Additionally, we also need to bear in mind that much of the modern chocolate industry also relies on modern slavery for its production and thus demands another side of welfare for those involved in its production.

Philanthropy was not obviated by the introduction of state welfare and the initial optimism of universality introduced after the Second World War, but still abounds today (Bekkers and Wiepking, 2011; Buchholtz and Brown, 2012; McGoey, 2016; Vallely, 2020). Indeed, the architect of the welfare state, William Beveridge, assumed that individuals and communities would remain involved in social service even when welfare was provided universally. Aspects of individual volunteerism among the general populace have characterised many elements of welfare and continue to do so, in the contribution of European neo-philanthropists such as Bob Geldof and Bono or through the Bill & Melinda Gates Foundation in the US (Breeze, 2005; Warden, 2021). Political calls for involvement in 'charitable' or 'good neighbourly' works may also represent a paradoxical desire to help and assist people at local and community levels while deflecting attention from governmental responsibilities or entrenching political popularity, as can be seen in David Owen's 'Good Neighbour Scheme' in the 1970s and Jesse Norman, Paul Blond and David Cameron's promotion of the 'Big Society' in the second decade of the 21st century (Hansard, 1976; Cameron, 2009; Blond, 2010; Norman, 2010). However, the determination to act on behalf of others also represents part of the human condition, the compassionate drive. These counterbalancing aspects of voluntarism expose the ambivalences inherent in our approaches to social welfare.

Charity, philanthropy and civil society

Histories of social welfare, personal social services and the British welfare state focus predominately on the legislative, political and economic changes and rationales for developing state-led or state-supported approaches to welfare policy and practice. In short, they focus on the evolution of the British welfare state (Harris, 2004; Fraser, 2017; Timmins, 2017). However, the history of modern welfare development is, as we have seen, more complicated and also includes the philanthropic activities of industrialists and capitalists, mainly in the 19th century, but also into the 20th century, seeking to improve the lives and conditions of their workers. While the underlying reasons for philanthropic actions are multifaceted and complex, deriving partly from concerns to maximise profit and sustainable production by ensuring the workforce is fit and able to undertake their tasks, there was also a humane and genuine compassion for fellow human beings in their actions (Jeremy, 1991). The work of these philanthropists has influenced community development initiatives, youth work programmes, and third sector activities as well as formal activities in the personal social services, community and care sectors, such as community need planning, youth offending programmes and so forth. Philanthropic and charitable activities certainly influenced the development of the welfare state whether or not one posits a teleological relationship between them, but they also continue today alongside state-provided and formal welfare provision. They represent a touchstone for those wanting to reduce state intervention and expenditure as was seen in David Cameron's government's calls for a 'Big Society' in the 21st century (Blond, 2010; Norman, 2010; Bochel, 2011). They have also underpinned aspects of a society that continues to be distrustful of centralised involvement in private life and supportive of individual charitable effort, perhaps as a reflection of individual self-responsibility expected of people (Prochaska, 2006). Moreover, they form part of a more radical critique from the political left dissatisfied with state welfare and its residual function (Bochel, 2020).

Gorsky (1999) employs Beveridge's (1948) definition of volunteerism or voluntary action, that it represents private actions that are not directed by state or other authoritative bodies, and involves philanthropic organisations, mutual societies and endowed charities alongside individual effort. Envisaging philanthropic effort as a stage in a linear development on the way to state welfare has been critiqued and 'deteleologised'. It is rather a 'moving frontier' in an ongoing interplay between state, market, volunteerism and family (Finlayson, 1990; Daunton, 1996).

Functionalist and class-based analyses have located philanthropy in class conflict and power relations to maintain the social order (Jordan, 1959; Owen, 1964; Forster, 1974; McCann, 1977; Thompson, 1991; McGoey, 2016; Vallely, 2020). While Gorsky (1999) suggests that the employment of sociological and anthropological studies of gift-giving chart a shift towards principles of reciprocity he also recognises that the ritual element involved represents a means of asserting authority and re-establishing social relations based on differentiation and gratitude (see Kropotkin, 1902/2021; Mauss, 1967; Vallely, 2020). We may understand this ritualised aspect in respect of state welfare as a form of social contract that demands gratitude and structures power relations to maintain the status quo, something that McGoey (2016) critiques in respect of the Gates Foundation.

The terms philanthropy and charity are used in multiple ways which perhaps reflect some of the ambiguities associated with them. Concepts of differentiation, distinct evaluations of groups based on underpinning notions of giver and recipient, and elements of trust influence the ways in which gift, giver, receipt and receiver are perceived, making philanthropy, volunteerism and charity ambivalent concepts that attract praise and opprobrium in equal amounts. For instance, working-class involvement in voluntary action showed a degree of social consensus but also entrenched normative social power and control (Vallely, 2020). As we saw in Chapter 2, Singer's (2005) example of soup kitchen provision ('*imaret*) shows how Ottoman power and loyalty to the Sultan was enhanced by the daily act of giving food to the poor. A further example demonstrating monarchic power and control in a British context is seen in the ritualised giving of Maundy Thursday monies to the poor. Such ancient and ingrained rituals portray ludic elements of our ambivalent relationship to social welfare. On the one hand, we recognise and laud the beneficence of the giver and yet, on the other, we see the recipient of that charity as being less worthy or even tainted by the necessity of reliance on such actions. It also involves belonging, being beholden and indebtedness. The game that we engage in through these ambivalent weightings not only allows the status quo to continue but further entrenches societal acceptance of inequalities and, thereby, the need for a disparate range of social welfare provisions.

As noted, the focus on voluntarism, at an everyday individual level, and its philanthropic counterpart as a role of the wealthy, has increased again since the introduction of austerity measures in 2010 and further enhanced in 2015 when state expenditure has been further reduced while welfare needs have grown. Briggs and Foord (2017), for instance, argue that food banks have assumed an unquestioned and central place in social welfare but represent a welfare underpinned by rising conditionality, sanctions and a distrust of financial welfare claims (see Veasey and Parker, 2021). For Briggs and Foord, the food bank can also act as a challenge to those neoliberal discourses that privilege the roll-back of state intervention in favour of civic and individual responsibilities when the suffering of citizens, including nurses and teachers and not only the traditional poor, is brought into sharp relief (Harris, 2021). However, the moral, ideological and practical discourses illustrated in these conflicting approaches to voluntarism betray ambivalences in the public mind of the need for welfare and the welfare claimant, and render less problematic, to this way of thinking, the religious, moral and voluntary aspects of it (see Jawad, 2012).

Social status and prestige are important for assuming and maintaining power and control in society. Warwick-Booth (2019, p 45) reinforces the point that such authority and influence can be gained from 'charitable giving, philanthropic endeavours and the "presentation of gifts"' (see also

Prochaska, 2006). The ambiguous rationale for, or function of, 'gift-giving' is well recognised as noted earlier (Mauss, 1967), and it illuminates the complex relationship between doing 'good works' and exerting control over the social world. For instance, the philanthropic associations connected with the Rothschild Buildings in the East End of London in the late 19th century inspired Jewish and Christian women and impoverished people in the community to operate a range of support, including feeding the hungry, caring for the sick, providing education and child care. Caroline Colman, wife of the Liberal MP James Colman, who owned the Colman's Mustard Carrow Works in Norwich, set up schools, technical classes, sewing and cooking classes, and Sunday schools, alongside supporting a local hospital, distributing food hampers at Christmas, operating a lending library, sick benefits, clothing clubs and almshouses for pensioners. Prochaska (2006, p 23) stated that these activities demonstrated '[a] shrewd and effective combination of charity and sound business, which in the nineteenth century were so often intertwined. Mrs Colman's aim was "to raise the moral as well as the commercial standing of the company"'.

The religious foundations of philanthropic social welfare have long been recognised (Jordan, 1960; Heasman, 1965). It is generally recognised that the link between religion and the state endured longer in Catholic countries where involvement of the state was reduced until recently (Payne, 2005). However, Prochaska (2006) sees religion and public works as inextricably linked, even claiming that the 'elevation of works' (p 7) derived from the adoption of non-conformist theologies, the growth of individual responsibility and dislike of governance intervention in private life. This Weberian approach indicates that religiosity and charitable giving were both important in the development of the more formal structures of social welfare:

> In centralized welfare states, it is easy to forget that a nation's political condition depends to a large extent on the creative chaos of its associational life, on the myriad actions, typically unexceptional and little publicized, undertaken in local communities by self-governing churches, charities, mutual aid societies, clubs, and other institutions that operate outside the state. (Prochaska, 2006, p 9)

The principle of subsidiarity that has developed in German welfare provision encourages individuals and small organisations to do what they can before looking towards wider state help (Frampton, 2019). For example, the Catholic welfare agency Caritas undertakes welfare work that the state contracts out to it as part of the wider social protection and social services system.

Woodroofe (1962), in contrast to Prochaska, saw the expansion of 18th-century philanthropy as the result of minimal state provision, recognising that philanthropy and voluntarism gradually receded throughout the 19th century as state aid and intervention grew. She argued that the importance of philanthropy, by the politically and economically powerful, was seen in its fragmentation, as this could be used as a buffer against collectivism and democratic change, which were feared and associated with communistic thought and revolution. Although more complex than Woodroofe's binary and linear approach appears, the principle of welfare as a means of offsetting revolution or social unrest has permeated the histories of welfare policy and practice (see Chapter 5). There is certainly an unspoken class-based discourse that informs the consideration of and support for voluntarism. Moreover, Tait (1995) argued that voluntarism and philanthropy acted to promote an 'all-in-it-together' mentality, something that still continues to influence social sensibilities in an attempt to contain pressures for more radical change. This 'all-in-it-together' trope was seen in the British government's response to the 2020 COVID-19 pandemic, which failed to acknowledge the different ethnicities, health statuses, living conditions, levels of resources and needs of people. Even the requirements of a national lockdown had differential effects on people claiming benefits, on low income or with emerging needs (Parker and Veasey, 2021). Again, it suggests why our relationship with social welfare continues to rest in ambivalence in Britain, where suspicion of state involvement in private lives is rife and infuses the thoughts of those who would most benefit from increased state pensions, for example. In this way class control and the balance of power relations in favour of the rich and powerful remains.

Chocolate, flowers and key philanthropic families

At first glance it may be assumed a somewhat trite conceit to link chocolate, flowers and welfare. If you search 'chocolate' AND 'welfare' on the Internet you are likely to come up with links to rabbit welfare through chocolate (Make Mine Chocolate, nd), especially at Easter, or links to the nutritional value of chocolate and its health benefits (Lomax, 2017). However, the long legacy left by philanthropic Quaker business families who created Britain's chocolate industry is still to be seen, for instance, in the development of a garden city in Bournville for the Cadbury workers. It is not only the Cadburys' concern for their workers that links chocolate and welfare, but includes the Frys' campaign for prison reform, especially for women in prison, for nurse education and improved social conditions; and also Seebohm Rowntree's concerns for the hardships experienced by workers' families in York and the development, alongside Charles Booth in London, of the social survey, used as a political tool to highlight the plight of people in poverty. And yet, the positive aspects of charitable giving and human compassion through the chocolate industry are tempered by the colonial and exploitative contexts in which the trade is set. Robertson (2009, p 7) puts this well: 'Perceptions of Rowntree and the other Quaker chocolate firms of Terry's, Cadbury and Fry as "enlightened", "model firms" may be held in tension with the imperial and colonial origin of key factors of production such as sugar and cocoa.'

When we consider flowers, we extend the boundaries of philanthropic reach to include the development of spaces, worker well-being and the creation of garden cities. In Cadbury's case this was associated with chocolate and the development of Bournville, whereas in Kingston-upon-Hull, James Reckitt's garden village was developed around the area of Reckitt's pharmaceutical and household product industry after workers and their families were found living in insalubrious accommodation. Again, a Quaker approach drove this philanthropy. The Lever brothers in Cheshire took non-conformist, but not Quaker, religiously inspired philanthropy into their soap business in developing Port Sunlight on the Wirral (Jeremy, 1991; Macqueen, 2005; Rees, 2012). These improvements to social conditions often came with religious, social and behavioural requirements, which echo contemporary critiques of power and social control through philanthropy (McGoey, 2016; Vallely, 2020), but were no less genuinely inspired (Macqueen, 2005).

The story of chocolate is shrouded in the prehistory of the Americas, reflecting the colonial and imperialist legacy that pervades our histories in the West. In Coe and Coe's (2013) history of chocolate there is an important focus on the symbolic association between chocolate and human blood. While this coupling goes back to the Maya and Aztec people, as can be seen from the Madrid Codex which depicts the Mayan gods piercing their ears to spill blood over the cacao pods, the European story is associated with brutal colonisation, slave labour and exploitation – profit through the shedding of blood (Robertson, 2009). The mistreatment of cacao workers was recognised in the 16th century when 1537 Pope Paul II Farnese published *Sublima Deus*, a papal bull, to excommunicate anyone enslaving the Indigenous people of South America, while excluding Black slaves. However, as Coe and Coe indicate, the institution of *encomienda*, a kind of indentured service, secured the continuation of forced labour for the *encomenderos*, if they ensured that the Indigenous peoples converted to Christianity. It seemed that religion could be used to defend the exploitative behaviour of the colonising powers.

The rising popularity of chocolate across Europe ensured the trade grew. This burgeoning commerce was serviced by Black African slave labour with slave ships from Spain, Portugal, France, Holland, Denmark and England working a three-way trade system in which ships carried manufactured goods to African slave depots, bartered the goods for human cargo and then transported these people to sugar, cacao, indigo and tobacco plantations in the colonies, after which they returned with plantation produce, meaning that 'the chocolate sipped by Europeans from Pepys in London to Cosimo

III in Florence came largely from "Zaracas" cacao groves worked by slaves' (Coe and Coe, 2013, p 186).

The association between chocolate and slavery, interspersed by genuine religious philanthropy, has continued not only through the São Tomé and Príncipe 'Cocoa Scandal' in the early 20th century (Robertson, 2009), to which we will return later in this chapter, and the sugar trade (Walvin, 1997), but through to 21st-century concerns for child labour in African plantations (Odijie, 2020). Coe and Coe (2013, p 264 state that the 'conditions decried in the 19th century by those honest Quakers – the Fry and Cadbury families – still exist. Those who enjoy mass-produced chocolates with *forastero* cacao might ponder who produces them'. However, on a more positive note, philanthropic work also continues in the chocolate trade. From Josephine Fairley's development of Green and Black's fair-trade 'Mayan Gold' chocolate in the 1980s to the small Guatemalan producer, Rain Republic, moves to end child exploitation, encourage education and promote fair means of production have increased. Indeed, there is now website dedicated to 'slave free' chocolate, a site which, paradoxically, does not include Cadbury's, Fry's (now part of Cadbury's), and Rowntree's (Slave Free Chocolate, nd).

Prison reform

Prison reform gained the attention of religiously inspired reformers, concerned for both the physical and spiritual health of prisoners, such as Josiah Dornford and Jonas Hanway in the late 18th century (McGowen, 1995). However, it was John Howard's account of the prisons that he visited in Britain and, later, throughout the rest of Europe, that influenced prison reform. He advocated structure, rules and cleanliness alongside a sympathetic religious approach, combining the principles of 18th-century rationalism with a deep religious faith. Howard's work *The State of Prisons in England and Wales*, published in 1777, and his evidence to the House of Commons in 1794, was important in leading to legislative change and humane reform, particularly the Penitentiary Act 1779:

> There are prisons, into which whoever looks will, at first sight of the people confined there, be convinced, that there is some great error in the management of them: the sallow meagre countenances declare, without words, that they are very miserable: many who went in healthy, are in a few month changed to emaciated dejected objects. (Howard, 1777, p 7)

Howard's zeal was echoed by fellow reformer George Onesiphorus Paul in his 1784 book *Thoughts on the Alarming Progress of Gaol Fever or Typhus*. Paul campaigned successfully for healthier environments after reporting that 'I constantly found a number of persons committed for bastardy,- for default of paying small penalties,- for vagrancy and other trifling offences,- associating with notorious criminals who were infected with the gaol-fever. The consequences of this inattention were such, as must naturally follow' (Paul, 1784, p 6).

Religious zeal and voluntary campaigning coalesced in developments in state provision. The appetite for reform by the state was aided by 18th-century political changes (May, 2006). The prison population grew significantly after Britain lost the means to send prisoners to the American colonies following the War of Independence in 1776. Australia was not used as a place of transportation until 1787, and the need to house prisoners of the wars with France between 1793 and 1815 strained the existing prison estate (May, 2006). Thus the building of prisons was something of an imperative and in this context the physical and spiritual health needs identified by reformers began to be addressed. It also illuminated the intertwined aspects of state policy, provision and voluntary effort.

By separation, confinement and focus on spiritual and behavioural conformity, Howard's prison reforms, encapsulated in the 1779 Penitentiary Act, exemplified an attempt at the creation of what Foucault (1991) would call docile bodies, made so through the means of correct training and discipline that would become second nature. The religious *habitus* of the late 18th century, which inspired philanthropic and voluntary action, had the effect of exerting the beginnings of a subtle disciplinary power in which prisoners would measure themselves against the assumed rules of the institution and, indeed, wider society. However, this power was exerted over the religious reformers as well, whose actions were guided by what was accepted to represent the religious and morally correct approach to voluntary action and political campaigning. It reflected religious and social normativity and a long process of embedding (Hardman, 2007). It is also important to remember that calls for reform did not come from the people experiencing prison and the distress identified there but by those with the power and resources to identify issues of note and to set the terms of the reform agenda. This is important in reinforcing those unspoken discourses of what might be considered right action and appropriate reform and who deserved it and when.

Elizabeth Fry and women prisoners

Elizabeth Fry, part of the Fry chocolatier family of Bristol, was part of this drive towards reform that was inspired by a deep religious motivation moving from gay to plain Quaker sensibilities (Skidmore, 2005; Opperman, 2015). She was a prosperous Quaker woman who campaigned for prison reform in the early 19th century after observing the conditions in which women and children were kept in Newgate prison and wishing to stop the cycle of recidivism (Opperman, 2015). Her observations led her to set up the Ladies' Association for the Reformation of Women Prisoners in Newgate in 1817 and she advocated with other women to change the law to ensure segregation of the sexes, and the introduction of education to assist rehabilitation. Prison reform legislation was passed in 1823 in the Gaol Act. However, her reforming work continued through the creation of the British Ladies' Society for the Reformation of Female Prisoners, which worked to improve standards and conditions for women prisoners and develop programmes of moral treatment (Zedner, 1995). Alongside her work in England, she also campaigned for sex segregation and the removal of male guards in French prisons where many inmates became pregnant at the hands of their captors. Her key ideas on prison reform were enshrined in her 1827 work *Observations on the Siting, Superintendence, and Government of Female Prisoners* (Fry, 1827), in which she articulated her broad concerns for women's welfare:

> During the last ten years much attention has been successfully bestowed by women on the female inmates of our prisons. … But a similar care is evidently needed for our hospitals, our lunatic asylums and our workhouses … there are departments in all such institutions which ought to be under the especial superintendence of women. (cited in Skidmore, 2005, p 147)

Fry also investigated conditions in asylums and on convict ships bound for Australia (Zedner, 1995; Opperman, 2015). She started a nursing school, a soup kitchen and campaigned for better housing for the poor and education for women.

The fact she was wealthy and came from the independent thinking tradition of Quakerism helped in her unusual campaigning role. McGowen (1995) illustrates how Quaker activism was widespread in prison reform. William Allen, the owner of a pharmaceutical business in London, first began visiting Newgate in 1813 to be joined by Fry the same year. Fry's brother-in-law, Samuel Hoare, visited Coal Bath Fields prison. Their religion was key to activism in prisons, which promoted the idea that people were able to improve and change with the right help, and that punishments reinforced rather than prevented criminal behaviour. However, this non–conformist approach was not altogether appreciated by prison chaplains (who were Church of England, the established church), many of whom promoted separation from the world and nature through imprisonment as key to Christian reform and change. Benthamite utilitarian approaches to reform also promoted impersonal, disciplinary techniques rather than the relational methods rooted in belief in the power of religion that informed Quakerism (Zedner, 1995; Skidmore, 2005).

Fry's non-conformist background allowed her to be influenced by American co-religionists who visited London and Newgate prison in 1813 while her influence inspired a group of Quaker women in Philadelphia to begin prison visiting and campaigning for reform. Elfleet (2019) argues, however, that the gendered discourses driving Fry's work on penal reform for women are reflected in contemporary debate. While there are, undoubtedly, differences between Fry and 21st-century reformers, Elfleet suggests that there remains an identification of intrinsic problems or deficiencies within women prisoners that should be addressed through more gentle, gender-specific penal regimes; that these women should take personal responsibility for their betterment and engagement with penal rehabilitation measures. These regimes may not be as benign as superficially presented, however, as they serve to reinforce gender stereotypes and display a functional element designed to preserve the status quo.

Cadbury, Bournville and Rowntree

Bailey and Bryson (2006) explore George Cadbury's deep faith and how his Quakerism inspired the development of Bournville Model Village in 1893, which offered low-density housing not restricted to factory employees but mainly for them, something that was recognised early on and evident in his upbringing (Gardiner, 1923; Hall, 2017). There was recognition that poor housing was contributing to worker ill-health and having a concomitant impact on productivity as a result. George Cadbury's Model Village was different to earlier faith-driven philanthropy in focusing on the aesthetics of the design and the importance of this in relation to well-being. This approach was somewhat at odds with elements of his Quaker upbringing which was based on self-denial and eschewing all luxuries. The development of the business from tea and coffee to chocolate, promoted as something pure, led to the factory being moved from insalubrious inner-city premises to a greenfield site. This move suggested that hard business acumen sat alongside his philanthropic side and made complex the reasons for his concern for the welfare of his workers (Coffman, 2006). Economic considerations drove him to acquire land surrounding the factory because the success of the business was proving attractive and high-density housing was likely to grow up around the factory. He bought the land personally, releasing houses on long leases. The complex reasons underpinning his treatment of workers was also shown in the early use of tannoyed music in his factories, also used in the Rowntree chocolate factories, from the late 19th century onwards. Ostensibly, there was a welfare function in reducing monotony on the production lines, but, allied with that, was a concern to increase productivity and, therefore, profit (Robertson et al, 2007). It was evident also in Cadbury's focus on educational provision for his workers, something which George's brother Richard devoted himself to as part of his Quaker faith (Wordsworth, 2020). Education, decent conditions and housing were designed to enhance personal fulfilment, improvement and capacity alongside encouraging greater economic functionality and offsetting unrest (Gardiner, 1923; Smith et al, 1990; Bull, 1991).

Rowntree is associated with women workers' welfare, developing a Women's Employment Department in 1896 that took an interest in women workers' health, morality and general well-being (Titley, 2013). In 1905 this approach was further embedded by the development of a Domestic School designed to address concerns that the employment of women in the chocolate factories would lead to a loss of skills important to maintaining family life. The school was renamed in 1943 as the Girls' Continuation School as the importance of general education grew. There was also a focus on financial benefits for women as well as men, including sick pay and pensions. However, since married women were not allowed to continue in permanent positions the effects of these benefits were limited. Married women were taken on as seasonal workers from 1912, and provided with an evening 'housewives shift' in 1959, but not until 1962 were married women allowed to take permanent positions and, therefore, benefit from the sick pay and pension schemes. Despite this, Robertson's (2009) interviews with retired women showed an appreciation of the welfare provision and of job prospects in the 20th century.

As noted earlier, unlike the plain Quaker asceticism associated with a repudiation of aesthetic pleasantries and images, Cadbury was a patron of the Arts and Crafts movement and managed to combine his Quaker puritanism with architecturally attractive but not flamboyant buildings by developing it as public rather than individual art. According to Bailey and Bryson (2006), Cadbury's passion for housing reform was tightly connected to his Quaker values of self-reliance, thrift and dignity through reconnecting people with nature by providing gardens as spaces to produce food. His religiosity underlay his desire to improve the moral character of the working classes, providing suggested rules for healthy living for residents based on his Quaker principles of simplicity, temperance and restriction, although he interpreted his Quakerism quite liberally, deviating from traditional evangelical forms.

It was not just George Cadbury who was involved in promoting the welfare of Cadbury's workforce, his wife, Elizabeth Taylor Cadbury, was also active in the development of Bournville village, the elementary and infant school provision for workers' children and the promotion of local government medical health services in schools (Hall, 2017). Smith (2012) saw this as reflecting a specifically gendered perception of aspects of welfare, which, of course, is something that influences contemporary discourses in which gendered perspectives can influence the value and worth accorded to certain activities (see Chapter 6).

Robertson (2009) identifies the romanticism in pioneering discovery narratives of chocolate that were used by Rowntree, Cadbury and Fry to offset the realities of exploitation, inequalities and the brutal aspects of colonialism. The important philanthropic legacies for local towns, cities and workers, such as the new town of New Earswick near York, stood in stark contrast to small donations made in cocoa producing regions in Africa and suggest localism and profit are important considerations to keep in mind when assessing the Quaker contribution to philanthropy and the growth of social welfare.

The history of chocolate in Britain, and its associated cacao production, was linked to the slave trade at its outset from Sir Hans Sloane's visits to the slave plantations in Jamaica in the early 18th century. However, Quakers had developed anti-slavery positions early on after challenging slavery with coreligionists and developing an abolitionist stance within the movement (Stillion Southard, 2016; Rediker, 2017; Chenoweth, 2019). Hasian (2008) recognised that the Cadbury family had, as Quakers, supported a range of anti-slavery measures but in 1908 it was suggested that the businesses were profiting from Portuguese colonial African slaves, or forced labourers, to buy cheap cocoa. William Cadbury sued *The Standard* newspaper for reporting the story, as he thought, inaccurately. The court files are interesting for their depiction of different perspectives (see Gardiner, 1923). Cadbury trusted the Portuguese plantation overseers to make incremental changes to improve standards whereas critics wanted immediate radical change (Satre, 2005; Hasian, 2008). While by modern standards we may consider Cadbury's response somewhat half-hearted, the manufacturer was scrupulous in visiting cocoa producing plantations to ensure that workers were treated fairly (Gardiner, 1923; Higgs, 2012). It seems there was an ambivalent relationship between the philanthropy and humane approach to business taken by the chocolate producers and the relationship to earlier slave-based cocoa plantations and forced labour of the 19th and 20th centuries (Off, 2014).

James Reckitt and garden villages

Isaac Reckitt created the household product company in 1840, becoming Reckitt and sons in 1879. The Reckitt Benckiser Group Plc remains a major employer today. James Reckitt, one of the original sons of Isaac, took the helm of the business. He was a dedicated Quaker which led to him devoting much of his later life to social causes in Hull, helping to set up the Hull Royal Infirmary, and what later became the University of Hull. He also supported the Sailors' Children's Society and campaigned for public libraries in the city. His biggest social action, however, was to create a garden village for his workers in East Hull.

The Hull Garden Village Company bought 140 acres of land with James Reckitt putting in two-thirds of the £200,000 cost in return for reserving two-thirds of the properties to be built for his workers. The project took shape between 1899 and 1914 at a time of prosperity and recognition of public health consequences of insanitary and cramped urban conditions. The garden city movement, started by Ebenezer Howard as a means of marrying town and country, influenced the design and development of the project which opened in 1913 with 600 houses (Ashworth, 1968), although Lever had set out his vision of architectural difference somewhat earlier (Sutcliffe, 1981).

Pietrusiak (2004) believes that Reckitt's philanthropy was influenced in part by a fear of social unrest and developing a healthy workforce to ensure productivity and economic gain. He was also influenced by his own experiences at school as a child and his own ill-health. The rise of the Labour Party at the turn of the 20th century had raised fears of revolution among liberal politicians and Winston Churchill and Lloyd-George both pointed to the problems that would result if social reform were to be ignored. Ashworth (1968) linked this fear to Reckitt's fear of Marxist revolution. Pietrusiak (2004), however, sees a more complex background in his motivations. The Reckitt family were descended from French Huguenots and the impact of the French revolution was still being discussed in society. Family background and the rise of socialism combined with genuine religious concern for the well-being of the working class.

Okamura (2004) argues that the development of garden villages, by Reckitt, Rowntree, Salt, Ackroyd and others, aided by the development of philanthropic trusts, such as the Peabody Trust (1862), Guinness Trust (1889), Sutton Housing Trust (1900) and Samuel Lewis Trust (1906), were instrumental in raising questions about the complex relationship between charity and social welfare. This is something that has not diminished with the increase of state welfare and continues today (see Briggs and Foord, 2017). The unresolved relationship provides a means for governments to return to advocating civic society and voluntarism at times of fiscal distress and, perhaps more insidiously, creates a mindset in which charity as gift-giving to the 'not-quite-as-worthy' other becomes optional and dependent on fulfilling certain conditions of acceptance and obeisance to the status quo. It allows the poor and those in need to remain in these conditions without a general clamour for change because actions that are voluntary are privileged over those that are state-mandated.

Rowntree, Booth and the social survey

Seebohm Rowntree, the son of Yorkshire Quaker and chocolatier Joseph Rowntree, enjoyed the wealth his family owned and his directorship of the chocolate business. This, alongside his Quaker principles, led and allowed him to undertake a large-scale social survey of poverty in York. He is most remembered for the comprehensive study *Poverty: A Study of Town Life* (Rowntree, 1901). The study owes a great deal to the survey that Charles Booth was undertaking in London at the same time. It demonstrates many methodological flaws compared with today's data collection as Peter Malpass's (2012) comprehensive review shows but it also reminds us of the impact of private landlords and capital on the structural position of the poor. The survey had been employed earlier to evidence poverty as seen in the survey of the Glasgow Parish of St John's by the evangelical Scottish cleric and academic Thomas Chalmers (1780–1847) (McCaffery, 1981; Furgal, 1987).

Rowntree, with one paid interviewer and a small band of volunteers, undertook 11,500 interviews covering the population of York's poor and to ask the question whether people are poor because of some deficiency within themselves or for other reasons. Charles Booth's poverty maps of London are equally ambitious in coverage. While we can draw attention to the methodological infelicities and naïveté of the surveys, both represent the dawn of a new way of approaching poverty and understanding the structural aspects of it. They were possible because of individual wealth, and stem from so-called 'benign capitalism', as, indeed, does the philanthropy of the Quaker reformers.

19th-century charitable bodies

Moral and religious principles drove many of the charitable innovations of the 19th century as we can see in Mrs Ellen Ranyard's mission, through the work of Dr Barnado, William Booth and the Salvation Army, the Police Court Missionaries and within the Charity Organisation Society.

The relief of poverty and destitution and the 'rescue' of prostitutes characterised these predominantly middle-class activities, which were often underpinned by Christian ideals undertaken by women as a practical expression of religious devotion (Burt, 2020). The goals of moral welfare were to develop character and employability and the focus on individuals emphasised the moral responsibility and, indeed, culpability of those receiving support. The Charity Organisation Society, established in 1869, and Mrs Ellen Ranyard's Bible and Female Mission, established in 1857, worked by gathering facts about clients and their situations allowed charitable workers to evaluate the deservingness of those coming to them, and where deemed appropriate to make plans and provide help or referral according to perceived needs.

The Charity Organisation Society was established in the midst of increasing chaos in the numbers, remit and responsibilities of charitable bodies. It worked to introduce regulation into charitable distributions by assessment of claims made by deserving individuals. The work was designed to provide the administrative means needed to prevent pauperism, to eliminate handouts and to encourage thrift. Using concepts derived from Poor Law they separated clients into two groups, the 'helpable' (those with moral fibre to become industrious and law-abiding) and 'unhelpable' (the feckless or ill, and disabled). Those deemed undeserving were directed to the Poor Law (Skinner and Thomas, 2012).

In the late 19th century women from many of these charities were active as 'friendly visitors', a system of personal moral influence which originated in Boston in the US. This movement ignored social conditions and became increasingly unpopular. The Charity Organisation Society and religious friendly visiting was subject to criticism by the burgeoning social reform movement which assumed that state provision was a necessary defence against the arguments of moral culpability promulgated by the Charity Organisation Society.

Political approaches from social reform movement ideas that recognised the impact of social and economic conditions had their origins, in part, in the Settlement Movement. In 1884 the Reverend Samuel Barnett founded the Toynbee Hall settlement which offered support, teaching and arts for poor people often offered by young men attending university but living among the poor. Women were also involved in these approaches (Oakley, 2019).

Towards the end of the 19th century other voluntary agencies important for the development of social welfare came into being. The Salvation Army was founded in 1879, and the Police Court Missionaries of the Church of England Temperance Society, who later became probation officers, formed in 1876.

Continuing philanthropy, charitable giving and civil society

There is a long history of civil society reaching back to Plato and before. In UK politics, however, prior to the emphasis on 'Big Society' in Cameron's Coalition government, two things stand out. First, the 1976 Labour government introduced a 'good neighbour scheme' to recapture a cooperative spirit redolent of wartime Britain in preparation for the Queen's Silver Jubilee in 1977 (Hansard, 1976). The impact was short-lived and earned no reference in discussion of the 'Big Society' concept although it shares many comparisons in terms of content and political context which required distraction from global fiscal problems and cutting back or austerity. The second pronouncement came, ironically, from former social worker and Conservative government minister, Virginia Bottomley, in the 1990s in a statement making the implication that a force of 'streetwise grannies' could undertake 'social work' (Parker and Doel, 2013). Lady Bottomley's ideas did not gain purchase on the sector but perhaps reflected a common-sense assumption among many of the general public that gave impetus to 'Big Society' beliefs and provided an unspoken belief in the redundancy of state provision (Bourdieu, 1977).

There have been broad attempts towards engaging citizens in civil society. Hirst's (1993) 'associative democracy', on which Blair and Gidden's 'Third Way' and Cameron and Letwin's 'Big Society' are loosely based, was built on the perception that the expanding welfare state had lost ground, legitimacy and effectiveness to the growing influence of market and corporate interests (see Breeze, 2005). Associative democracy embraced both marketisation of welfare and democratisation by including citizens in decision-making, believing that this would make social welfare more responsive to social need (Westall, 2010).

The 'Third Way' never really moved beyond early New Labour policy rhetoric although the focus on working one's way out of poverty was maintained as a useful deflective mantra (Pierson, 2021). Mechanisms which sought to instil citizen involvement were trialled in the National Health Service (NHS), with some success. For example, in the late 1990s and early 2000s, citizens' juries and citizens' councils had been formed to engage and consult citizens on NHS tendering and rationing issues (Dunkerley and Glasner, 1998). The 'Big Society' concept, however, did not hide its attempt at mobilising citizen engagement and replacing the role of the state. By using the emotive words of First World War General Haig, in a 2010 Conservative Party conference speech, Prime Minister David Cameron sought to mobilise British citizens by suggesting that 'your country needs you' (Mulholland, 2010).

The 'Big Society' agenda, as promoted by the Conservative-led Coalition between 2010 and 2015, had appeal in times of austerity when welfare spending was restrained but social need increased. Philosophically, the 'Big Society' concept developed from Tory disillusionment with state welfare, which, it was argued, had not produced a caring, supportive society in which people expressed concern and care for one another, but rather created a selfish, individualistic society that left communities isolated and disadvantaged alongside leading to a life of dependency and reduced individual and corporate responsibility (Murray, 1990; Cameron, 2009; Jones, 2012). These concerns had, from Margaret Thatcher onwards, permeated Conservative Party thinking, but represented a sharp shift from the post-war welfare state consensus (Fraser, 2017). Paradoxically, although the individualistic agenda promoted by New Right monetarism was ignored, it seemed that developing concern for a more caring and compassionate society was hijacked by those who saw an opportunity to reduce welfare expenditure and promote individual responsibility for care needs (Page, 2011, 2018). The focus represented a deflection presaging the later 'alternative facts' discourse arising in the early days of the Trump presidency in the US.

Economic arguments for civil society initiatives abound in the Conservative Party's 'five pillars' towards shifting power from the 'Big' state to local communities (Cameron, 2009):

1. communities should be given a tangible share in local economic growth;
2. local government should be free from central government control – while not dealing with the tensions inherent within this;
3. local people should have more power over local government spending and resource allocation – which seemed politically driven as a means of derailing initiatives that might support non-Conservative Party priorities;
4. local people should have more power over spending priorities;
5. regional government should be removed – again a political initiative to remove an 'expensive' tier of bureaucracy which tended to favour the Labour Party rather than the Conservatives.

The 'Big Society' idea was included in the Conservative Party Manifesto (Conservative Party, 2010a, 2010b) and a three-point priority area plan was delineated in the 2010 document *Building the Big Society*, although the detail was not fully worked through. Public service reforms included the third sector taking a greater role in tackling social problems, especially at a local level, partly funded by releasing monies from dormant bank accounts. Communities were to be given control over local facilities, planning and the accountability of local public services. Behavioural economics would be employed to create volunteering opportunities and philanthropy.

The policy intended to reduce the state and tiers of government, something perhaps that resonates with many on both left and right and with public concerns to reduce unnecessary expenditure. However, there was little fine detail given in the thinking, except perhaps a proposed National Citizen's Service scheme for 16-year-olds (Norman, 2010; Stott, 2011). While not gaining significant popularity (Stott, 2011), the 'Big Society' idea continued to be promoted through the online Lottery-funded Big Society Network, a body that fell into disarray following allegations of funding misuse (Mason, 2014). There were also calls for greater decentralisation of power and the facilitation of charity and philanthropic development towards the 2010 election as a means of promoting the Big Society concept (Norman, 2010).

Norman (2010) promoted the message that developing a new compassionate society transcended the problems of left and right in politics; a message that many people disillusioned with party politics could grasp. Also, Blond (2010) suggested that communitarian civic concern could seek to redistribute capital and capacity from the centre of government to local communities. His critique of market economics 'as a mask for the justification of the restriction in the freedom of others by the advancement of self' (Blond, 2010, p 185) indicated another more moral approach to the economy that was conveniently ignored in the Big Society debate. Lord Wei played on public fears of a 'broken society' to be mended by mass participation in the 'Big Society', predicated on the assumption that people have not only the drive and energy to engage but also the time to devote to such which allowed the Cameron government's focus on neoliberal market forces (Stott, 2011).

Austerity and promotion of markets and consumerist values diluted the potential impact of the 'Big Society'. Later it was overshadowed by Brexit and continued disquiet about welfare expenditure, social and health care (Pierson, 2021). The ideas underpinning it were, as Jordan and Drakeford (2012) admit, a shift from the economic model followed by New Labour previously and the prevailing hegemony of the market championed by Margaret Thatcher and interpolated into New Labour's policies. However, the focus on local communities writ large in 'Big Society' concepts ignored the necessity of national frameworks and welfare planning needed to tackle large-scale social problems. Jordan and Drakeford (2012) suggest that in order to tackle such matters a Basic Income Scheme and adequately funded National Care Services would first be necessary (see Chapter 8).

Debates around civil society and 'Big Society' are organisational and moral (Greve, 2015). The contemporary welfare mix concerns a (shifting) balance in organisation between state, market and civil society (family, third sector). The various iterations of 'Big Society' sought to increase the role of civil society in providing welfare services which means relying more heavily on families, volunteers and third sector organisations without acknowledging the discourses underlying this shift. This ignores the contraction in income experienced by UK charities under austerity which, in turn, has a deleterious impact on what they can provide (Clifford, 2017). Moving towards such an organisational mix also requires the adoption of a discourse that shifts moral responsibility onto individuals and away from state provision.

Contemporary philanthropy, such as that espoused by musicians Bob Geldof or U2's Bono, often raises suspicion and ambivalence reaching back to Maussian perspectives of authority and superiority because of its association with celebrity status and super-richness. However, it has always been part of human social action, was retained in Beveridge's vision for a universal welfare state, and stems from deep-rooted beliefs concerning the importance of acting for the social good, whether social action in Geldof's case, or religious belief in Bono's (Vallely, 2020).

The position following the June 2016 'Brexit' referendum result brought questions of welfare into sharp relief again although the concept of a 'Big Society' is almost absent (Chapter 9). The focus now concerns the reduction of welfare spending, and continued pathologisation of those requiring welfare, support and care. The construction of the despised 'other', as we saw in the previous chapter, allows the government to deflect attention from individual need, structural conditions and to reduce expenditure by apportioning blame.

Conclusions

Philanthropy has an ambivalent character. It is driven by underpinning religiosity and genuine humanitarian concern but also by business and economic matters, both of which construct discourses of care within particular bounded parameters. Quaker abolitionist principles have been strained by associations with slavery, despite Quakers not being directly involved themselves. Fear of social revolution has also driven philanthropy as a means of protecting benign capitalism and ownership. These associations between genuine compassion and ownership and economic growth illustrate the ambivalent relationship we have with welfare yet in a more subtle way that we found in respect of moral binary distinctions discussed in Chapter 3.

5

War: the paradoxical crucible
of welfare reform

War may not be something that one would immediately associate with welfare, although it may perhaps appear, on a superficial level, to be a fairly simple concept to define. Wars are conducted by nations or states against other nations or states, and the actions of war have been mandated by at least one of the states' governments. Oppenheim's (1912, p 60) classic definition states: 'War is the contention between two or more States through their armed forces for the purpose of overpowering each other and imposing such conditions of peace as the victor pleases.' Warfare, therefore, concerns engagement in and the prosecution of armed state struggle. However, it is not quite so simple. Wars can be large or small, involve many or just two nations and the violent actions of armed militia may be conducted by groups other than nations or states. They may be historical and perhaps not always ended by treaty (for instance, the, possibly apocryphal, story of Berwick-upon-Tweed on the English–Scottish border remaining at war with Russia because of its omission from the peace treaty signed in respect of the Crimean War [see Kiely et al, 2000]). It is also the case that war, while usually concerned with open expression of hostilities by states towards one another, is also enacted between or against stateless peoples, or between groups within a state as a 'civil war'. Dinstein (2017) exposes many of the tensions in this slippery concept from his analysis of war recognising the many uses of the term, and the difference in use by domestic states and international law. However, as a violent contention between two opposing groups war will result in an increase in need and demand for certain social and citizen entitlements, notably those concerned with social welfare, health and security. Indeed, one can think back to developments in health care emerging from the Crimean War and celebrated in the figures of nursing pioneers Mary Seacole and Florence Nightingale.

Dinstein (2017) also acknowledges its use as a figure of speech in common parlance when describing any serious struggle in which people or states engage, such as the 'war on drugs', 'poverty' or 'disease'. This metaphorical use of the term 'war' is employed to describe the serious and exacting nature of people battling against adversity, while creating morally weighted oppositions. As such, it links directly to social issues that require welfare support to address them.

According to McDonald (2013), war and peace represent increasingly distinguished concepts in emergent modern societies from the 17th century to the Second World War, but recent shifts towards 'securitisation' blur these boundaries and we now face permanent and pervasive situations of war across all social life, which engenders its own particular social needs. The 21st century has seen an increased vulnerability to attack from state and non-state combatants for many people across the world. Alongside this, military personnel leaving the services are likely to have a range of social needs from employment, social security, housing to specialist health and disability care. Many of the displaced people, asylum seekers and refugees that come to Britain as a result of conflict and war represent an additional demand for housing, education, health care, social protection and support.

This chapter examines the place of war and warfare in demanding and creating the conditions for the development and reform of social welfare in Britain. We will briefly consider the place of war in engendering broad social action throughout history. However, we start our analysis in earnest, if only briefly, from the time of the American War of Independence when large numbers of British military personnel returned to Britain needing work, food and support. Following the French revolution and the Napoleonic wars we continue this exploration, linking the fears of revolution, the needs of returning service men and those widowed and orphaned with other drivers for change and reform of the Poor Laws. It is also important that we consider the outcomes of Germany's war with France leading to unification under the Prussian Otto von Bismarck in 1871 as marking the beginning stages for systematised welfare reform through his social insurance system that was, to an extent, emulated in early 20th-century Britain under the Liberal government of the day. Alongside these changes, the Boer War and First World War illuminated the poor health and nutritional state of the soldiery and added another lever to calls for state support (Mitton, 2012). The drive for a bigger role in state provision continued after Boer into both the First World War and in preparations for the Second World War (Harris, 2004). Recognition that poverty and social problems were the result of external and structural factors and not moral fecklessness and personal failure began to reshape welfare provision. By the Second World War political demand for social reform, greater equality and social welfare support had grown and common wartime experiences led to calls for change at a national and universal level, resulting in the formation of the British welfare state after hostilities had ended. The effects of warfare and violent conflict in driving social change and welfare development did not end at this point and have continued to champion demands for greater social welfare and fairer treatment for military personnel engaged in conflicts overseas and for those seeking refuge in Britain from war, conflict and violence in other countries. The paradox of destruction, and resilience and sustainability, is considered as a feature of welfare policy psychology, leading as it does to a further consideration of ambivalence.

War, conflict and welfare demands

War and conflict have, throughout history, created welfare demands for those left behind, those bereaved, where living spaces are ransacked, crops and livelihoods destroyed, and for those returning disabled and injured or simply demobbed. The burden of care has for many fallen on women who were more likely not to be combatants but to have responsibility for dependents in need. Alongside the needs created by destruction, misfortune and difficult times, developments and enhancements in care and welfare have taken place. We have known that social and technological innovation takes off at times of national need, necessity being the 'mother of invention', to paraphrase Plato's *Republic*.

Harris (2004) reviews aspects of social development during times of war. He explores how Andrzejewski (1954) relates social policy development directly to the ratio of military participation. Where participation is high there is a tendency towards egalitarian social policies and a reduction in the scale of social inequalities. A principle of cooperation is enacted between people in society experiencing the same levels of national threat. Three reasons are developed to explain this phenomenon:

1. the displacement effect in which people will accept methods of raising revenue that would be deemed unacceptable at other times, such as higher taxes and demands on private ownership;
2. new governmental obligations arise, such as war pensions, debt interest and reparation; and
3. an 'inspection' effect results in which government and people are forced to see social realities and needs more clearly (Peacock and Wiseman, 1961).

Titmuss (2001b) agreed with this thesis of consensus driving social policy but it has been questioned. Abrams (1963) and Lowe (1976) acknowledged that evidence from the Boer War (1899–1902) promoted a focus on national efficiency but suggested social reform was not sustainable and failed after the First World War with spending on welfare being reduced after 1918 as the emphasis on egalitarian principles was replaced by a focus on class and individual differentiation.

Obinger et al (2018) and Obinger and Petersen (2017) consider the ways in which warfare and welfare state development may be causally linked while recognising that this, at first glance, appears counterintuitive, with war being associated with mass destruction and welfare with the construction of well-being. However, considering welfare state development after the

Second World War, it may be suggested that increased state intervention in welfare provision represents an unintended consequence of total war. This paradoxical relationship has, as we have seen, long been recognised (Porter, 1994), destruction demands its counterpoint, welfare, reform and rebuilding.

Building on Andrzejewski's (1954) thesis, Obinger et al (2018) identified a number of possible causal links between warfare and welfare that are recognised in the Second World War and subsequent development of welfare states. They identify three phases in respect of the war – war preparation, war mobilisation and post-war legacy – each of which is related to short- and long-term social policy development. When preparing for war in the 1930s, concerns rose for population health, social security, the replenishment of the population and increasing skills. These concerns resulted in policy developments in public health, social rights, a youth and maternalistic family policy and education reform. The austerity of the war years, in which the need for resources to prosecute the war led primarily to retrenchment in welfare provision, later resulted in the development of post-war planning while the state gained experience in organising direct intervention in people's social lives and the population experienced greater collective and shared experiences and democratisation. These experiences came to fruition post-war in codified democratisation, increased rights and entitlements and universalism in social protection. Next we turn to consider the development of welfare as a result of or reaction to times of war, conflict and revolution.

The late 18th century to Poor Law reform

Fifty thousand troops fought on the British side during the American War of Independence, all receiving rations that were greater than could be expected in civilian life (Hagist, 2012). Many died in the war and not all troops were British but came from many different European countries, so not all would have sought to return to Britain following their defeat (Conway, 2010). However, it is likely that significant numbers returning were suspected as having been contaminated with revolutionary ideas and welfare demands resulting from their experiences of being looked after as part of the militia as much as having fought for Britain.

As Hobsbawm (1973) argued, in the year of the French revolution, 1789, Europe was predominantly rural, people were less sturdy, tall and heavy, while travel and communication was more prolonged and exacting. The reaction to feudal agrarian practices led, over time, to the dissatisfaction that resulted in the French revolution. Alongside this, the beginnings of moves away from agrarian society, cottage industry, and towards urban development and industrialisation, known later as the 'industrial revolution' (Griffin, 2018), or the great transformation (Polanyi, 1944), began to characterise European changes. In turn, this also evoked fear and reaction in the ruling classes in

Britain who feared the onset of potential revolution. Politics and the political economy were harnessed during the 18th and 19th centuries to guard against revolution. Daunton (2008) examined the changing social and economic world. He found that new social and political formations required measures to contain revolution and fear of it. Questions concerning the employment of returning militia, appropriate resources for those in poverty and need were underpinned by these fears and welfare reactions were affected as a result.

Between 1795 and 1796 there were discussions in the House of Commons of agricultural conditions and famine. Samuel Whitbread proposed a minimum wage but the prime minister, Pitt the Younger, spoke against this, introducing his own Bill in 1796 ostensibly to aid the poor but also to quell fears of revolution (Fukagai, 2005; Martin, 2011). The Bill allowed for children over the age of five to work long hours but also suggested extra material support for non-self-supporting poor men with more than two children and for widows with more than one child. The Bill was defeated in 1797 and Malthus argued strongly against what he saw as the Bill's population inflationary potential. However, the fear of revolution was clearly influencing policy development at this point.

The fears of revolution expressed were not groundless. In the second volume of Thomas Paine's *The Rights of Man*, he not only advocated revolution and republicanism but also outlined a programme of social welfare that was universalist in approach (see Chapter 8). Mary Wollstonecraft took forward his enthusiasm for revolution through her *Vindication of the Rights of Woman*, expressing to former bishop and revolutionary diplomat Talleyrand, her own radical views snubbing rank and hierarchy: 'After attacking the sacred majesty of Kings, I shall scarcely surprise by adding my firm persuasion that every profession, in which great subordination of rank constitutes its power, is highly injurious to morality' (Wollstonecraft, 1796, p 26). This may well have tied together social welfare and fear of radical change – something that underpinned reactions to welfare reform over many years and still exerts an influence on social and political commentators (Thompson, 1963). Fears of revolution, social discord and reactions to them, grew during the long period of war between Britain and France, 1793–1815, which was broken only briefly in the early 1800s, and during the war with the United States from 1812. They contributed to discussion around reform of the Poor Laws which eventually took place in 1834.

Fear of social unrest permeated the reactions to and reform of the Poor Law and the development of social policy throughout the 19th century. This was also a feature of other European societies and can be seen to underpin Otto von Bismarck's social insurance reforms in the recently united Germany after 1871. Changes to the Poor Laws and social welfare, prompted by fear of the development of communist thought and revolutionary fervour expressed throughout Europe in 1848, and in Britain through the voice of the Chartists and other calls for political reform (Hobsbawm, 1973; Claeys, 2001), protected the populace and government against calls for more radical or revolutionary reform. Sitting alongside a genuine desire to improve conditions, whether on humanitarian or economic grounds (or more likely a complex mix of both), fear focused the policy direction in Britain. When consensus developed during periods of conflict, especially during the First and Second World Wars, social policy development progressed (Burchardt, 2001; Titmuss, 2001b). Fraser (2017) believes that fear of Bolshevism led some to demand repression on the scale seen after the Napoleonic wars but Lloyd George pushed forward an ambitious social programme to prevent the conditions for revolution developing in the first place.

First World War

The degeneration in health and stature of the populace was identified as a central factor in the British army's poor performance in the Boer War (1899–1902) in the Fitzroy report (Fitzroy, 1904). The decline was put down to the results of industrialisation and increased urbanisation and was met by an increased emphasis on developing national efficiency for the next military generation through the provision of school meals and child-focused welfare reform forming part of the Liberal government's promotion of Bismarckian social policies (Fraser, 2017; Obinger et al, 2018).

Fraser (2017) suggests the drive for national efficiency on a massive scale underpinned many of the changes taking place during the First World War. It was aided by the population sharing a common purpose, near nationalisation of key industries, and a willingness to accept greater taxation and curbs on profits. He recognises the so-called failure of social reform in the post-war years but states the wider role of the state did not completely subside as the subsequent welfare programmes indicated. Harris (2004) acknowledges that the war reduced extreme poverty because of the increased levels of employment, many children being better fed and better dressed. However, he also states that the cost of living rose while pensions, at first, remained static, causing some degree of hardship to many. The costs of social welfare were more acceptable in times of national adversity rather than peace-time, indicating our ambivalent relationship with welfare.

Smith (2010) explores the two-edged aspects of a particular element of social welfare. The National Insurance Act 2011 introduced state social welfare into Britain in a way that presaged the welfare state after 1948. However, no widow's pension was provided at the outbreak of war. The enactment of a war widow's pension in 1916, the first non-contributory pension and one for women, appears, at first sight, as a positive social protection of so many women who lost husbands in the First World War. Using case study material, Smith shows how the introduction of this welfare action was used, however, to subject women to close scrutiny that led to the withdrawal of the benefit from those deemed to have displayed infidelity or misbehaved. Smith argues that this demonstrates a new bureaucratic relationship between state and citizens that continues in contemporary British social welfare. Those in receipt of benefit are treated as the 'other', as suspicious and legitimate targets of surveillance. This entrenches pejorative conceptions of those in receipt of state welfare and especially misogyny (see Chapters 3 and 6).

Alongside the National Insurance Act, the development of a National Health Insurance scheme in 1913 also foresaw the increased role of the state in health care provision. Sturdy (2002) sets this against a backdrop of concern that the Poor Law was failing industrial society and that the ill-health of workers was weakening national economic and military interests. While he acknowledges the growing role of the state in welfare provision, Sturdy also recognised the continuing influence of business interests and the diverse voices of different philanthropic and voluntary organisations in the development, agreement and provision of state provision, a delicate balance of economy, nationalism and compassion. The changes auguring the welfare state later in the century resulted from economic and military anxieties rather than from the demands of an increasingly enfranchised working class; concerns for human need and distress took second place.

The Defence of the Realm Act 1914 gave the government powers of rationing in respect of the population and to assume control of industry. The development of wider state apparatus allowed and required a deeper focus on welfare. In 1917 the Ministry of Reconstruction was formed under Dr Christopher Addison as a means of moulding a better future after the war. The focus here was not on returning to the way things were before the war but to identify ways of improving health, housing, education and unemployment insurance (Fraser, 2009). Indeed, the war had introduced separation allowances for servicemen's wives following complaints from Poor Law Guardians who wanted to stop claims from those who received no money from servicemen abroad (Smith, 2010). There was a move to raise pensions which also set the principles for post-war change (Harris, 2004). The Adkins Committee (Departmental Committee on Old Age Pensions) raised and extended provision.

The First World War had reinforced earlier national concerns expressed during the Boer War over the poor physical condition of people. This, in turn, led to calls for greater health and social reform and a number of measures were brought forward. While the Maternity and Child Welfare Act was passed in 1918, full-scale health reform was restricted by vested interests from the Poor Law Boards, Friendly Societies and private industrial insurance schemes. However, by 1919 the Ministry of Health was formed, which brought a degree of state involvement on a national scale, although reform to the Poor Law was shelved until 1929. Despite these changes the effects of the health improvements were fairly modest (Harris, 2004).

Christopher Addison, a former medical doctor turned politician, was appointed Minister for Reconstruction in 1917 and pushed forward his approach to housing reform, attempting to meet Lloyd George's bold claim of building 'houses fit for heroes'. Addison's Act 1919, or the Housing and Town Planning Act, gave local authorities a duty of remedying housing deficiencies while also offering them subsidies. However, the financial benefits of the end of the war were rapidly overshadowed by expense and need in all areas and the bold ambitions that Addison had could not be met. Addison did not curb his programme and was subsequently sacked from government. In total, however, 213,000 homes were built. Addison left the Liberal Party and took his reform agenda into the Labour Party where he employed the future prime minister, Clement Attlee, as his parliamentary secretary.

Education formed part of the post-war social programme under H.A.L. Fisher, a former university vice chancellor, whose Education Act 1918 established the principle of appropriate free education, foreshadowing the 1944 Education Act (the Butler Act), which was again passed in wartime. Under the 1918 Act, fees in elementary schools were abolished and the school leaving age was raised to 14. The Education (Provision of Meals) Bill 1914 rescinded the 1906 limitations on what local authorities could spend on providing food for pupils and focused attention on health and well-being as part of legitimate national concern (Harris, 2004).

Welfare policy and provision grew at the end of the war. Moves towards greater state provision, standardisation of services built on nationally recognised needs for a healthy and fit workforce and military force for when it was most needed were not seen as outlandish and became equated with the prevention of revolution rather than potentially leading to it.

Interwar years

Unemployment never fell below one million between the two world wars and was sometimes as high as three million. This put an enormous burden on unemployment insurance schemes and contributed to the desire to build an efficient systemic approach to the problem. Addison had planned for an out-of-work donation that was non-contributory and set at a subsistence level with a dependent allowance as well. The thinking behind such suggested changes embedded the principle, according to Fraser (2017), that the state had a responsibility to look after its citizens in times of unemployment, something expressed well by the influential writer J.B. Priestley (1934) in his *English Journey*. Harris (2004) saw this in the recommendations for the abolition of the Poor Law system of administration, which although fiercely resisted by those within it, presaged the future direction of state-provided welfare service. However, the cost of the scheme and concerns expressed about its effects on workers meant it was never implemented. Rather a new form of contributory unemployment insurance was rushed through under the Insurance Act 1920. Fears of revolution, this time Bolshevism, were again part of the reason for this scheme which acted to support unemployed people in a similar way to outdoor relief.

The programme of reforms begun before the First World War in 1906 by the Liberal government continued into the interwar years. Despite budgetary setbacks and restraints, these developments led, in the Second World War, to 'the political and social determination to overcome enormous difficulties and in its wake the spirit and practice of universalism affected the course of social policy' (Fraser, 2009, pp 245–246).

Second World War

In studying the social policy history of the Second World War, Titmuss (2001b) was surprised by the lack of accounts of the impact of war on social organisation and life. Indeed, he had to go back to Plutarch's history of the Peloponnesian wars to find such. However, modern warfare is different. The Second World War was a total war involving everyone, which, in turn, led to a common concern for the health and well-being of all. Food shortages, rationing and subsidies applied to all whether rich or poor; evacuation demonstrated the ways in which the poor lived; the needs of wartime production led to an almost communistic division of labour (Fraser, 2009). Universalism was seen as meeting the needs of all people for shelter, protection and food and a replacement of the traditional poor relief by a rights-based universal approach (Marwick, 1988). Questions of social welfare represented a concern for the national interest in the face of a common external enemy rather than a concern to maintain the status quo and social hierarchy against internal agitation. This indicated a change in the underlying rationale that made welfare more palatable to more people across society. Titmuss (2001b) saw the change to increasing participation of the populace in modern warfare as leading to various stages of social interest throughout the 20th century.

First, biological interests focused on ensuring sufficient numbers of men (it was gender-specific at the time) being available for battle. This led to an emphasis on social administration measures such as national censuses and interest in social trends. Second, qualitative standards of military recruits came to the attention of the state in terms of physical, functional, psychological and social attributes, and, in the US initially, the adoption of Freudian psychoanalytic techniques in recruitment and assessment of fitness. Two things resulted from the increased interest in qualitative standards. There was an increase in military demand for the 'brightest and the best', which concomitantly led to increasing numbers of people being rejected from military service or moved out of such and into social settings in which they then required social services and care in general society. Titmuss (2001b, p 74) states: 'The social costs of the Boer War and the First World War, as measured by expenditure on pensions, widows' benefits, medical care, rehabilitation, sickness claims, rent subsidies and national assistance, represent a substantial proportion of the social service budget in the 1950s.'

The third interest shifted the concern for the health and well-being of people in the military to a concern for the whole population and particularly children who were still seen as the next generation of available fighters. The interest in health and physical fitness of soldiers in the Boer War encouraged the concern for universal citizen health that resulted, ultimately, in the birth of the National Health Service (NHS) in 1948. The poor physical health, sickness and mortality of troops led to a questioning of the idea of continual social and material progress. This resulted in inquiries which led to the first school medical service and meals in elementary schools in 1906 alongside campaigns to reduce infant mortality (see Fitzroy, 1904). The concerns repeated themselves in the First World War and saw the introduction of the first hints of a free NHS at the point of need in the treatment and prevention of venereal disease. In the Second World War, this was taken further through the Emergency Medical Service that served as a NHS prototype (Hart, 2015).

The social measures taken during the Second World War centred on meeting the primary needs of the whole population irrespective of class, creed or military status (Titmuss, 2001b). The increasingly universal focus led to early emphasis on planning for post-war reconstruction, the removal of the Poor Law, and a consensus around social democracy, a process that Titmuss describes using Falls' (1941) concept of 'demostrategy' or offering something better to look forward to after the war. This was enacted through the Beveridge report and subsequent development of the welfare state. Klausen (1998) recognises the continuities between warfare and the welfare state in the immediate years after its development but identifies changes in post-war planning as social stabilisation took hold and new priorities emerged.

The evacuation of children during the war was also important in highlighting grave inequalities across society, showing the urban poor children as unkempt, ill-clothed, undernourished and often incontinent. To an extent this pricked the social conscience, although, as Fraser (2009) acknowledges, it may have entrenched some discriminatory attitudes as well. Grier (2001) notes that the six years of the Second World War were recognised as exacting a significant toll on children but also allowed for research into the ways children experienced distressing circumstances, displacement and substitute care. Coupled with changes in family composition and rising divorce rates, so interestingly captured at the time by Folsom (1945), an observer of British life from the US, children's experiences acted as a driver for childcare reform. In 1944, Lady Allen's letter to *The Times* illuminated fragmentations in services and divided responsibilities for different aspects of child care (Holman, 1996; Grier, 2001). A year later, in January 1945, the death of Dennis O'Neill, a boy fostered out but inadequately supervised by the authorities, added to the call for child-care reform (see Chapter 9).

In 1946, the Curtis Committee, which had been set up in the wake of O'Neill's death, chaired by Myra Curtis, reported on all forms of child care (Care of Children Committee, 1946). Evidence to the committee was particularly scathing of the existing system, drawing attention to the placing of young children in Public Assistance Committee institutions for adults and even older, infirm people, and a general lack of child-centred, nurturing care.

The Curtis Committee made 60 recommendations in total and called for a single government department to take central responsibility for all children in need of substitute care. At local authority level, it was recommended that children become the sole responsibility of an ad hoc committee who were to be assigned a Children's Officer who would be answerable to that committee. The Curtis Committee also recommended that foster parents were carefully selected and assessed as appropriate to the task. This began to standardise care and to create a system of child-care social service which was concretised in the 1948 reforms.

Interestingly, a welfarist approach to juvenile delinquency was continued during and immediately following the Second World War (Smith, 2013). Delinquent behaviour was believed to result from broken families and social deprivation and a rehabilitative and welfare driven approach was considered best for dealing with it. This was challenged by some, however, who favoured a more punitive approach, especially to boys, and the use of corporal punishment also increased during the period. Two faces of social policy ran together, reflecting continuities in welfare provision and ambiguities underpinning their expression that were so starkly illuminated by welfare provision and care at a time of great destruction. Each reflected particular political and moral discourses vying for ascendancy in the development of social welfare.

While certainly nuanced, the Second World War was fundamental in the crystallisation of welfare state development (Sullivan, 1996), although Jones and Novak (1999) argued this was but a brief respite to a harsh and punitive history of social policy that quickly reverted to type particularly during Margaret Thatcher's administrations after just 30 years of relative acceptance. Titmuss (2001b) draws attention to the democratising impact of food policy in which rationing was universal and without privilege. Universalism in policy and practice was bi-directional between the military and the general population and led to ensuring that military personnel had access to education, music, drama and the arts, from which they had been previously discouraged.

If global war was the crucible in which fundamental welfare change was initiated, we must ask what of later times of conflict? It is to this question that we now turn, using the example of the second Gulf War or the Iraq War although recognising there have been multiple conflicts in between and that the Korean War had an early impact on the costs of the welfare state (Timmins, 2017).

The war in Iraq

The Iraq War at the turn of the 21st century represents a different form of conflict to the two world wars considered previously. It is a controversial period in history for the politicised deployment of the British military. It was undertaken in the context of the history of the welfare state, universalism and New Right attacks on the prevailing consensus, and occurred around the reintroduction of austerity, residual entitlements and the rediscovery of the 'shirker', the blameworthy individual as we saw in Chapters 2 and 3. The war also had a significant impact on the civilians who were citizens in the immediate theatre. A refugee crisis comprising two million Iraqis ensued, requiring help and assistance from the international community, international non-governmental organisations, Iraqi non-governmental organisations and those from Jordan and Syria (Harding and Libal, 2012), and demanded increased funding and support for social policy initiatives (Alzobaidee, 2015).

In Britain returning veterans have demonstrated housing, mental health and general welfare needs. These are accounted for in the same way as other citizens' needs given the democratising effects of universalism in the creation of the welfare state. Indeed, Ministry of Defence (2019) figures show that 97,566 people are in receipt of disablement pension, with 53 per cent over retirement age, and 14,626 in receipt of widows' or widowers' pension with 89 per cent over retirement age. These are not insignificant numbers. Disablement pensions cost the economy £506.8 million and widow(er)s' pensions £190.5 million in the year 2018–2019. However, given retrenchment, austerity and changes in attitude towards social protections a great deal of the need has been left unmet. This perhaps shows an effect that has turned full circle and now demands support from services charities such as the Royal British Legion, the Soldiers, Sailors, Airmen and Families Association, and Help for Heroes to name a few; often well supported by the public. This links with a mixed economy of care but also the fragmentation of care and welfare and its residual, stigmatised status at state level, although something that attracts greater public support in the main. Ambivalence around the discourses of desert versus non-desert can be used politically to ensure public support for charitable work offsetting demands for greater formal support, although the attitudes influenced by such discourses are fluctuating (Baumberg, 2013; House of Commons Library, 2022).

There is greater recognition, generally, of the impact of trauma on veterans' mental, physical and social health and social security needs (Scullion et al, 2021; Scullion and Curchin, 2022). However, in combat troops, it remains an issue to be addressed in the chain of command rather than by health professionals and policy (Huck, 2014). Greenberg et al (2011) outline two approaches that have begun to be taken to meet combat military meant health needs. Third location decompression (TLD) seeks to place combat personnel in a safe, third space before returning home to accustom them to a different, less stressful environment relaxing with peers. This is usually a military base in Cyprus and is reported to be useful in reducing emotional problems. Trauma Risk Management is also employed, in which combat personnel are encouraged and supported in talking about their experiences and in seeking help so as to reduce stigma and shame later if a need for help arises, although stigma still remains (Green et al, 2010; McAllister et al, 2019). However, mental health needs in the community post-discharge compete across the population for reduced and stretched services. Unmet need can often lead to other social problems.

Homelessness has become a substantial social problem and increased significantly since austerity measures and cuts to public spending following the 2008 financial crisis. The Ministry of Housing, Communities and Local Government (2019) report on the working of the Homelessness Reduction Act 2017, which amended the Housing Act 1996, giving extra powers to prevent and relieve homelessness, suggesting that homelessness among veterans was low, about 0.72 per cent of the total recorded (1,780 homeless veterans of 246,292 homeless people). The No Homeless Veterans campaign (nd), however, suggests this figure masks a much higher hidden total of more than 3,500 (Curry, 2019). The group campaign to take a coordinated approach to work, family, health and well-being which is popular among the general public but is undertaken at a time when the demonisation of those in need again dominates the social policy landscape (O'Hara, 2020).

The number of campaigning groups on behalf of veterans is significant and it is not too wild a claim to suggest ex-military in need are considered the deserving poor when approached through the binary oppositional lens of neoliberal austerity. They could also be considered, however, as the non-deserving when considered as anti-social nuisances with mental health, substance use and housing problems because of the association with personal choice and responsibility. The ambivalence with which social welfare is seen depends on the moral lens through which observers survey the field.

Conclusions

War and welfare are interlinked in complex, continuing yet changing ways. Welfare may be increased in order to wage war; it may be used to compensate citizens for wartime experiences; it may be enhanced post-war to rebuild economy and society and to prepare for future wars. Warfare may be considered to be a catalyst for change; a crucible in which shared experiences and solidarity are forged and in which egalitarian and universal provision becomes acceptable.

These interconnections involve fear of revolution or of the other, conflict and social unrest, which have led to two opposing responses: liberal reform or harsh treatment. War has acted as the crucible in which universal reform measures and a democratisation of state aid has come about, and done so during a period of near political consensus. However, differential treatment measures for different groups have been supported at times of austerity. These political informed changes have diluted and fragmented approaches to welfare and illustrate the tension between public support and fundamental disagreement with social welfare provision. It is an ambivalent performance of social governance that benefits, controls, blames and moulds according to the moral discourses of the day.

6

Gendered perspectives on welfare

Women have been and remain integral to the development and delivery of care and social welfare but have an ambivalent relationship to it, sometimes being side-lined and hidden, sometimes being obliged to undertake roles they may otherwise choose not to, and sometimes being constrained by essentialist notions of gender characteristics that reflect unspoken assumptions about women's 'natural' caring natures. Thane (1978) recognised that women are often hidden within or excluded from histories of social welfare policy, which:

> largely neglect, as most historians of social policy do, the especial problems of poor women. Women however were a majority of the population, were less able to help themselves when unmarried or widowed due to low wages and employment opportunities, and were if married, less likely to receive benefit when unemployed than men, and could rarely be members of self-help organisations such as friendly societies and trade unions. (Thane, 1978, p 19)

It is interesting to note, also, that this exclusion appears to be related to assumptions of patriarchal privilege. One chapter in Thane's collection is indexed as relating to women because it deals with family allowances (Macnicol, 1978). Women are cast as dependents, family-bound, children-focused and caregivers, but not as individuals in their own right.

Women have held a central place in welfare in terms of provider role, catalysts for change but also recipients of patriarchal givens and normative expectations. This ambiguous and somewhat contradictory positioning of women should be seen in the context of gender-power relations and feminist approaches to formal and informal welfare practices and philosophies. Religious thinking and political or social ideologies drive welfare policies and practices in respect of gender.

There are early examples of gendered differences in caregiving. For instance, there was the expression of gendered essentialist ideas of caregiving in which women in the early Christian church assumed nurturing and serving roles while men tended towards more physical ways of offering support such as digging graves. Then in renaissance Italy we witnessed a change from flexible informal approaches to masculinised administrative ones. In a study of documentary evidence from Bologna, Terpstra (2004) charts the gendered tensions between traditional poor relief which allowed for occasional festivities and well-being (female) to the new culture emphasising restraint, discipline and efficiency (male).

Orme (2001) indicates that gendered perspectives in poverty relief and charity were implicit within services which, themselves, were based on familial assumptions in which women were expected to be financially dependent on and supported by men. Women were responsible for care within families as daughters, mothers and wives. When women were outside of those relationships they often came under the purview of the workhouse and Poor Law officials. Orme posits that the beginnings of differentiation and stigmatisation of particular groups, in this case women, rested within this unquestioned organisation of charitable and Poor Law relief, and that this continued 'throughout the twentieth century which ultimately led to "welfare" approaches to such groups which maintained them in a state of dependence' (p 37). Oakley (2001) indicates that there was little awareness of the role of gender differentiation in social policy affecting life chances before 'second-wave' feminism in the late 1960s and 1970s. This begs an analysis of gender relations in social welfare based on ambivalence; welfare has improved and, indeed, saved lives, but it has also entrenched power-based and patriarchal assumptions throughout history.

This chapter considers the impact of welfare on women and of women on welfare throughout history and into the present. We trace women's treatment under the Poor Law, especially that of unmarried mothers and the laws of bastardy. We then chart women's involvement in charitable work, political activism and calls for change before examining some of the ambiguities of the welfare state for women, showing the uneasy relationship between welfare and gender that continues through caregiving roles.

It is important to add a note on terminology. While sex, as a category, is biologically determined at birth, gender is socially constructed relating to social, political, economic and health inequalities and behaviours based on labels of masculinity and femininity (ONS, 2019; WHO, 2022). Shaver (2019) considers gender to represent the primary feature of those institutions comprising welfare states which, in Bourdieusian terms, both form and maintain gender relations. Gender is embedded within the forms, functions and ideologies of social welfare and links to questions of differential roles and treatment in paid work and unpaid work, and to care, family and autonomy.

Women under the Poor Law and 'bastardy'

Slack (1990) associates the rising population, from before 1520, with rising prices while food supplies and employment failed to keep pace. Wages lost value in the 50 years before 1630 and illegitimate births, crime and vagrancy rose. In this context poverty was defined as a threat to be policed and punished as seen throughout Tudor times and clearly in the later 1610 legislation *For the Due Execution of ... Laws ... Against Rogues ... and Other Lewd and Idle Persons* which allowed for houses of correction to be built in every county for paupers of all descriptions. However, there were also initiatives, continued from the previous era, from religious philanthropists to develop a more compassionate social welfare, generally along moral grounds: 'alliances of godly magistrates and ministers sought to remodel their little commonwealths, and they used the management of the poor as a tool for that purpose. If idleness were rooted out, drunkards, bastard-bearers, hedge-breakers and other rogues would disappear' (Slack, 1990, p 16).

For married women whose husbands were in receipt of parish relief, a child often simply meant an increase to that dole (Brundage, 2002). Unmarried women who were pregnant or mothers experienced significant problems under the Poor Laws while the fathers of these children did not (Griffin, 2013). Brundage (2002) describes attempts by the Poor Law overseers and magistrates to determine a child's paternity and to apportion financial responsibility to the father. However, the bastardy laws took a large amount of time and exacted considerable cost. While illegitimacy was frowned upon and from the early 17th century to the extent that a woman could be sentenced to one year in prison chargeable to the parish, this legislation was little used. In practice yet more brutal tactics took hold. Poor Law officials and overseers, in the Poor Law days, were known to bribe women to go to other parishes or even more overt male violence towards women with them being abducted and dumped in another parish so near their time that they delivered there. A child was deemed to be the responsibility of the parish in which it was born unless paternity could be determined (Charlesworth, 2010a). Women, therefore, would be questioned about putative fathers who, if accepted, would pay maintenance. However, if paternity was denied, a lengthy and costly appeals process could be initiated, but was often ignored because of the expense involved.

Brundage (2002) suggests the cheapest solution was often sought rather than to pursue paternity claims. With the change in the Poor Laws in 1834 came the opportunity to change bastardy clauses. Negative feelings had been building towards unmarried mothers over many years. These prejudices were often ignited, according to Brundage, by Malthusian and Evangelical fears of demographic and moral collapse, with misogynistic belief pitching women as culpable and men practically blameless. Thus in the 1834 Act, it was suggested that illegitimate children were to be made the sole responsibility of their mothers, and that affiliation proceedings, against putative fathers, were to be stopped. These changes were rejected but the result was the same in that it became much more difficult to claim maintenance from fathers.

Slack (1990) acknowledged that settlement gave place to people but for women it was not always easy to prove derivative settlement from husband or parents, which illuminated the status of women as dependents and therefore of less worth than men. Indeed, Charlesworth (2010) explained that when a woman married she automatically took her husband's settlement and lost her previous status. This was problematic for illegitimate children where paternity could not be established. In most cases illegitimate children took their mother's settlement. Because this was an area of some contest, the Poor Relief Act 1814 allowed for an illegitimate child being born in the workhouse to take the mother's settlement, extended to all illegitimate children in the 1834 Act.

Englander (1998) reports the ambiguous position of women under the Poor Law in which women, in general, were considered to be non-wage-earning dependents of men, with no autonomy. Women had to follow husbands into or out of the workhouse because of this assumed dependency. However, the assumed culpability of licentious and seductive behaviour under the bastardy clauses suggested agency. The two contradictory positions maintained patriarchal privilege while consigning women to the position of blameworthy 'other', whether as a dependent and, therefore, costly, or as an irresponsible seductress of men. Shame was employed against unmarried women, which allowed for enhanced punishment and less eligibility (Englander, 1998).

The prison record in Table 6.1, taken from Dorchester prison in March 1834 before the implementation of the Poor Law (Amendment) Act later in the year, shows the harsh treatment, through imprisonment, of three women and infants for bastardy and only one man. That the women were committed by members of the clergy, including one by the aptly named Rev J. Bastard, shows the moral-religious approach that underpinned control of the populace by gender. It also indicated that poor relief as social welfare was considered residual and a last resort to be given to blameworthy individuals. Welfare was associated with wrongdoing and therefore a duty on 'decent society' to treat these failings with disdain and punishment.

Williams (2013) describes the impact the new Poor Law had on unmarried mothers when, *de facto* if not *de jure*, given sole responsibility for the child. Affiliation proceedings were made much harder demanding corroborating evidence and costs to be paid by a parish if it was unsuccessful. The outcome of this was not only to reduce the number of applications but also to stigmatise illegitimacy further because assistance became based on the principles of Poor Law deterrence and less eligibility.

Gibson (2018) suggests that it was the correlation between paternity, property and social order that increased 18th- and 19th-century concerns about the moral and economic impact of illegitimacy. This reflects a patrilineal, patriarchal society in which men controlled women's sexuality and reproduction to preserve property rights and ownership.

This 'moral collapse' stance and hostility towards unmarried mothers has featured in governments over time (Forman-Cody, 2000), and has been

Table 6.1: Dorchester prison record, 5–9 March 1833

When brought to prison	Name	Age	Parish	Trade	Condition	By whom committed	Crime	Stature	Hair	Eyes	Complexion	Marks
5 Mar 1833	Silvester Wilkins	15	Bridport	Shoemaker	Single	Jos Grundy Esq. Justice of the Borough of Bridport	Arson	5' 4" ¾	Brown	Grey	Sallow	Dimple chin. Several large pocks on his face. A large cut on the back of the left hand diagonally, on the left thumb to joint.
"	David Curme aka David Fudge Curme	17	Bridport	Printer	Single	Jos Grundy Esq. Justice of the Borough of Bridport	Arson	5' 8" ¼	Flaxen	Blue	Fair	
"	John Stainer	18	St James Shanton	Labourer	Single	Rev R. Blackmore; Chas Bowles Esq.	Assault	5' 5" ½	Dark brown	Hazel	Fair	A mole near the corner left jaw. Stammers a little.
"	Jane Read and infant	40		Labourer	Single	Rev R. Blackmore; Chas Bowles Esq.	Bastardy					
"	Caroline Harris and infant	22	Stalbridge	Glover	Single	Rev H.F. Geatiman; Rev J. Bastard	Bastardy					
"	Eliza Balson	42	Whitechurch Canonicorum	Weaver	Widow	Rev F. Goforth; James Hussey Esq.	Stealing an ass					

Table 6.1: Dorchester prison record, 5–9 March 1833 (continued)

When brought to prison	Name	Age	Parish	Trade	Condition	By whom committed	Crime	Stature	Hair	Eyes	Complexion	Marks
""	John Lawrence	25	Mere Wilts	Labourer	Married	Chas Bowles Esq.	Bastardy	5' 6" ¾	Dark flaxen	Grey	Fair	Two pock marks on the right eye brow.
8 Mar 1833	Anne Barber and infant	29	Wimborne	Labourer	Single	H. Bankes Esq.; Rev Loughly Esq.	Bastardy					
""	James Ward	22	Leary Bank near Wellington Salop	Collier	Single	Sir John Smith Bart	Vagrancy	5' 2" ¾	Black	Grey	Swarthy	Burnt all around his snout and left side of face.
9 Mar 1833	John Middleton	17	Bridport	Shoemaker	Single	Jos Grundy Esq. Justice of the Borough of Bridport	Arson	5' 2" ¾	Dark brown	Dark grey	Fair	Slight appearance of a cut on the back of left hand. A burn on the back of the ... thumb right.

reflected in the literature of the day such as Harriet Martineau's (1839/2021) *Deerbrook* which examines the place of women in the mid-19th century. Gibson (2018) draws parallels with Margaret Thatcher's comments in 1988 that single young women were becoming pregnant deliberately to gain housing benefits and welfare benefits (see Dench, 2010). Her minister, John Redwood, took forward this demonisation of single mothers, especially teenage mothers, when he suggested adoption rather than benefits or reduction of benefits if adoption was refused (Arai, 2009). These discourses of vilification were continued into John Major's government in the 1990s, accusing single mothers of increasing welfare costs and putting children into a life of crime, deflecting attention from structural causes underpinning welfare and crime (Atkinson et al, 1998; Carroll, 2017). The discipline and control of women became so embedded within unspoken discourse that women Poor Law Guardians themselves sometimes called for the compulsory detention of single mothers to prevent further issue (Bartley, 1998).

Increasingly, the Poor Laws gained a popular reputation for being ineffective in reducing poverty and acting as a spur to overpopulation. Kelly and Ó Gráda (2011) suggest, however, that they did relieve poverty and even helped to lower the fertility rate and lowered the remarriage rate of widows. The disparity between popular mythology and reality reflected the embedded belief in the moral culpability of the poor and needy, where punishment was often seen as a protection or talisman against becoming such oneself. The long-standing antipathy to unmarried mothers is an easy way of reinforcing moral culpability and fecklessness in a group often solely dependent on meagre state benefits and charity. This blame engenders a demand for gratitude from recipients who subsist on the largesse of those who were often responsible for their situation. Power relations come to the fore, as does misogyny, all geared towards strengthening patriarchal control, economic and political power.

The legislation and practice relating to single women, mothers and widows illustrates the ways in which care often took second place to control. The development of formal welfare systems seemed to have a functional element that maintained power relations and structured the workings of society along normative patriarchal lines. The ambivalence experienced by women recipients of welfare was of help and support that kept one alive, that accounted for basic needs, but which also subjected them to a strict regime reinforced by moral diktat often internalised by women themselves. The self-replication of disciplinary power bolstered the system of moral welfare at voluntary and state levels.

Surveillance and the Poor Laws

Smith (2010) employs the concept of state-sanctioned bureaucracy to examine the surveillance and moral policing of war widows (Foucault, 1972,

1991; Sarangi and Slembrouck, 1996), making an association between the surveillance and moral attack on single mothers in the 1990s which focused on reducing welfare costs and channelling behaviour along normative lines (Atkinson et al, 1998; Arai, 2009). From the 1908 Children Act parents began to be policed over neglect which allowed the surveillance of the poor and especially women who were charged with responsibility for the moral and physical well-being of children as the building blocks with which society could continue the colonial project of empire (Skeggs, 1997).

There was considerable suspicion about the way the New Poor Law was introduced as a means of monitoring the poor and controlling fertility and sexuality through segregation of families and sexes in the workhouse to the bastardy clauses in the Act. Hall (2009) saw this in the anonymous *Book of Murder*, the two pseudonymous pamphlets written as anti-Poor Law invective (Marcus, 1838/2019.). There was the suggestion that the laws were developed to control the working classes, based on Malthusian principles, and sought to reduce their population by infanticide. The Chartists saw an association between the New Poor Laws, the Anatomy Act 1832 and the ideas of Malthus (1798/2015). This perceived control over women's bodies and fertility, by men, has infused the history of social welfare, often hidden and tacitly accepted without question.

James (2018) describes the shifts in power and control under the New Poor Law amplifying Foucauldian notions of rule, regulation and regimes of power as more subtle. Using punishment books, required following the 1847 Consolidated General Order, his case study of punishment in the Ampthill workhouse in Bedfordshire affords insights into the ways in which punishment of women and abuse of inmates could be challenged and addressed. In fact, James describes a negotiated and relational concept of power that can be understood in terms of resistance and disciplinary power in which perceived abuses are challenged.

The National Insurance Act 1911 shifted a degree of welfare responsibility from the Poor Law Guardians to the state. This was replicated in the war widows' pensions in which the state took on the role of husband and expected self-surveillance and discipline from the women who were subjected to suspicion and questioning, before their moral acceptability and claims were recognised. They had to prove their husbands had died in the war effort, details were then checked and, in the National Archive records, ticked with blue pencil once confirmed. Women then had to sign a truthfulness declaration. If a woman deviated from the expected behavioural sobriety and discretion benefits could be halted. Smith stated:

> As a direct effect of the First World War, this moral policing of the population carefully masks underlying parsimonious ideology and patriarchy. ... Any woman who digressed (or was suspected of

digressing) from this moral role would be liable to have her wider discursive role of pensionable war widow questioned and investigated. The constant surveillance of these women for the duration of their pensions reflects an underlying fear of the State subsidising undeserving citizens. (Smith, 2010, p 532)

This reflected a fear of looking after illegitimate children. The moral taint of illegitimacy, beliefs about 'bad blood' and concern for the empire, alongside patriarchal privilege and male-line inheritance, underpinned welfare practices and reinforced the tropes of deservingness and undeservingness. It was not until 1987 in the Family Law Reform Act that the legal distinction between illegitimacy and legitimacy in children was removed, reflecting changes in family composition in the 20th century that saw an increase in cohabitation rather than marriage (Gibson, 2018).

While there seemed to be a general shift towards greater welfare acceptability, the change was more one of form from overt antagonism towards illegitimacy and single motherhood towards moral self-surveillance and behavioural monitoring according to normative patriarchal expectations.

Hidden women in welfare and women hidden in welfare

Thane's (1978) perspective that women were hidden from view in discussions about and the implementation of social policies holds true throughout history unless it concerned overt moral punishment. Early philanthropic effort was directed towards moral reform such as the Magdalen Hospital for 'poor, young, thoughtless females' in 1758. In the Old Poor Laws, the number of recipients, in general, appeared to be skewed towards women with a shift towards men in the mid-18th century. Southern and eastern records and northern and western ones examined by King (2000) showed the skew to favour women when looking at the regular pension lists as well. Despite this, in the 1834 Poor Law outdoor relief was cut back for women of all statuses (Englander, 1998; Brundage, 2002); they were not the main concern of the Poor Law which focused on able-bodied men and, thereby, marginalised women, assuming them to be non-wage-earning dependents with no autonomy from their husbands (Englander, 1998). Thane (1978) reports that 166,407 women were in receipt of outdoor relief in 1871 which had reduced to 53,271 in 1892. Women were also most likely targeted for cutbacks in outdoor relief as indicated in the Manchester Board of Guardian's Regulations on Outdoor Relief for 1875 which excluded single or able-bodied women, widows with no more than one child, married women with a husband in prison, deserted, or who had joined the militia, and those living with relatives from receiving relief.

McIntosh (2014) provides insights into poor relief in the 16th century, 1552–1563, through 30 collectors' accounts. While men outnumbered women and children in receiving payments at that time, both women and children received direct payments. Also, there was a move to providing regular support rather than sporadic relief. In terms of rate collection there were few women who held land in their own right and so comprised only about 6 per cent of those contributing. The Poor Laws positioned women as dependents and focused on adult males, a position which has suffused welfare legislation since (Digby, 1998). Yet women did work, received relief and contributed to the development of social policies and welfare. The hidden element precluded women from consideration in welfare development and entrenched women's precarious positions as both blameworthy when seen and dependent when not.

The use of local farm accounts shows women's wages and employment in agriculture in a way that offsets the problems of assumption and bias towards expectation and social mores that so often permeates printed records or official data such as censuses. Burnette (2004) recognises that while women were paid less than men there was a high demand for women labourers, who formed almost 10 per cent of the total and the gap lessened in the 19th century. Increased industrialisation and domestic industry were attractive to women, making those remaining in agricultural labour more highly sought after. It was difficult to determine whether the wage gap was based on productivity, that women tended to produce less than men, or whether it resulted from the devaluation of women. Verden (2002) identified regional and occupational differences affecting women in work. However, using the 1834 Poor Law Report and questions in appendix B to the report, she was able to locate the significant contribution made to family income by women and children's wages in some rural communities.

There have been questions as to whether women with young children should have been considered as able-bodied or not. The Minority Report of the Poor Law Commission 1909 described how the majority of outdoor relief was paid to women but 276 unions recognised the majority of women as able-bodied while a further 374 did not. The report of the Poor Law Guardians of 1 January 1907 indicated that in England and Wales 62,240 able-bodied people received outdoor relief, of which 59,712 were women. It was recognised that there were a small number without children, single, not old and without overt illness or disability but who were unable to work. However, the vast majority of these women were engaged in child care and, therefore, the Minority Report argued they should not be deemed able-bodied: 'We think that, in this matter, the practice of Scotland rather than that of England and Wales should be followed. Women having the care of children should, so long as such care is required from them, be wholly excluded from the category of the Abel-bodied [sic]' (Minority Report of the Poor Law Commission, 1909, Vol II, p 21). Brundage describes a moral element to relief that applied a 'calculus of character' to determine deservingness and level of receipt (Brundage, 2002, p 123).

In the 19th century, married couples and single women with several children were less likely to be forced into the workhouse, especially if they demonstrated knowledge of the law and a willingness to use it in maintaining their families (Brundage, 2002), although there was confusion in emphasis between acting as mothers in keeping the integrity of the family and being able to support themselves through work (Englander, 1998). The moralising functions of the Poor Laws were shown in sex segregation and prevention of communication of groups in the workhouse. Widows were increasingly dealt with outside the Poor Law. In part this was the result of war. In 1914 soldiers' widows, a burden on the parish in previous wars, were relieved by a separate National Relief Fund. Benefits were extended in the Widows, Orphans and Old Age Pensions Act 1925, initiated in 1923 when Neville Chamberlain served briefly as Minister of Health in Stanley Baldwin's government. There is a recognition here of a 'no-fault' discourse, but the underlying aspects reflect the tension between compassion and control. Widows, as legitimate recipients, were to be treated sympathetically while those in poverty for other reasons remained under the auspices of the Poor Laws and were to be controlled as moral suspects and thereby debarred from policy-making arenas and debate.

Providing and administering the Poor Law

Women's involvement in welfare, work and philanthropy has been widely studied (Prochaska, 1980; Hollis, 1989; Gleadle, 2001; King, 2004, 2010). In Chapter 4 we reviewed some of this provision, and in Chapter 9 we review the moral compass directing the Charity Organisation Society's and developments in social work which relied heavily on the impact of women. However, women have also been involved in the administration of formal poor relief. The first 50 years of the new Poor Law was administered solely by men. Women could hold subordinate posts, such as workhouse matron, teacher or nurse, but worked under the guidance of men (Englander, 1998; Brundage, 2002). The maintenance of patriarchal control is portrayed with comic genius by women's religious philanthropy patron Godfrey Ablewhite, in Wilkie Collins' 1868 novel *The Moonstone*.

Women worked with charities associated with local boards through such bodies as the Workhouse Visiting Society set up by Louisa Twining in the 1850s, although, similarly to formal welfare settings, many voluntary positions operated under male direction. Having said this, the significance of women's involvement in voluntary and philanthropic work was instrumental in the development of social welfare policy (Digby, 1998). Halliday (2017) uses the example of the Brabazon Employment Scheme extended to Glasgow in 1899 to show the significance of women's influence in changing and developing welfare policy, and to demonstrate how positively women's contributions were received by Poor Law officials and asylum doctors. Mary Jane Brabazon was active in philanthropy alongside her husband, and took a personal interest in the Brabazon Employment Scheme which provided meaningful employment to those unable to work. When the scheme was extended to Glasgow, women introduced the scheme into the poorhouses and asylums in which those unable to work were contained. This was well received and initiated changes to Poor Law medical relief.

However, it was not until 1875 that the first woman was elected to a Poor Law board, and women were only elected in any number after the democratisation of Poor Law elections in 1894 (Lewis, 1993). There were 1,289 women elected in 500 Poor Law unions by 1909 although distribution was uneven with more women elected in urban as opposed to rural areas (Crowther, 1981). Brundage (2002) points out that the introduction of women into the Poor Law system brought mixed results. In cases in which Charity Organisation Society representatives believed their mission was to reduce outdoor relief, this permeated a moralising influence to welfare, exemplified still in Priestley's 1945 play *An Inspector Calls* where Sybil refuses to help the pregnant Eva Smith (Priestley, 2001). However, women from all political standpoints were involved and believed that they brought particular gendered perspectives of compassion, attention to daily domestic detail, and intimate knowledge and understanding of the needs of children and young women.

Limited involvement in welfare did not stop women challenging men on policy, however. Louisa Twining campaigned against outdoor relief and for temperance when elected to the Kensington Board in the 1880s, and later to the board at Tunbridge Wells, while also campaigning for expanding and improving conditions and Poor Law medical services (Twining, 1898). As more socialist women were elected as guardians, especially after the formation of the Labour Party in 1900, more progressive attitudes towards outdoor relief developed. However, involvement was also used to promote women. Gertrude Green, the Fabian candidate for Greenwich in 1893, stressed women's particular contribution, while others, such as Emmeline Pankhurst, saw elections as preparation for political campaigning for suffrage and parliamentary office (Green, 1893; Pankhurst, 1914). Increasing roles for women stemmed from the growth in social research and humanitarian concern. For instance, Beatrice Webb and Helen Bosanquet, while coming from different political traditions, both contributed to the 1905–1909 Royal Commission on the Poor Laws, and Clara Collet made a career in the civil service after being a Poor Law guardian (see Oakley, 2019).

Only a handful of women served as Poor Law officials rather than guardians in the 19th century (Brundage, 2002). The first woman to serve was Jane Senior, daughter of Nassau Senior, one of the architects of the New Poor Law, who was asked in the 1870s to compile a special report on workhouse education. She recommended the creation of smaller units. Even so, women were expected to restrict attention to 'women's work'. In 1885 the Local Government Board appointed Miss M.H. Mason as assistant inspector for boarded out children. In 1910 the first women were appointed to the general inspectorate. Brundage suggests the increase in number of women in Poor Law posts was inextricably linked to the development of 'social work' roles (see Chapter 9). This in itself suggests the continuation of gendered thinking that cast caregiving compassion and support as women's concerns.

Ann Oakley (2019) charts a phenomenal yet hidden history of women in championing social reform and welfare at the end of the 19th and into the early 20th centuries. She describes the activities of key women who sought a radical change to the world ruled by men, militarism and capital. The achievements of women in welfare, peace, social work, education and so on was profound but under a patriarchal system often remained hidden. The power of men to silence women and to employ the systems of support and welfare to crystallise gender norms led to a range of assumptions on which the welfare state has been built.

However, not all women involved in social welfare projects were 'hidden' and there was a clear class aspect to their work. The Charity Organisation Society was staffed predominantly by women, although their work was directed by committees of men. These women were undoubtedly middle class and shared a moral vision to help the worthy and maintain traditional Christian values. Octavia Hill represents the values and sensibilities of the vaunted female archetype assisting families in a way that saw men working to support them financially and women to contribute housewifely tasks to maintain home, hearth and family and move towards self-reliance. The gendered element of charitable relief expressed itself in different directions. Not only were the women of the Charity Organisation Society directed by boards of men, they were visiting homes to deliver assessment for charitable help and therefore saw, mainly, women. Thus, practice became one in which middle-class women with different experiences in the world regulated and manoeuvred other women, mainly from the working classes, into 'right ways of being and acting' to preserve empire and society, and by default, the world of men.

Marks (1993) records campaigner Louisa Twining's bleak portrait of maternity services in the workhouse, which, until the 1880s when voluntary hospitals began accepting unmarried mothers, was the place many unmarried women went to give birth, seen in Hardy's description of Fanny Robin's death in childbirth while on the way to the workhouse in *Far From the Madding Crowd* (Hardy, 1874/2012). Looking at Bethnal Green, Poplar, Whitechapel and St George's-in-the-East unions and parish care where poverty rates were high at the turn of the 19th century, Marks charted improvements in antisepsis and the regulation and training of midwives. These improvements, alongside a reduction in stigma associated with poverty and illegitimacy in the early 20th century, reduced infant and maternal mortality. This was recognised in the Minority Report 1909 in which it was recognised that married and unmarried women in poverty used the workhouse as a maternity hospital as a matter of course. Midwives were first officially recognised in 1902, although from the 1870s Poor Law Guardians were engaging women trained in 'midwifery'. Under the Poor Law Amendment Act 1898 guardians were empowered to pay medical practitioners to undertake urgent medical care and midwifery work, although this was often challenged and disputed until responsibility was passed under the 1918 Maternity and Child Welfare Act to the local authorities if families could not pay. Marks concludes that:

> Much of the poor law policy was not sympathetic to the needs of women. ... Expectant mothers were not viewed as 'impotent' like the infirm or the elderly, and were often classified along with the able-bodied. Most women had to prove themselves destitute before they could any parish support for their conferment ... the great majority of pregnant women supported by the parish midwifery services were unmarried. Like that of the underserving poor, the moral conduct of unmarried mothers was regarded as questionable. (Marks, 1993, pp 533–534)

Family allowances

The concept of 'family allowances' is replete with national discourses that inculcate the notion that families 'ought' to represent the unit of support with the unspoken assumption that this concerns a heterosexual family with children, that the male is the breadwinner and the woman is dependent financially, socially and, by default, in all other ways. However, family allowances have gained support from both left- and right-wing political sensibilities. The former claiming a redistributionist element and the latter representing imperialistic, pro-natalist positions. Macnicol (1978) identified demographic and economic arguments at play. Those hoping to re-establish the primacy of nation, empire and race expressed concern about the failing birth-rate compromising the next generation of militia and contributors to economic growth, while campaigners, such as Eleanor Rathbone, drew upon interwar studies to demonstrate that large families were a major cause of poverty (Rathbone, 1924, 1940; Ford, 1934/2018; Pilgrim Trust, 1938/

2014; Tout, 1938; Rowntree, 1941). She fought for the allowance to be paid directly to mothers, which was rejected at first in the Family Allowances Bill of February 1945, but challenged by women MPs it was introduced as part of the Act when passed later that year.

The 1945 Family Allowances Act was directed primarily to child anti-poverty, influenced by the health concerns and minimum subsistence principles espoused by the Beveridge report (1942). However, Macnicol argues that a simple acceptance of this anti-poverty approach designed to control wages with the Treasury aiming to roll back these measures once the need had passed is misleading, seeing it originally as a temporary wartime scheme. The grudging acceptance of these measures were to manage the economy and to ensure that unemployment benefits were always lower than low wage levels and that the principle of 'less eligibility' was preserved. The Unemployment Assistance Board saw allowances as a means of addressing the problem of the 'poverty gap', which had been entrenched by the 1911 principle of insurance acting as supplementary rather than as full maintenance. Poverty reduction balanced with 'less eligibility' formed the planks on which family allowances rested. Macnicol (1978, p 196) suggests 'although Beveridge did genuinely see family allowances as combatting family poverty and encouraging parenthood nevertheless it was their "less eligibility" function that appealed to him most'.

Digby (1998) reports a shift in thinking from suffrage to 'maternalism', although Lewis (1983) recognises the concept as 'slippery', a double-edged sword, as the beginnings of an appreciation of gendered citizenship. Interestingly, she uses Eleanor Rathbone's (1924) turn from normative understandings in policy to one which takes a female focus to synthesise maternalist and equal rights feminism (see also Rathbone, 1940) that seeks to understand the world through women's perspectives rather than through those of men.

Questions of fertility, including child-bearing and child-rearing, have permeated discussions of welfare policy. Reductions of time spent in these activities leaves a greater amount of time for women to participate in the workforce which has significant implications for marriage, family and employment, and these changes were occurring after the Second World War when Bowlby's concept of 'maternal deprivation' was developed and when men were returning to the workforce and women's employment seen as representing the ills of society (Digby, 1998; Oakley, 2001). It was in this context that Titmuss addressed the Fawcett Society in 1952.

Titmuss recognised the shifts in roles and positions since securing suffrage, suggesting that the fall in birth rate, especially among the working classes, offered a 'revolutionary enlargement of freedom for women brought about by the power to control their own fertility' (Titmuss, 2001a, p 32). The impact on social policy is greater still because of increased life expectancy and as women tend to live longer than men. Titmuss also recognised that these changes were immersed in controversy and exposed patriarchal privilege: 'Few subjects are more surrounded with prejudice and moral platitude than an approach which perhaps deepens the conflict for the women themselves about their role as mothers, wives and wage-earners' (2001a, pp 39–40).

Welfare state typologies and gender relations

Gender inequalities have been written into welfare throughout history, as we have seen, so it is not surprising to see levels of gender stratification in the welfare state (Shaver, 2019). This is recognised in one of the first critiques of the underpinning suppositions of the welfare state in which Wilson (1977) debates the ongoing assumption of male breadwinner/female carer concepts as reflected in welfare provision, something that Lewis (1994) employs in her analysis, and permeates Briar's (1997) exploration of gendered welfare policies throughout the 20th century.

Esping-Andersen's (1990) three-category typology of welfare states, building on Titmuss's (1974) earlier comparative approach, remains a reference point for scholars of social welfare policy despite early criticisms of its Eurocentric focus (see Table 6.2).

Finkel (2019) adds that other typologies include a wage-earning welfare state such as Australia and New Zealand where state intervention is focused on realising a living wage rather than providing welfare. We must also note that Esping-Andersen's typology is Western, and indeed European, in focus and not make assumptions beyond context. Furthermore, it was initially criticised for its gender blindness (Daly, 1994, 2000; Kim and Choi, 2013), although later analyses contributed more to understanding gender equity and family policy issues, despite being more focused on care than wider

Table 6.2: Esping-Andersen's three worlds of welfare typology

Type	Characteristics
Residual/liberal	Opposes universality and comprehensiveness reserving state intervention only where individual responsibility and charity have failed to meet needs.
Conservative/corporatist	Social status and position affects eligibility. Welfare administration depends on the principle of subsidiarity which indicates a decentralised system with central government deferring the setting of social rules to local government, private and third sector agencies.
Social democratic	Comprehensive, universal, state-administered welfare programmes.

Table 6.3: Lewis' status typology of welfare

Type	Characteristics
Strong male-breadwinner states	Social and tax policies reinforce patriarchal families and discourage women's economic independence.
Modified male-breadwinner states	Patriarchal families are considered the norm but there is some support for women without partners.
Dual-breadwinner states	Economic and social independence for both sexes.

gender inequalities in income and poverty (Daly and Rake, 2003; Esping-Andersen, 2009; Aspalter, 2021a). The focus on paid labour and ignoring of care work was replete throughout these analyses.

Earlier, Lewis (1983) proposed a typology that still offers an alternative to Esping-Andersen's model. Her model categorises welfare-type by dependency and breadwinner status which permeates welfare systems and the thinking that drove their development, although, again, the focus is on economically productive labour (Orloff, 2009) (see Table 6.3).

Finkel (2019) suggests that the wartime rise in labour participation of married women was considered, at a social and political level, to be an aberration and so policies in the developing welfare states focused on male-breadwinner income and women staying at home to focus on social and familial reproduction as a means of 'getting back to normal', that is, a normative patriarchal hegemony. However, labour participation had fundamentally altered women's mindset and even some of the policies designed to keep women at home, such as family allowances and inclusion in state medical pension and disability plans, provided a degree of financial independence at odds with the gendered essentialist ideology of the developing British welfare state (Wharton, 2012).

Ellison (2014) points out a number of problems with the male-breadwinner assumption beyond the essentialist ideas of sex-related character, notably that families should be based on nuclear units, which are posited as being the best type of family arrangement; families should be heterosexual and monogamous; and that women are especially suited to caring and nurturing roles and naturally oriented towards such roles (see also Orloff, 1993; Shaver, 2019). A class aspect is also evident in the assumption that one wage is sufficient whereas in many cases this was not so.

Daly (2000) analyses how welfare states contribute to gender stratification and the differential distribution of resources which limit the potential of female participation in the labour market and reinforce normative gender relations. She points out that protections against unemployment do not cover the risks of single motherhood with entitlements focusing on adult males who are assumed to be primary breadwinners. Contemporary welfare states across the world also underestimate the burdens and costs of caregiving and its gendered nature. Moreover, as Lewis (1994) suggests, women provide and develop welfare as well as consume it which needs to be taken into account in a rounded understanding of gender and welfare (see also Beck and Thane, 1991).

Pensions make up a large part of the welfare state budget – £111 billion, or 42 per cent of the welfare budget, in 2017 (ONS, 2017). Fasing et al (2013) compare retirement incomes between Germany's corporatist conservative system and Britain's liberal regime. In both welfare systems single women have higher retirement incomes than continuously married women. However, while gender inequalities permeate both countries' welfare states, married women are less dependent on the male breadwinner role in Britain than in Germany. When comparing dual-career families in Britain and Finland, Repo (2004) finds that similar ways of constructing the social world and making sense of work and family are used by women drawing on cultural available ideologies. This creates different contextual meanings leading to Finnish women concerned with agency as a person in the system whereas British women stress the importance of feminist ideology in seeking gender equality and the need for welfare reform. The current state of pensions reflects gendered social practices – women take more career breaks and undertake more unpaid family work – leaving them disproportionately disadvantaged overall in respect of pension provision (Hinrichs, 2021). Pensions remain linked to paid work and the unquestioned inequalities within this remain unheard (Phillipson, 2013).

Wharton (2012) employs cross-national approaches to social policy to examine how national policies and cultural patterns shape and organise gender by incentivising and dis-incentivising work and caregiving behaviours. She concludes that while labour participation and family-type diversity have increased there is a structural lag in policy that betrays a remaining gendered essentialism in socio-political relations. If, however, we consider social democratic welfare regimes associated with Scandinavian countries we see a greater emphasis on universalism, individually focused benefits, low income inequalities and higher levels of gender equality, although women's participation in the labour market may still be gendered (Aspalter, 2021b).

Pascall (2012) recognises that, while the British welfare state was built with gendered assumptions in mind, there has been a shift towards gender equality. Kim and Choi (2013) see a positive shift in gender equality in all types of welfare state and focus particularly on the feminisation of poverty thesis first articulated in the 1970s by Pearce (1978). Pascall analyses how far gender equality has been achieved across a range of dimensions. The dependent married woman was seen by Beveridge as having a key role in reproducing the British family and British ideals, as well as producing the next generation of militia (see Chapter 5). This lay at the heart of welfare state developments and its assumptions in the early days. However, there have been fundamental changes in the way families are perceived, entered and maintained or otherwise. Divorce has increased, as have different family types and compositions, all of which challenge the concept of the stable, 'ideal' family structure in which a woman was dependent on a male breadwinner and content to be so (ONS, 2020a).

The equality legislation of the 1970s, notably the Equal Pay Act 1970 (implemented in 1975), the Sex Discrimination Act 1975 and the Employment Protection Act 1975 brought gender equality in employment and income centre stage. However, under Margaret Thatcher's and John Major's Conservative governments a more traditional gender-distinct approach was taken. It was mainly the EU and EU Court of Justice that demanded changes to these traditional gender and the male breadwinner assumptions that led policy development (or retrenchment). Korpi (2010) uses the Social Citizenship Indicator Program to examine 18 countries from 1930 to 2000 for changes in class and gender equality. To identify indicators relating to gender equality, Korpi used the concept of inequalities in agency and choice between paid and unpaid work. He recognised that many studies focus either on sameness of access to paid employment or comparative evaluations of traditional unpaid work in the home. Korpi follows Glucksmann (2000) in recognising the importance of the totality of necessary work that sees engagement in caregiving, unpaid work at home and paid work as important. Left-leaning, Nordic states have tended towards greater gender equality through welfare state development, moving towards a dual-earner/dual-carer model. Christian democratic countries have promoted the ideal type of mother at home, while more recently acknowledging the need for economic involvement and therefore facilitating part-time work, child-care services and parental, predominantly maternal, leave. Secular, centre-right countries, on the other hand, pursue market-oriented approaches that ostensibly left it to parents to decide, although they may introduce anti-discrimination legislation as well. What is omitted from these analyses is a consideration of custom and practice, of the unspoken assumptions that form the culture of the countries and thereby lead policy development and change and undergird perceptions of the acceptability or otherwise of these.

Welfare state types identified by Van de Velde et al (2019) differed slightly from Esping-Andersen's original typology including Southern and Central/Eastern regimes alongside liberal and Bismarckian ones. Looking at the prevalence of mental ill-health and gender differences, they found that liberal regimes had the highest prevalence and Central/Eastern regimes the lowest, while gender divides were greatest in Southern regimes and lowest in liberal ones. Unemployment and marriage seemed to be implicated in gender differences in mental health where traditional marital expectations led to greater mental ill-health, as did unemployment.

New Labour governments from 1997–2010 championed gender equality in terms of promoting female employment (Pascall, 2012). The setting up of Sure Start children's centres expanded child-care knowledge and family support and tax credits and child care tax credits assisted women in taking employment where child care was an issue. Gender equality was made a duty in 2007 and in the Equality Act 2010 this public duty was widened. Writing in the early days of the Coalition government, Pascall (2012) indicated that David Cameron attempted to make the Conservative party more gender inclusive but was prevented from increasing the numbers of women MPs by the numbers he wanted by local parties. The subsequent prime minister, Theresa May, followed a pragmatic approach rather than an ideological one (Page, 2018). Indeed, it was May who influenced Cameron's earlier desire to increase the number of women in becoming Tory MPs. She campaigned in the 2017 election on a manifesto of 'one nation' Toryism that saw a valid role for the state in social welfare. However, she continued austerity measures, expressed the desire to complete Brexit, and further entrenched populist anti-immigration measures. The 'just about managing' families she had spoken about helping seemed to disappear into the background during her premiership, replaced by concern for the 'squeezed middle classes' (OECD, 2019).

Contemporary demographic changes, for example the rise in numbers of people living with dementia (Parker et al, 2020), requires the development of sustainable policies relating to long-term conditions which still require a focus on gender equality. Work to reduce the unequal burden of unpaid domestic care on women and the creation of employment opportunities that meet welfare needs in a gender equal way (Esquivel and Kaufmann, 2017; Leichsenring, 2021). In Chapter 8 we will consider the potential effects of a Universal Basic Income on the ways in which we value and complete the totality of work and which offers potential alternative approaches to welfare, economy and gender.

Women and the current COVID-19 crisis: an equality issue

Experiences of recession and welfare reform are gendered depending on socio-political conditions, however, the pandemic heightened pre-existing structural inequalities (Women's Budget Group, 2021). The UK Women's Budget Group (WBG) published in April 2020 an important analysis of the different ways women and men may be affected by the COVID-19 pandemic (Women's Budget Group, 2020). While around 73 per cent of those affected by COVID-19 in England, Wales and Northern Ireland were men and the recession initially resulted in increased male unemployment and reduced incomes, it seems that existing structural disadvantages experienced by women contributed to a range of continuing gendered differences (Women's Budget Group, 2021). The WBG offered an evidence-based analysis of the disadvantages experienced by women and called for protections. In terms of employment, women formed the majority of health and social care staff coming into direct contact with COVID-19 (Bambra et al, 2021; Parker, 2021a). Young women were disproportionately affected by furloughs and redundancies from jobs in precarious sectors, especially hospitality and restaurants. In general, women are more likely to be in low-paid jobs, experience poverty and debt, and work in precarious industries.

Therefore, to protect women into the medium- and long-term, the WBG called for the government to collect gender-related data and ensure there are adequate social protections to keep workers safe, to ensure adequate social security and welfare benefits. The pandemic illuminated the stark structural differences in social and public policy in employment practice, social security and gender relations that continue.

Assumptions of the primacy of male breadwinner families remain (Veasey and Parker, 2021). When paid to a heterosexual couple living together, a joint payment, Universal Credit is put into the male's account by default. This entrenches female dependency, enhances male privilege and makes it difficult for women in abusive domestic situations to leave (Parker and Veasey, 2021). This was particularly important during the lockdowns of 2020 and 2021 when the numbers of reported domestic abuse incidence rose (ONS, 2020b; Bambra et al, 2021).

Conclusions

Gendered assumptions permeate social policy and welfare planning, development and provision and have done so throughout history. In British welfare it is the patriarchal system which holds precedence. This has normalised women's dependence on men, men as earner/breadwinner, and is heteronormative. Women's engagement in the labour market, education and autonomy has been cast as aberrant.

There are, however, examples of dual-earner, independent and more gender equal approaches to social welfare policy. The social democratic welfare states of Scandinavian countries offer such. Currently, in Britain, women's voice, autonomy and participation remains limited and, with an uncertain future under Brexit, difficult to determine.

Patriarchal hegemony has controlled and still controls the development and delivery of social welfare. This may seem an extreme perspective. However, if we look at who benefits from social welfare – whether that be armies, military might, politicians, business or, at the micro-level, the male breadwinner – the focus of welfare privileges male positions. This has perhaps become so ingrained that it is rarely given much thought. Indeed, because of the important drivers of immediate social need and want both men and women campaign for social welfare that adequately meets the needs of citizens. This does not detract from its connection with patriarchal privilege nor does the latter mean that social welfare is, therefore, inherently wrong. It acts, rather, as a clarion call for fundamental change.

7

Piacular austerity: sacrificing the poor for the rich

The notion of sacrifice is often used to justify immediate hardships in the hope of longer-term gain. However, it is usually those who are least affected by these 'sacrifices' that impose them on or require them of others. Such claims are made from positions of power in which assertions that 'we are all in it together' misdirect listeners from differences in experience, capital and resource. The concept of sacrifice is deeply rooted in the social consciousness, stemming from religious contentions of expiating wrong, and from struggle as a personal quality. It is often seen as necessary to achievement and is easily used, therefore, by those with political power to develop and implement policies and practices that enhance that power at the expense of those who are 'sacrificing' or being 'sacrificed'.

This chapter addresses the socio-political rationale for austerity measures and analyses this in terms of power relations and the social ritual sacrifice of the poor. Durkheim's concept of 'piacularism' as a collective social rite of mourning and Girard's subsequent concept of mimetic violence and the scapegoat are introduced as relevant conceptual metaphors for some of the ways in which social policies are enacted and supported to preserve a particular normative understanding of social life by sacrificing those considered poor, vulnerable and marginalised and loading them with social 'sin' that requires punishment and, in contemporary society, demands and legitimises the stigmatisation and punishment of those in poverty because they embody that social 'sin' (Katz, 2013). The use of these understandings is suggestive of violence (Ray, 2018). This is, indeed, useful as it brings home the everyday reality of many people sacrificed for the sake of established order, money and power. British society, just as others across the world, is not static and internal and external changes create novel demands which require changing the ways in which sacrifice takes place. The morally feckless and undeserving also shift according to the contemporary definition of the hate figure on the receiving end of such opprobrium. While the chapter focuses on austerity measures adopted in response to the 2008 financial crisis this does not imply that such measures are new or, indeed, that political decisions to sacrifice the poor and vulnerable have not been taken before and earlier examples will also be used.

We will first introduce the concept of piacularism, expiation, scapegoating and sacrifice after which we will examine some key points in British welfare history that evoke expiation and the sacrificing of the other, ostensibly for the wider whole, but representing a political decision based on power relations. Welfare reform throughout history hosts a plethora of examples of people in poverty being used as scapegoats to deflect attention from government failings or concerns. This is seen in the 1834 reform of the Poor Law and its further entrenchment of the concepts of deservingness and undeservingness through to our current approach to migrant workers, free movement when still part of the European Union and in response to refugees and those on benefits during the COVID-19 pandemic. These sacrifices have been made to maintain the status quo using politico-moral devices to set groups against each other while claiming allegiance through 'all being in it together' (Sanders and Shorrocks, 2019; Whitehead et al, 2020).

Piacular rites

We have seen in Chapter 3, concerning binary distinctions, that there is a political theology that divides the world into dualist relationships of good and bad. This conceptualisation of the world allows for the continued demonisation of the poor and, indeed, calls for the scapegoating of those in poverty as somehow morally culpable not only for their own situation but also for the socio-political problems seen within the world. This view permits those with political power to deflect attention away from structural issues that are expensive to address and visit the blame on others who have limited voice in counteracting the thesis. It also places those who are blamed into a position in which they can or ought to be sacrificed to re-establish balance and right in the social world. It is useful to rehearse Durkheim's thinking here.

In *The Elementary Forms of Religious Life*, Durkheim (1912/2001) suggested that ceremonies associated with coping with catastrophes that invoke fear and anguish often take a particular form. He used the term *piacular*, which suggests expiation or transformatory sacrifice, to describe these ceremonies. The word is taken from the Latin *piaculum* which has multiple meanings such as victim, sacrifice, atonement, punishment, crime or sin. In Durkheimian terms, the piacular rite represents an expression of community solidarity in times of crisis. This model has been used to understand acts of terrorism and the sacrifices of civil freedoms demanded of citizens in a country to protect them from terrorism (Worrell, 2013), but we can extend its reach to address fiscal crises, poverty and the receipt of welfare benefits.

In Durkheim's anthropological review of Australian aboriginal peoples, he found that in their mourning rites deep sadness often turned to anger and, subsequently, to ritualised violence against oneself or against certain prescribed other members of the group. He understood these as communal displays of suffering in which the self-inflicted pain and wounds express explicitly that one is suffering. However, they also represented a duty imposed by the group, an obligation to lament that appears to be performed out of respect for custom rather than because of any individual affective state: '[I]t is not simply to express an individual grief, but to fulfil a duty to the feeling that the surrounding society does not fail to remind him of in the event' (Durkheim, 1912/2001, p 297).

We can extend this in our contemporary welfare practice, purporting that the expression of shame, unworthiness and gratefulness for being in receipt of welfare benefits is not simply an individual act signalling a perceived failing, but it is required by those in society not in receipt of benefits so that the causes and results of poverty are assuaged and not visited upon the non-recipient other. This provides a powerful socio-political justification for the introduction of austerity measures which generally have a greater impact on minority groups, women, people in poverty, on low incomes, or in receipt of benefits than on those who impose the measures. In this way, the 'poor' are sacrificed for the benefit of the 'rich', or at least those who align themselves with vested interests and the status quo.

Durkheim found that grief is intensified when it is expressed collectively, which allows a transformation to take place through the rite of mourning. Collective grief can be seen as ritualised in the binary oppositions within society that classify the 'striver' against the 'skiver' and the 'deserving' against the 'underserving'. The 'mourned for' are those who have in some way failed morally and found themselves in the position of having to claim welfare benefits; a feared group because of their diminishment, moral culpability and because of the mystique that surrounds them. These strong emotions are encouraged by those with political voice to further entrench their positions against those in need.

The rite, and especially the shedding of blood in many of the rituals Durkheim relates, is understood as sacrificial. Traditionally, that sacrifice deflects an evil or expiates a misdeed now exemplified, even embodied, within the deceased. But Durkheim goes further in his explanation, suggesting the rite itself, without supernatural ascription, is seen to effect a change, working through the collective forces that are set in motion. Since misfortune threatens the collectivity or social group as a whole, sharing and intensifying the anguish allows the group to ameliorate the effect through the rite of punishment inflicted by expiation as a manifestation of public anger. This directly relates to the experience of the demonised other, those in poverty claiming benefits especially in times of financial crisis. The collectivity requires the amelioration of their potential misfortune by demanding the sacrifice of those who embody that unfortunate position; the miscreant who is perceived as 'taking from' rather than 'contributing to' society and the amelioration of the financial problems of the country. Thus they attract and receive public anger against their moral culpability and need. In turn, this assuages the need for structural change to address the experiences of poverty and allows political power to enact austerity measures that reduce public spending and ensure that vested interests in those powers are preserved.

Durkheim suggests that religious life gravitates around two opposing but also sustaining forces or poles – the pure and the impure, the sacred and the profane. The place of these forces on the poles can change through the ritual, the unclean becoming an instrument of purification: 'The victim immolated in expiatory sacrifices is laden with impurity, since it has been heaped with sins that must be redeemed. Yet once it has been slaughtered, its flesh and blood are put to the most pious uses' (Durkheim, 1912/2001, p 306). We can see a similar social process happening within the realm of social welfare and health. The outrage against 'benefit cheats' and 'scroungers' was supplemented, during the COVID-19 pandemic, by a concern to admonish those who break the rules on social distancing or staying at home, considering the individual to be the problem and not considering the inequality gulf and structural problems such policies expose:

> When society encounters circumstances that sadden, anguish, or irritate it, it exerts pressures on its members to bear witness to their sadness, their anguish, or their anger through expressive acts. It imposes in them something like a duty to weep, wail, and inflict wounds on themselves or others, for these collective demonstrations and the moral communion they express restore to the group the energy that events were threatening to take away, and this enables the group to recover itself. (Durkheim, 1912/2001, p 307)

However, the process of anger and outrage can also be understood to address the situation in which the sacrifice of the welfare recipient allows wider society to assume a position of moral uprightness, to be part of the non-stigmatised, those 'hard-working families' as opposed to the undefined others in government pronouncements as we saw in Chapter 3 and to maintain a sense of collectivity.

There are other ways of understanding sacrifice that also offer useful perspectives on the social opprobrium visited upon people in poverty. Girard (1972, 1986) suggests that disparate people who are all vying for the same thing, adequate resources, are united when they join together to punish an agreed scapegoat. There is a communal participation in the execution of violence against a specific enemy – in our case metaphorical, and sometimes actual, violence against the unemployed, the disabled, the sick, the needy. Girard importantly states that the coming together against the scapegoat must be unconscious. The scapegoat must be considered monstrous and evil and not an 'innocent' scapegoat such as in the biblical story underpinning Passover in Leviticus 16. The ritual re-enactment of scapegoating of the poor ensures that there is seen to be one righteous, pure and normative community in which the other must be punished to ensure community survival. Thus, sacrifice is functional and paradoxically the sacrificial poor are needed in society to fulfil the role of scapegoat. This is echoed in popular food activist Jack Monroe's (2022) coruscating analysis of government policy to reduce expenditure by imposing hurt on those in poverty. The three elements of employing violence to reduce violence, in Girard's view, are: the codification of central prohibitions; the creation of rituals that enact redemptive violence and patterns of required conformity; and the killing of the scapegoat. These violences are enacted in respect of those who require benefits. The systems are complex and codified, specifying punishments for non-conformity and non-compliance akin to the conditionality and sanctions applied to current benefits. Rituals are required in which those claimants are exonerated and expiated or found guilty and sacrificed. The sanctions on these people are imposed to 'kill' the scapegoat and to redeem society (Weaver, 2001).

The concept of sociological hetarchy concerns a paradoxical fusion or interdependence of full economic deregulation, atomised individualisation, domestic political futility or anomie that sits alongside the growth of state apparatus and surveillance technology. This is something we have seen in abundance since the Brexit referendum in Britain, the election of Trump and his term in office in the US, but developed earlier alongside neoliberalism. Individuals are atomised – divorced from responsibility for others which allows for reporting and surveillance of those, paradoxically, not following rules. We can see examples of this in reporting of so-called benefit fraud, 'illegal' immigration and breaking COVID-19 lockdown restrictions.

The tightening of immigration rules and the Windrush scandal also illustrate this sacrifice. Amelia Gentleman, sister-in-law of former Prime Minister Boris Johnson and award-winning *Guardian* journalist, tirelessly excavated the scandal arising from Theresa May's 'hostile environment' for ('illegal') migrants to the UK (Gentleman, 2019). This example demonstrated the indiscriminate targeting of immigrants as a source of welfare extravagance, of the undeservingness of some, and therefore required an approach that showed them to be unwelcome, shameful and to be expelled.

The Windrush generation were invited to Britain to ensure that essential services were supported as there was no one else to undertake those jobs. So, people from former British colonies were invited to take on these roles. Many settled and made Britain their home. The hostile environment created the conditions to make these invited people and their descendants unwelcome scapegoats of a system in austerity. The threatened and forced expulsion of many reinforced a ritual sacrifice to 'take back control', a myth promulgated by those with resources and power in the country. The myth has turned on those creating it during the 2020 COVID-19 crisis, which exposed just how much the National Health Service (NHS) relies on migrant and second- and third-generation migrant workers at all levels.

The historical sacrificing of the poor

The ritualised demonisation of the poor has been enacted throughout history as a means of purging the feared contagion of poverty and unworthiness. The public humiliation and whipping of the vagabond and the distinction of deserving and undeserving demanded a response with community expiation gained by chasing out the feared other (see Chapter 2). As calls for reforms to the Elizabethan Poor Law grew, so too did the enactment of power over those in poverty. While Malthus and others called for the removal of welfare benefits or Poor Law relief, the physical punishment of those calling for reform in favour of those people in poverty or with no recourse to the franchise was seen at Peterloo in 1819, in the 'Swing' riots of 1830 and embodied in the Tolpuddle Martyrs in 1834. These actions, continued following the introduction of the New Poor Law in 1834 in the arrest of anti-Poor Law campaigner Rev Joseph Raynor Stephens, for example, represented ritualised responses to guard those with the means to set the terms of the argument and to sacrifice those who carried the sins of poverty. These responses continue and are clearly exemplified in the austerity measures introduced as a result of the 2007–2008 financial crash.

Austerity and welfare reform in the 2000s
Policy

After stepping down as leader of the Conservative Party, Iain Duncan Smith formed the Centre for Social Justice. However, there was a swift change in his character from someone who, on seeing the deprivation in Easterhouse in Scotland, vowed to address such poverty and conditions, to becoming the Secretary of State for Work and Pensions who presided over the most punitive sanctions in British welfare history (Slater, 2012). Using Proctor's (2008) concept of 'agnotology' to describe the manufacture of doubt and ignorance, Slater details how Duncan Smith's Centre for Social Justice created doubt about the structural causes of poverty, deprivation and unemployment to effect a swing back to popular belief in the moral culpability and failings of individuals in order to reduce welfare costs by introducing more punitive conditions and sanctions on benefit receipt. This change was predicted by Vis et al (2011) after a short period of investment immediately after the financial crisis. This political shift to deceive was seen in the use of terms such as 'broken' and 'breakdown', especially in respect of families, used so often that it became accepted and then used as a rationale for tackling poverty through moral regulation and reform of the individual and through promotion of marriage and family rather than on a concern to address structural causes. Welfare conditionality and a workfare focus that started with New Labour could then be recast through an agnotological lens to create a public recognition of blameworthiness and fault among the poor, which justified 'less eligibility' and punishment (Slater, 2012). This long history of punishment expresses itself in a double regulation of the poor through state action and popular opprobrium (Piven and Cloward, 1971; Waquant, 2009), and allows individuals to construct a spoiled self-image accordingly that requires self-regulation and sacrifice (Goffman, 1963; Foucault, 1984, 1991). Stigma and suffering become 'inscribed on the body' (Frost and Hoggett, 2008, p 452) and the sacrificial victim becomes marked out.

Machin (2020) analyses the UN Special Rapporteur Paul Alston's 2018 report on poverty and human rights. Using McConnell's (2010) policy evaluation framework Machin outlines how welfare reform, as a political choice, exacts a high human cost on people in poverty and those who are vulnerable. Amplified welfare conditionality, although having a longer history than the current round of austerity measures and benefit reductions, has increased poverty. Machin reports Alston's analysis that austerity is based on misguided values that have increased rather than alleviated poverty. The morality argument concerning poverty individualises blame and removes the focus from the structural roots of poverty Ih have disproportionately affected minority ethnic groups, people with disabilities, women and children. Wright et al (2020) interpret this punitive approach through sanctions and conditionality as causing symbolic as well as material suffering, and identify it as state-perpetrated harm, not dissimilar to our own understanding of structural abuse (Parker, 2021a; Parker and Veasey, 2021). This vilification and blame aligns with the conditions necessary for ritualised violence, through state action, against the scapegoat in Girard's (1972, 1986) conception (Wright et al, 2020). Acceptance, therefore, of welfare conditionality and sanctions for non-compliance represents a recognition of the moral culpability and fecklessness of claimants in respect of their own poverty and marginalised positions while allowing the legitimised violence of non-claimants (see Dagilyte and Greenfields, 2015).

The moral discourse of welfare has been brought into sharp relief when comparing domestic benefit claimants and EU migrants. Under a purported focus on 'fairness' an attack has been levelled against a 'dependency culture' through political speeches and the promotion of those discourses through the media into mainstream, everyday understandings (L.D. Morris, 2019). Domestic benefit claimants on their own are pilloried, but can be used symbolically in contrast to migrants where the pilloried becomes the deserving poor unfairly treated by migrant claimants who 'take' their benefits (Dagilyte and Greenfields, 2015). A new approach was taken to welfare spending following the financial crash of 2007–2008 that was embedded within legislation (Taylor-Gooby, 2018). The Treaty on Stability, Coordination and Governance in the Eurozone, which introduced a 0.5 per cent cap on deficits, closely followed by the UK, was reinforced by strict conditions imposed in joint European Central Bank, International Monetary Fund (IMF) and EU loan packages. This demanded draconian public spending cuts, a restructuring of the public sector, increased privatisation and tax reform. For Jordan and Drakeford (2012), the crash and the subsequent austerity measures introduced highlighted the failure of the assumed benign goals of global capitalism to produce increased equality. It was met by a shift in income redistribution and change in the roles of social care to regulate and discipline people and to exert power over those with lower incomes. This is echoed in Bhattacharyya's (2015) thesis that post-crash austerity represents a political strategy, which is imposed rather than enacted by explicit consent as a 'hegemonic project' (p 11), creating a distinct tonal shift from Thatcherism in which consent for spending cuts, retrenchment and self-imposed hardships was sought. Garrett (2018, p 10) explains this as 'semantic recalibration' in which Conservative protestations to tackling injustices and inequalities are belied by imposing harsh austerity measures and public spending and welfare cuts that disproportionately affect people on lower incomes while claiming there is a collective need to 'tighten one's belt'.

The introduction of austerity measures seems from an individualised perspective to be 'common-sense' – if you have not got the money to pay for something you cannot buy it. Indeed, as Hill and Irving (2020) point out, the cost-cutting, public service reduction measures established by national governments, regional and international organisations after the crash were promoted as a logical strategy for economic recovery. However, such a message fails to take into account the differential experiences of people in which not paying for public services had a monumental effect on those in need but had little or no effect on those with means. It is false and mealy-mouthed to pretend that everyone experienced austerity. It sacrificed the poor for the benefit of those with business and other vested interests (Mendoza, 2015). Some lives were considered less valuable than others. This is seen in the ways in which the British media, tabloid in particular, pounced on the chance to run stories of single examples of fraudulent benefit claims, of scrounging and of unworthiness as austerity measures were introduced after 2010 rather than reporting on wider societal elements (Chauhan and Foster, 2014).

Eckersley and Tobin (2019) recognise that most studies on austerity focus on the impact of budgetary cuts and public sector restraint, but do not usually consider how policy directions overall have changed as a result of these actions. Using Bauer and Knill's (2012) concept of 'dismantling by arena shifting' they describe how the pursuit of low visibility policy dismantling allows more profound changes in public sector involvement while avoiding the blame for cuts in public spending and services. 'Dismantling' is wider in scope than cutbacks or retrenchment (Pierson, 1994), although changes to welfare provision, children's services, adult social care and so on are often framed in this way. Such shifts in policy capacity lead to more subtle changes in discourses of government and policy action than those occurring under Thatcher's terms which construct the arenas of practice and allow both significant shifts and reductions in public spending and avoidance of blame for unpopular cuts; government becomes a matter of 'it is what it is'.

Joy and Shields (2018) identify the worldwide growth of interest in social income bonds as part of this shift in the policy narrative. Social income bonds use austerity measures to increase their popularity and to gain the consent of the general public for reforms of public services. However, as Joy and Shields point out, there is no research evidence to show they are effective in addressing embedded social problems. Most social income bonds represent a form of philanthro-capitalism that further privatises state welfare and gains public support in times of austerity and spending reductions. It is also a means of exacting a monetary sacrifice from people that bolsters those with political power. By moving provision from the state to private, economics-oriented organisations the role of the state in public welfare is further eroded.

Hill and Irving (2020) recognise that the current round of austerity has reduced social citizenship entitlements, public spending, public sector jobs, and has removed public subsidies on food and fuel, raised taxes such as value added tax (VAT) and introduced public sector pay freezes, all of which have a disproportionate effect on people in poverty and on low incomes. The lack of growth arising from these policies has increased material inequalities. However, they suggest this has also led to changes in public narratives on collective responsibility and solidarity and now the welfare state is considered too costly and should target only the poorest and neediest in society. This shifts the concept of the welfare state from qualitative provision of universal citizen entitlements to an economic political strategy. Social divisions across age, class and gender have widened as these entitlements have shrunk and universal perspectives have been replaced by more nationalist and populist agendas such as 'welfare chauvinism' (van der Waal et al, 2010), which allows blame and stigma to grow and which requires sacrifice to offset – through conditionality, sanctions and blame.

Of course, austerity did not start in 2010 nor result solely from the 2008 crash, as Mendoza (2015) points out, but arose through the neoliberal development of global economic force designed to keep the global economy afloat regardless of the impact on individuals. The IMF offered loans to struggling nations on the basis of selling assets, predominantly to developed nations, and in return for controls on public spending through the Structural Adjustment Programme (SAP). Austerity represents a form of SAP that services the national debt. The bank bailout was taken in the UK to prevent the collapse of investment banks and ensure their continued profitability against the interests of ordinary citizens. The debt was serviced by tight control of public spending justified on the basis of necessity, a lie illuminated by the ability to respond to the COVID-19 crisis through business funds, self-employment finance, increased Universal Credit and so forth. The sacrifice of those in need allowed those with capital and power to maintain and even increase it at the expense of others. This willingness to sacrifice the other deviates from the collective ritual that Durkheim describes and adds a new complexion to the notion of the expiation. The poor and those in need are seen to embody that which is feared – poverty, need and lack. Thus, these people are sinful and demand to be punished, making the system of benefit reform righteous and necessary to protect the public interest, aka the interests of the rich. The collective approach to demonising the sacrifice is aided by the tabloid press, itself controlled by the rich and controlling the mass, who identify the sins of the sacrifice and the need for its ritual punishment through reduction of benefit, ostracisation and humiliation. This is further compounded by televisual media in such programmes as Channel Four's *Benefits Street* or the late *Jeremy Kyle Show* (see Jensen and Tyler's [2015] discussion of 'benefits broods').

Austerity measures have taken the sacrifice to the ultimate extreme with people dying before receipt of benefit whether that be Universal Credit Personal Independence Payments (PIP) or other. In answer to a parliamentary question asking how many people had died waiting for PIP the Department for Work and Pensions (DWP) indicated that between April 2013 and April 2018 there were over 3.6 million applications made; of these, 4,760 claimants died between their case being referred to, and returned from, an assessment provider; 73,800 claimants died within six months of their claim being registered; and 17,070 claimants died after registering but prior to the DWP making a decision on their claim (UK Parliament, 2018).

In respect of Universal Credit, the numbers dying are hard to determine with the DWP not collecting adequate data and not reporting these (Topple, 2020). What is clear is that the numbers of people dying while trying to claim benefits are significant, that benefit cuts and restrictive regulations are to blame, and that these represent sacrifices to reduce the economic cost of social welfare during a time of fiscal constraint. Austerity measures have exacted a high price across many areas. Martin et al (2021) estimate that over 50,000 extra deaths could have been linked to austerity measures in social and health care between 2010 and 2015, while overall deaths linked to austerity between 2012 and 2019 have been conservatively estimated at 335,000 (Walsh et al, 2022).

Torfs et al (2021) compare the effects of austerity measures across different European countries to explicate the increase in reported unmet health needs as a result. However, the burden of the effects was experienced differentially and not just seen as affecting lower-income groups. Policy choices in Ireland have protected lower-income groups with the major effects being felt by middle-income groups. This suggests that austerity policies represent a political choice and that health inequalities can be mitigated by certain policies.

The 'Great Recession' of 2008 was met, in many countries, by reduced public expenditure, often in health care (Torfs et al, 2021). To a large extent Britain protected its health-care spending with a real annual average growth of 3.94 per cent between 2008 and 2014. In policy terms, however, there was a reduction in health-care professional salaries. These cuts, driven by budgetary constraint, increased health inequalities already noted in the Black report (1980). When Marmot first reported in 2010 inequalities were noted as rife with people living in impoverished areas having a life expectancy seven years lower than those living in wealthier areas (Marmot, 2010). In the ten-year follow-up report these inequalities continued unabated with geography and region as well as wealth contributing to poorer health outcomes (Marmot et al, 2020). Those working in health care saw wages reduced in real terms and represented a sacrificial lamb slaughtered with impunity, as those experiencing health inequalities were more likely to be poor or economically unviable. When we see, as in Ireland, measures being put in place to protect low income groups, it seems that unmet medical needs no longer affect them disproportionately when compared to higher income groups.

Disability

Harris (2014) argues that the change from Disability Living Allowance to PIP, to assist with those additional costs of living arising from disability and introduced by the Welfare Reform Act 2012 ss 77–95, placed disabled people in the same context as other benefit claimants. Thus, numbers of disabled people claiming benefits were reduced and those still doing so were cast in the blameworthy category of 'underserving', a product of the discourses driven by an agnotological approach that prevents critical questioning (Slater, 2012), a change echoed also in Gregory's (2017) research on the 'gig' or 'on-demand' economy in which alternative work opportunities were considered to be available. Increases in conditionality and sanctions are purportedly designed to encourage people into work. However, Ceolta-Smith et al (2018) found little evidence that these welfare reforms have been effective, or perceived as such by frontline workers, in supporting disabled people and those with long-term health conditions into work. Harris (2014) argues that these changes breached the rights of disabled people to independence. This was affirmed by the United Nations report in 2016 that found a systematic violation of rights and a disproportionate adverse effect of welfare reform on disabled people, which the UK government (2016) rejected. Entitlement is based on individual assessment by approved health-care professionals and is subject to periodic review (Machin, 2017). These changes promoted independent reviews to question the role of private assessors and to call for greater accountability and quality control in those assessments (Gray, 2014, 2017). These changes reflect the homogenisation of diverse groups as 'claimants' which has become synonymous with those negative labels identified in Chapter 2 as workshy benefit fraudsters who deserve their punishment and therefore should be sacrificed for the greater good of 'hardworking families' and 'taxpayers'.

Employment and mental health

Historically, welfare has been implicated, by those with adequate resources, in creating a poverty trap in which individuals are financially better off out of work. Attempts to address the perceived incentives to remain unemployed, associated with the Speenhamland system of outdoor relief, were harshly drafted in the Poor Law (Amendment) Act 1834 in terms of 'less eligibility'. These actions have been replicated in the removal of Family Income Support in the 1970s and family credit in the 1980s and addressed through individual blame, the creation of punishment through sanction, and behavioural conditionality for receipt in the Welfare Reform Act 2012 and the introduction of Universal Credit (Larkin, 2018).

Beatty and Fothergill (2018) identify that welfare reform during austerity has produced savings, albeit unequally, across the country, but despite the increased conditionality and sanctions appears to have done little in reducing unemployment. They state that welfare reform has been predominantly concerned with reducing public expenditure in the most deprived and impoverished places rather than trying to deal with the social problems exacerbating these issues. Dwyer et al (2020) show that there is little evidence to suggest that conditionality helps people into employment but significant evidence to show its deleterious impact on mental health. Initiated by New Labour in 2008, the Employment and Support Allowance (ESA) replaced incapacity benefit, disability related income support and Severe Disablement Allowance and introduced elements of conditionality and workfare. However, in their study of welfare conditionality, it was the change brought in by Universal Credit that merged Jobseeker's Allowance and the ESA and removed the 'limited capacity for work' payment worth £29.05 per week that was experienced by disabled people as especially problematic. Increased conditionality and fitness for work assessments were considered uncaring and insensitive, exacerbating the mental ill-health of respondents. All this indicates a willingness to sacrifice the vulnerable and poor to reduce state expenditure and protect the interests of those who have.

Austerity measures affect those on the lowest incomes, women and children, those in social and private rented housing, with the biggest losses occurring in older industrial areas, less prosperous seaside towns and some of the London boroughs. Earlier Harmitz (2013) described the impact of the Welfare Reform Act 2012 on the London borough of Newham from the perspective of a local charitable organisation, Community Links. The charity held regular in-depth interviews about the changes to welfare with 16 local people over a three-year period. Levels of awareness of changes, the introduction of Universal Credit and PIP, the household benefit cap and under-occupancy charges were low and generally misunderstood but there was a lack of trust in the reforms helping those who were unemployed or in poverty.

The impact of employment on the mental health of lone mothers between 1991 and 2008, using the General Health Questionnaire and data from the British Household Panel Survey, is associated with supportive welfare policy reform (Harkness, 2016). Unlike men, employment on its own does not appear to be indicative of improved mental health in women, especially lone mothers, no doubt because of the often ignored factors of women carrying greater responsibility for child care. However, New Labour welfare reform did appear to improve mental health when taken alongside increased employment (Waldfogel, 2010). Between 1999 and 2003 financial incentives to take up employment were offered through Working Family Tax Credits and child-care support. In 2003, this was replaced by Working Tax Credits and Child Tax Credit, although this also saw an increase in compulsion towards work through the implementation of six-monthly work-focused interviews. Poor mental health rates for working mothers with partners changed little with these reforms alone, but lone mothers' poor mental health decreased considerably after the reforms and if they gained employment – between 12 and 18 per cent when welfare benefits were combined with employment. When austerity measures have reformed welfare by targeting certain groups, and when employment is more precarious, poor mental health outcomes may rise again, but lone mothers represent a traditional target for sacrificing to ensure others are supported – a moral approach.

Housing

Manzi and Richardson (2017) recognise the impact that austerity measures and market-led provision have had on housing professionals. Coalition and post-2015 Conservative government policies have marginalised the social housing sector and consolidated a shift from welfare professionalism to more market-friendly managerialism, which has led to a delegitimised housing sector that no longer serves poorer residents and potential residents but works to abstracted and impersonal market rules (Jacobs and Manzi, 2013; Manzi,

2015). This represents an ideological shift reinforced by discourses of the feckless, undeserving aspects of those requiring social housing. Daly (2018) confirmed the impact on workers when examining staff in a small agency working to resettle homeless people. Cuts to welfare and support and welfare reform reduced provision, or even saw the deletion of services, and shifted it in agencies to a more impersonal market-driven notion of care towards 'embodied austerity', in which the relational values of staff were destabilised and conflicted. The changing realities of work reflected the precarious, underfunded arena in which it was practised. Targets, monitoring and surveillance led to changed relationships within organisations and between staff and the people they served.

Food banks

Lambie-Mumford and Green (2017) report on data from the Trussell Trust Foodbank Network that shows austerity measures and reduction in welfare benefits have led to an increase in the number of children in families being supported by food banks. In areas of high deprivation, where there is a high risk of poverty, the number of children reliant on food parcels has grown. This demonstrates a shift from the concept of universal social security and support to a system dependent on charitable support. This indicates governmental willingness to sacrifice those most vulnerable to poverty in its move away from a focus on child poverty to family conceptions when delivering or planning welfare. The effects of welfare reform have been particularly harsh for children. Using data from the Trussell Trust Foodbank Network, Lambie-Mumford and Green reported the increase of children relying on food banks and recognised the association with deprivation, arguing that this results from a shift away from the structural drivers of poverty.

Why are governments willing to sacrifice the poor and why do they choose to do so? Othering of the expendable deflects attention, but it also highlights an ideological rationale to privilege markets above people. Austerity measures were built on understandings of poverty and the privileging of particular welfare solutions and not just as reactions to the financial crisis. Lambie-Mumford and Green (2017) suggest that behavioural explanations grew while structural explanations have been replaced by notions of individual failings, which, in turn, has further entrenched the binary oppositions we dealt with in Chapter 3 of 'deserving and undeserving' welfare recipients. The Conservative ideology of 'civil society', which took shape in the 'Big Society', emphasises the importance of charitable organisations as opposed to state provision of welfare as seen in changes to housing provision (Manzi, 2015).

In psychosocial terms the public support for those requiring food bank support forms another sacrifice – leaving gifts to assuage guilt and fear of contagion from food poverty, alongside the heartfelt compassion being expressed through these charitable actions. It also begins to hide and obviate state responsibility by individualising poverty and deflecting attention from structural drivers of inequality.

COVID-19 lockdown and sacrifice

While Chapter 10 will deal more fully with COVID-19, it is important to consider how pandemic policies continued the sacrificial element of welfare delivery. 'Stay Home, Protect the NHS, Save Lives' – the mantra of the 2020 COVID-19 lockdown in the UK. The policy of lockdown, shutting businesses, schools, transport and putting in place rules of 'social distancing' – perhaps better described as 'physical distancing' as its practice is anything other than social – came late after a suggestion that catching the disease might create 'herd immunity' to protect the wider population in the future (Aschwanden, 2020). While not a popular decision, it seemed to be generally accepted that lockdown was necessary to reduce overload on an already stretched and under-resourced NHS. The NHS had experienced resource cuts since the introduction of austerity measures along with other public services. The message to stay in was reinforced by the pleas of overworked medical and nursing staff, through emotional videos and press releases. However, the lockdown was broken by the Chief Medical Officer for Scotland, by cabinet ministers in England alongside those who were subject to press scrutiny for holding parties, for sunbathing in the park, having barbecues or meeting with friends.

The police took their new powers seriously; flying drones to picture and shame ramblers in Derbyshire, to break up groups in parks, to move on those who sat in parks and to tell people they couldn't sit in their front gardens. The Coronavirus Act 2020 gave the police sweeping powers to enforce the lockdown, but brought to the fore questions of trust in the police, heavy-handedness and a focus on social inequalities. This came centre stage during the weekend of 13 March 2021 during the vigil mourning the murder of Sarah Everard when police officers were accused of heavy-handed policing tactics that echoed the violence attendees were protesting against. The police were found guilty of breaching protesters' rights in a judgement by Lord Justice Warby and Mr Justice Holgate in March 2022.

Complaints against lockdown measures on the lives of the most vulnerable in society, including women and children in dysfunctional and abusive households, disabled and older people with underlying health conditions and people on low incomes demonstrate politically unacceptable risks of poverty and growth in socio-economic inequalities (Lyne and Parker, 2020; Hantrais and Letablier, 2021; Parker, 2021a; Veasey and Parker, 2021).

Experiencing a lockdown when one has family, social media technology, space and a garden is different to experiencing it in small-roomed flats, or with partners who are potentially or actually abusive. People in poverty and need suffered more under lockdown than those with means and adequate resources (Bambra et al, 2021). Everyone was said to be in the fight against the rapid spread of COVID-19, but not everyone was in it in the same way (Bambra et al, 2021). The government made provision for people and businesses experiencing hardship but this did not filter to those in most need as quickly as needed, and the levels of provision for the poor had been reduced consistently over the previous ten years, making the experience more profound. The poor were sacrificed for the nation through a policy designed to help alleviate the worst ravages of the disease. This is reinforced when looking at education.

Eurydice (2020) was a European network of 43 national units based in the 38 countries operating the Erasmus+ programme developed to assess the impact that school closures had on children. The study found a number of positives in relation to reorganising teaching online and continuing to offer educational provision. However, there were a number of negative impacts recognised which were exacerbated within families with less access to resources or the means to provide children with the necessary resources to learn online. Indeed, existing inequalities were increased even in professional working households working from home. Women took the bulk of child care/home schooling and antisocial hours, while male partners took the prime daytime hours for their work (Ashencaen Crabtree et al, 2021).

Food banks were unable to make deliveries to those hungry and unable to buy food. They began to run out of food and yet the focus remained on the working of the lockdown policy rather than on the burning questions of social justice and adequate incomes for all. On 19 March 2020, when the schools were closed during the first lockdown, the Department for Education (2020) issued guidance to ensure that children receiving benefits-related free school meals would continue to receive meals or food vouchers while not in school. This guidance seems supportive but changes and U-turns during the summer and subsequent lockdowns saw the government back down to pressure and reinstitute free school meals only after a popular campaign by Manchester United footballer, Marcus Rashford, while measures to support businesses experiencing hardship continued (Fareshare, 2022). This suggested that business interests took precedence over the well-being of children from low-income families, these children were expendable, sacrificed for broader economic goals.

Conclusions

For centuries there has been a deep social demarcation between those in possession and the ones they have dispossessed (O'Hara, 2020). This builds on a legitimated ritual sacrifice of those in need or poverty (undeserving) for the supposed collective good of the rest (deserving). This is not a willing sacrifice but a cynical, albeit often unconscious, political sacrifice. It unites the majority of citizens against others, deflecting attention from structural problems and governmental responsibilities and imputing these to the sacrifice who is, therefore, rightly punished. This form of socio-political strategy of sacrifice fragments society and maintains the power of those with vested interests in society. It is far from a wish to provide universal welfare for all.

8

Universal Credit versus Universal Basic Income: strange bedfellows?

The inclusion of the word 'universal' in Universal Credit (UC) is a baffling misnomer that seems to represent a long-standing desire to simplify the administration and reduce the costs of social protection benefits within a system that can be applied to those eligible for receipt of such. The benefit is not universal and reflects the shift towards reinstating means-testing of benefits that has characterised the welfare state since its inception. The universal application of state provision is exemplified, however, by most proponents of a Universal Basic Income (UBI), something paid to everyone regardless of need, resource or status. This chapter will consider one of the 'holy grails' searched for throughout the history of British social welfare, the need to reduce administration and bureaucracy in social security and welfare. Alongside this, we will introduce and explore historical calls for (universal) basic income. These may seem a strange combination to debate together in the same chapter. However, our central concern lies with social security/ social protection in general. We consider Poor Law dole and outdoor relief, alongside philosophical treatises on proto-basic income schemes to chart the twin aims that have often infused formal policy directions from both poles of the political spectrum: the need to simplify benefit systems and to find novel ways of ensuring a more equal or equitable distribution of income. Both desires are underpinned by political ideologies.

Universal Credit? Ways of reducing welfare administration to address poverty

UC was introduced to replace four other benefits and two tax credit schemes: Child Tax Credit; Housing Benefit (HB); Income Support; income-based Jobseeker's Allowance; income-related Employment and Support Allowance (ESA); and Working Tax Credit. It was meant to simplify the process and thereby reduce costs by replacing disparate benefits and systems by a single approach to welfare benefit (Gov.UK, nd). However, when it was implemented it was administered in different ways according to personal status and geography.

Citizens are eligible for UC if they are unemployed or in work but earning a low wage with the benefit tapering as more is earned. The HB component is paid directly to the claimant rather than to landlords, which has caused some concerns and problems as living on a low wage has forced some people into making choices to spend money allocated for HB on quotidian living costs (Wilson, 2019). Under some circumstances, claimants could ask for the HB element to be paid directly to a landlord. Rather than benefits being paid weekly, UC is paid monthly (or twice monthly in Scotland) with a view to mimicking in-work payment conditions. Thus, the thrust of the UC policy is geared towards paid employment which, in itself, is almost an unquestioned given that reflects an underlying and unspoken antipathy towards the unspoken and mistaken assumption that social welfare involved getting 'something for nothing'. Questions relating to the value of different forms of work and activity, such as child care, looking after relatives who are ill, disabled or in need, or undertaking voluntary work, for instance, are rarely voiced when considering benefit reform such as UC.

UC was developed and proposed by Iain Duncan Smith in 2010 when he became minister for work and pensions. Following a report by the Centre for Social Justice, 'Dynamic benefits' (2009), the concept was adopted by the Coalition government and found its way into statute in the Welfare Reform Act of 2012. The process of introducing it into welfare payments in practice was slow and fraught, with people initially waiting up to six weeks for payments although this time lag decreased over time (Walton, 2018). However, in 2015 Chancellor George Osborne announced a £5 billion cut to UC, which further exacerbated many of the problems experienced by recipients of it.

The concept of UC was ideologically driven, as Duncan Smith's foreword to 'Dynamic benefits' indicates:

> As leader of the Conservative Party I frequently encountered significant social breakdown and dysfunctionality across the country. I met people trapped by dependency and left behind by society.
>
> This emerging underclass lives in communities consistently defined by five characteristics, which become the pathways to poverty: family breakdown; educational failure; drug and alcohol addiction; severe personal indebtedness; and economic dependency – caused by intergenerational worklessness.
>
> The CSJ has published more than 350 policy solutions to reverse this breakdown – breakdown which costs society more than £100 billion a year – and move people out of poverty. At the heart of these solutions is recognition that the nature of the life you lead and the choices you make have a significant bearing on whether you live in poverty. Policy-makers regularly fail to understand this, instead viewing poverty through a financial lens only. (Centre for Social Justice, 2009, p 4)

UC has been seen in similar ways to other means of reducing the complexity of social security/protection benefits, and tapering income at the lower end in standardised ways a little like negative income tax, which Bowman (2014) describes as a graduated universal benefit that decreases with earnings. However, Bowman goes further and describes it as equivalent to a basic income, which it is not because of its conditional and means-testing characteristics. The potential of UC as a measure in the fight against inequalities is echoed by such stalwarts of social policy as Bill Jordan (2012), who see UC as reform of the tax-benefit system and a necessary first step along a rather tortuous road towards Universal Basic or Citizen Income. However, while UC appears, superficially, to be a sensible move in welfare reform by reducing complexity and simplifying the system (Jordan, 2012), it has many critics who highlight its shortcomings (Wright et al, 2016). It is digital by default and thereby constructs exclusionary criteria for people already experiencing marginalisation in society through disability, low educational attainment, unemployment and poverty (the 2016 Ken Loach film, *I, Daniel Blake*, shows dramatically how these problems can mount). There remains a built-in waiting time for receipt of benefit which, like work, is paid in arrears, and this has increased the use of food banks and increased suffering considerably (Booth, 2019).

The concept of welfare conditionality is not a new idea, and in UC reduced benefits with conditions are deployed to encourage recipients to engage in work-seeking or work-maintaining behaviours. This aligns with the deserving/undeserving debate in which claimants are only considered worthy if they are actively, and can prove it, looking for employment, or working in low-paid employment. Thus, someone who is unable to work for a range of reasons – ill-health, caregiving responsibilities and so on – may be open to sanction, meaning a reduction in benefits (Pennycock and Whittaker, 2012; Puttick, 2012; Dwyer and Wright, 2014; Reeve, 2017; Fletcher and Wright, 2018; Cheetham et al, 2019).

Between April 2020 and the end of September 2021 UC was increased up to £20 per week to help claimants through the COVID-19 pandemic. It was estimated that 690,000 people were protected from poverty by this measure (Winchester, 2021) although here it seemed to help single parents and workless families more than those in work because of the taper rate. Withdrawal of the increase was significant for many people and, according to Griffiths (2021), illustrated structural problems with UC. Poor communication from the Department for Work and Pensions to claimants meant that many were not aware the uplift was temporary, did not receive the full amount, and were unprepared for its removal. In the autumn budget of 2021 the taper rate was reduced from 63 per cent to 55 per cent. This action served to help those in work but not those out of work (Kirk-Wade, 2022).

UC has been developed as a means of reducing welfare costs, through decreasing administration and bureaucracy. However, it has done so at the expense of people in vulnerable, precarious and impoverished circumstances (see Chapter 7). The roll out of UC exposes the privilege of those setting the agenda and portrays a fundamental lack of insight into the lives of welfare recipients (O'Hara, 2020). UC indicates that the discourses constructed by those with the power to set the terms of the argument about welfare benefits, reform and those in receipt of benefits have been internalised and believed. The rationale driving the introduction of UC echoes the familiar calls that so attracted Edwin Chadwick in the Commission underpinning the Poor Law (Amendment) Act 1834, cutting costs by less eligibility, reducing benefit administration and complexity and introducing punishment conditions (sanctions and conditionality) to address the individual moral failings of those claiming or in receipt of benefits. This was something taken up by Richard Titmuss in his defence of redistributionist social policies (Titmuss, 2001a). However, there have also been calls for a different approach that, also, takes some of its justification from historical thought, debate and practice. We shall now turn to consider the concept of (Universal) Basic Income.

Universal Basic Income: novel schemes from different perspectives

There are a number of income support schemes that appear somewhat similar that have been categorised as UBI. The concept of negative income tax represents one such approach. It was proposed by the right-wing economic thinker, Milton Friedman, as a means of reducing the welfare bill to the state in the US and assisting people in poverty. UBI differs from this and other similar schemes, including minimum income guarantees and tax credits, because, suggest van Parijs and Vanderborght (2017), it is unconditional and not means-tested. Haagh (2019) argues against negative income tax because, like the underlying philosophical base for UC, it focuses on employment and sanctions and is concerned with encouragement towards paid employment. Rodríguez-Fernández and Themelis (2021) argue that UBI is preferable to the guaranteed minimum income schemes that have developed throughout the EU under the Maastricht Treaty 1992 as the former rests on the principle of citizen rights rather than economic competitiveness.

UBI is a non-means-tested income at a certain level applied to everyone. It has supporters from across the political spectrum, with some suggesting this could replace all cash exchanges and welfare benefits in way that simplifies the system as UC was intended to do (Murray, 2013). However, introduced without redistribution, for instance, by taxing wealthier citizens is unlikely to do anything other than retrench the position of those on lower incomes (Fitzroy and Jin, 2018). As such it remains a politically controversial concept.

Standing (2016) understands the concept of a citizen's basic income as a way of addressing many of the administrative and bureaucratic hurdles that UC was designed to overcome but often, unwittingly, reinforced. He suggests that UBI represents a means of 'consolidating many existing transfer schemes and replacing others that are riddled with complexity and arbitrary and discretionary conditionality' (Standing, 2016, p 200). Malcolm Torry (2016, 2018) describes universal income as a citizen's right, linking it directly to the concept of citizenship (Marshall, 1949/1992; Dwyer, 2004). He defines basic income as a 'citizen's basic income (which is) an unconditional, automatic and non-withdrawable payment to each individual as a right of citizenship' (Torry, 2018, p 123), although he would concede differential payments according to age. Despite differences in the concept, the universality and unconditionality of it is stressed: 'A universal basic income (UBI) would see a tax-free, unconditional and non-contributory weekly income paid to every individual as of right, irrespective of how much they earned or their work status' (Downes and Lansley, 2018, p 1).

There are arguments about UBI as a replacement of benefit or as an independent income. UBI is promoted as non-conditional, in terms of income, spending and behaviour (Standing, 2017; van Parijs and Vanderborght, 2017; Haagh, 2019). It is a stable income that is both individual and universal. For Standing (2017), it is income and not benefit and therefore it will not replace welfare systems, and it is a cash rather than in-kind payment (van Parijs and Vanderborght, 2017). Sameroff (2019) acknowledges these features but considers it as a replacement to most existing welfare benefits. Stephens (2019) also poses that question in relation to the New Zealand/Aotearoa welfare system, suggesting that a conditional system akin to UC would be preferable because of increased costs. UBI is controversial, radical and multifaceted as a concept which could replace some social security systems, lower dependency on and reduce problems of low take-up of means-tested benefits, remove people from the existing poverty trap when taking up employment, reduce stigma and save exorbitant costs in administering social security (McDonagh and Bustillos Morales, 2020). Haagh (2019) suggests, however, that it is not compensatory but a fundamental part of a socially developmental welfare system.

Two approaches are taken to UBI, egalitarian and libertarian approaches, the latter advocating the break-up of the current welfare state system and nudging people into 'correct' behaviours and work (Murray, 2006). Libertarian ideals are often associated with the political right – suggesting that land is owned by no one and therefore can be exploited by anyone. Sameroff (2019, p 146) argues against the 'boundless idealism' of UBI expressed by Bregman (2018) and others, and even suggests it could be conditional if used in a clear political way. This seems to misunderstand the basic principles involved in UBI. Standing (2017) takes an egalitarian approach more associated with the political left and suggests the land is owned by all and UBI represents universal compensation; an instrument of democratisation that would reduce the influence and excesses of rich and powerful people. Haagh (2019) describes this as a democratic humanist approach.

There is a long history to basic income (van Parijs and Vanderborgt, 2017; Downes and Lansley, 2018; Torry, 2018). Downes and Lansley (2018) take the debate back to 483 BCE when the distribution of income from a rich seam of silver discovered in Athenia was discussed. One suggestion was to distribute equally among the 30,000 Athenian citizens akin to the social dividend from oil revenue offered to Alaskan citizens today. This was not adopted, rather the income was used to support building the Athenian navy. Standing (2017) also traces the history of UBI back to Ephialtes and Pericles in Athens, but also to its medieval roots in the Charter of the Forest, part of the Charter of Liberties/Magna Carta, which gave rights of common to ensure subsistence.

Historically, there are differences as to whether payment should be universal or conditional. The concept was cited as a means of reducing theft and murder in Thomas More's fictional *Utopia* (1516/1910), which advocated UBI as a means of dealing with growing crime: the Portuguese protagonist, Raphael Hythlodaeus, submitted to the Archbishop of Canterbury that stealing should not be a capital offence but that universal income should be given to all (van Parijs and Vanderborght, 2017). Ten years later Spanish-Flemish scholar Johannes Vives offered a detailed proposal to the mayor of Bruges for civil investment in poor relief. There was a brief trial of food and relief being given for work in Ypres but this developed around the concept of a right to work. Johannes Ludovicus Vives made his arguments directly to the authorities rather than through fiction in his *De Subventione Pauperum* (1526) (see Sherwood, 1917). He advocated payment to those who were deemed to be deserving paupers demonstrated by their willingness to work and so maintained eligibility criteria rather than universality. These developments influenced Thomas Cromwell's Tudor Poor Laws, which, in turn, underpinned the Elizabethan Poor Laws (van Parijs and Vanderborght, 2017). At this time there was a concern for able-bodied persons working to secure a living and a fear of idleness seen in John Locke's criticism of poor relief as failing in this regard in *On the Poor Laws and Working Schools* (1697; see Fox Bourne, 1876). This was maintained in legislation in the 1723 Workhouse Test Act.

However, modern historical arguments are considered to have started in Thomas Paine's claims for agrarian justice in 1795 in which he argued for every person over 21 years to be paid £15 'coming of age grants' and all over 50 years paid £10 basic income. Paine expanded the common inheritance approach devised by the 4th-century Saint Ambrose of Milan. In England, Thomas Spence suggested the payment of a social dividend, while on the continent in the 19th century, Charles Fourier, Joseph Charlier and Francois Huet promoted an unconditional cash transfer. However, this was overtaken by the rise of communism and social democracy, with Marx, himself, later proposing common ownership.

The controversial 1795 Speenhamland system supplemented wages, as a counter to the fear of revolution. It has been criticised for keeping wages low by trapping people in poverty. While based on employment principles rather than a UBI, Bregman (2018) suggests the Royal Commission Report on Speenhamland, confirming contemporary criticism of poor relief, was wrong, and the system was in fact successful. William Pitt attempted, and failed, to introduce a Speenhamland-type system nationally, facing criticism from such as Edmund Burke (1729–1797) for removing Christian duty and placing it in state hands.

Thomas Malthus built ideas around those of Joseph Townsend's (1786/1817) *Dissertation on the Poor Laws*, which posited that poor relief encouraged idleness and procreation among the poor. This was echoed in Frederic Morton Eden's *State of the Poor* (1797). Malthus (1766–1834) wrote in his *Essay on the Principle of Population*, in 1798, that state aid restricted the work ethic and by so doing increased the number of the poor. He suggested poor relief should be withdrawn and the poor left to charity and their own devices (Book 4, chapter 8, s 7). This antipathy to state aid was reproduced in many of the political, economic and philosophical thinkers of the time including David Ricardo in his *Principles of Political Economy and Taxation* (1817); Georg Wilhelm Friedrich Hegel, on the continent, who discussed the English Poor Laws in his *Elements of Philosophy of Right* (1820) (Wood, 1991); and one of the progenitors of sociology, Alexis de Tocqueville, who suggested that the Poor Laws were no longer degrading enough to coerce people into work in his *Memoir on Pauperism* (1835/1997). These are ideas that have permeated criticism of social welfare through history as the rich blame the poor for their lot (Bregman, 2018). Utilitarian philosopher Jeremy Bentham was less radical in his *Second Essay on the Poor Laws* (1796), but predicated support on the basis of workfare. These critiques from the powerful greatly influenced the 1832 Royal Commission and its proposals for restricting outdoor relief to the impotent poor only. As the New Poor Law took hold, John Stuart Mill moved closer to UBI, in his 1848 work *Principles of Political Economy* (1848/2004), recognising the structural problems with the Poor Laws but advocating for a change to obligation-free justice, like Charles Fourier in *La Fausse Industrie* (1836/2017), but one which was means-tested.

The concept has been debated and developed, underpinning Poor Law and welfare state developments throughout Europe (even in novels such as Edward Bellamy's *Looking Backwards* [1888] and William Morris' *News from Nowhere* [1890]). A second wave of interest in UBI took shape after the First World War. For instance, C.H. Douglas in the 1920s proposed the social credit movement, recognising something needed to be done to address the increasing social divide resulting from technology. Bertrand Russell argued, in *Roads to Freedom* and *In Praise of Idleness*, that leisure was a good in itself, moving away from the concept of employment and workfare. These ideas for changing work and paid labour were replaced by the paid employment-focused welfare state, although UBI advocates remained. Through the 20th century and into the 21st century a number of UBI experiments were undertaken and interest in the idea has been shown across the political divide including the philosopher Bertrand Russell, economists J.K. Galbraith, Friedrich von Hayek and Milton Friedman, civil rights activist Martin Luther King, sociologist Charles Murray, businessman Mark Zuckerberg and politician Barack Obama. In the UK the Green Party and Scottish Nationalist Party have shown interest in it.

When Beveridge was developing his ideas on social insurance, Lady Juliet Rhys Williams, a member of Beveridge's committee, published an argument in favour of a system akin to non-contributory basic income although the social insurance system prevailed at the time (Rhys Williams, 1943). Later, in 1982, her son Brandon Rhys Williams, a Tory MP, again campaigned for basic income as a way of simplifying the complexities of the social security system. Again, this focused on paid employment and conditionality rather than income and universality. These ideas were not taken forward. The nearest the UK has come to adopting a UBI, according to Torry (2016, 2018), has been the Family Allowance Act 1945.

Downes and Lansley (2018) identify four waves of interest in UBI since the early 20th century. After the First World War the development of a basic social security safety net was considered as a way of tackling the severe economic insecurity of the interwar years. The interest grew again in the second half of the 1960s through calls in the United States for a negative income tax and Nixon's Family Assistance Plan, 1972. This differed from universal, unconditional payments as it was based within the existing tax system and would be means-tested as people earned more, but the debate concerned the development of universally applied income security measures. The Alaska Permanent Fund was set up as an investment of revenue from the Prudhoe Bay oil field that would pay dividends to all citizens of Alaska, however.

In 1986, the third wave of interest took shape within the formation of a cross-European, and pan-global, Basic Income Earth Network (BIEN), a group committed to the debate about basic universal welfare who developed the concept of basic income as 'a periodic cash payment delivered to all unconditionally without a means test or work requirement' (BIEN, 2022). This was preceded by the development in 1984 of the Basic Income Research Group, now the Citizen's Basic Income Trust (Torry, 2018).

A fourth wave of interest took hold after the 2007–2008 financial crash. The increased automation of labour represents an argument for shortening working hours and introducing UBI while increasing work precarity demands it (Bregman, 2018). There have been experiments with introducing basic income approaches in some places, and most recently in Finland, Canada and the Netherlands from 2017, but limited application to date (see Rhaphael et al, 2019). Bregman (2018) reviews the evidence from the Mincome experiment in Dauphin, Manitoba, alongside Nixon's earlier Family Assistance Plan, that suggest money would be spent well, providing long-term health benefits and saving money in the long run. Ruckert et al (2017) review the impact of UBI pilots on the health of citizens concluding their importance to improvements in child health and development, educational attendance and attainment, mental health, care and housing security. From the 2008 financial crash, however, Torry (2016) and Downes and Lansley (2018) report a flurry of reinvigorated interest. Downes and Lansley believe this has been driven by the processes of deindustrialisation and austerity that has resulted in increased work insecurity or precarity (Standing, 2016), by concomitant increases in automation and the new machine age, and especially by pre-existing social security systems being inadequate to deal with recent social and political changes and increasingly conditional and punitive. The Welsh Government (2022) announced a three-year pilot offering £1,600 unconditional basic income to 18-year-old care leavers as a means of enhancing life chances.

Although there are different perspectives, basic income, in general, moves us directly away from the retributive, moral high-ground approach of welfare conditionality and workfare. Other important aspects of this in human terms concern the reduction of stigma (Calnitsky, 2016). UBI guarantees provide a more robust safety net, reduce dependency on means-testing, policing, sanctioning, and can assist in producing a fairer, less harassed society. Paradoxically, this maybe one of the causes of resistance to introducing or contemplating UBI. Unconditional, universal income would remove a very useful scapegoat used to offset blame and hardship, to place these on the demonised 'other', and to confirm collective solidarity so that those with social, political and economic power maintain it (see Chapter 7).

Bregman (2018) states that things are getting better for human beings in the world, aided by welfare states. Following Wilkinson and Pickett's assertion (2011) that economic growth is less effective than equality for dealing with social problems, Standing (2017) argues for social justice as well as economic security as justifications of UBI. As Standing comments, Thomas Paine saw the collective wealth of society as something to be equally distributed as a national inheritance for all – a social dividend:

> A basic income can thus be conceived as a social dividend paid from the collective wealth of society created and maintained by our ancestors and as a shared return on the commons and national resources that

belong to all. This reasoning supports basic income as social justice rather than as a response to poverty per se, and contrasts with the system of entitlements based on direct contributions that was to emerge in social insurance schemes in the nineteenth and twentieth centuries. (Standing, 2017, p 27)

Bregman asks the important question raised by some commentators, often without acknowledging the underlying discourses privileging paid employment: Why should we give money to people for 'nothing'? Van Parijs and Vanderborght (2017) review the ethical objections against able-bodied people living off the work of others, arguing this is no different to rich people having leisure time and not having to work, and represents a sharing of the privileges and bounties of the land. Given that basic income tends to increase reciprocity and greater levels of undertaking work that would otherwise be unpaid the objection does not work. Also, means-testing is costly, complex, increases stigma and may reduce work.

Haagh (2019) considers that UBI provides individual rights and also strengthens social cohesion by stabilising the human condition, giving existential security and a basic sense of independence to citizens. She believes that the democratic case is important for civilisation as an enabler of human development and social cooperation rather than a replacement for the existing benefit system. In this way UBI reduces waste and inefficiencies by promoting social development. UBI acts against coercion and conditionality and therefore meets the humanist principles of justice and fairness (van Parijs and Vanderborght, 2017).

Standing (2017) suggests that UBI represents a share in inherited wealth. Wealth is often created because of laws and regulations and systems and therefore should be shared. Standing (2017) also insists it meets the Rawlsian principle of fairness in its impact on reducing the poverty trap for the most insecure. He also suggests an ecological imperative in shifting time from resource-depleting activities in work to reproductive and communitarian activities, which could strengthen civil and political engagement – especially if fossil-fuel taxes are used to offset costs. Bregman (2018) agrees that less time spent in working hours or in resource-costly jobs reduces CO_2 emissions, leads to fewer accidents and less inequality. This is important in terms of the climate crisis.

UBI offers a means of reducing poverty without stigmatising people or making them more insecure but focuses on rights (Rodríguez-Fernández and Themelis, 2021). It is unconditional, avoids the destructive deserving/undeserving debate, overcomes the poverty trap as low-paying jobs need not be taken, and trusts people to spend as they will (Standing, 2017; Haagh, 2019). UBI reduces inequalities as long as anti-poverty and welfare measures remain in place.

Standing (2017) identifies economic benefits and health improvements including communitarian developments, assisting caring roles, increasing leisure and promoting small entrepreneurial developments. Empirical evidence from trials indicate physical and mental health improvements, reduced drug and alcohol use and therefore reduced public expenditure. Health benefits are also emphasised by Sircar and Friedman (2018) and Raphael et al (2018), who argue strongly for the retention of existing welfare programmes alongside UBI. Health benefits are contingent on income. Haagh (2019) also highlights that UBI formalises an individual's status as a citizen. Bregman (2018) employs the 19th-century French economist Frédéric Bastiat to consider *ce qu'on voit et ce qu'on ne voit pas* when looking at potential gains. The hidden economy relates to unpaid work, caregiving and community effort, which UBI encourages and allows as people have stability and potential time to devote to these essential aspects of society.

In respect of objections levelled against pursuing UBI, Standing (2017) uses Hirschmann's three rules for testing new social policy ideas – futility (wouldn't work); perversity (unintended negative consequences); jeopardy (endangering other goals). He argues that unless UBI is tried we will not know whether it works and what consequences there might be, but we do know some of the underlying philosophical reasons why it should be piloted (Standing, 2017; Sameroff, 2019). Some objections relate to detail and focus rather than universality. For instance, arguments in favour of universal public services shift from income to aspects of citizen entitlement and enhancing well-being (Labour, 2019), while the New Economics Foundation argues for better work–life balance and conditions alongside increased minimum income scales (Button and Coote, 2021). While such service provision would be universal it differs from UBI in its emphasis on paid work as the starting point. The arguments for UBI are not obviated by the New Economics Foundation recommendations.

Contemporary calls for universal/citizen's basic income

There is no single agreed model of universal or citizen's basic income. It has been promoted as a means of revising the tax and benefit systems but also as a precursor to a post-capitalist and post-work world. As a system of collectivised citizen wealth it remains controversial. McDonagh and Bustillos Morales (2020) understand UBI not just as a means of revising social welfare policy but as a fundamental shift in the ways in which society is organised. They understand UBI as a measure that addresses some of the serious shortcomings resulting from neoliberal capitalist societies and promoting a fairer, more just way of living. Stubbs (2020) also argues for UBI as a central plank of social protection that can respond both to local needs and global welfare. That welfare is a global concern has been shown through the

COVID-19 pandemic. Standing (2017) recognises that arguments against UBI suggest that people would be able to spend the money on drugs, alcohol and tobacco or make other unhealthy choices. However, the reduction of poverty and hopelessness is seen in experiments to reduce such behaviours. It seems that people in receipt of UBI tend to use the money for children's education, food and support, stigma is reduced and the removal of the poverty trap actually incentivises work. McDonagh and Bustillos Morales (2020) also argue that women are helped by UBI although the assumption that women are predominantly responsible for unpaid work has potential drawbacks in terms of reinforcing expectations.

Another objection is that it is cost prohibitive if UBI is provided at a level that is sufficient to meet basic need. This does not factor in all current welfare administration costs and the unseen costs relating to health, substance use and premature death that affects people when facing social inequalities. Wilkinson and Pickett (2011, 2019) demonstrate the association of great social equality with healthier, less stressful societies in which lower life expectancy, homicide, suicide, physical and mental ill-health and substance use problems are mitigated. Their work also addresses the objection that UBI could crowd out other social spending such as that provided for health care. The latter two objections show the size of funds that can be freed up by governments in the UK and across the world; although this is targeted towards business and economic continuity rather than towards individuals.

UBI represents a simple, direct and efficient form of income security in place of unemployment benefits. Given that it is not linked to work or work-seeking behaviours, it includes all people – those who cannot work for reasons of health, disability and so on as well as those with caregiving responsibilities. In this sense it is a feminist approach to welfare provision with the divide between public and private spaces being eroded. Stubbs (2020) believes that with a system of progressive taxation in place, and further targeted support for those in greatest need, UBI could reduce social and economic insecurity for many. There would be a need to develop other eco-social policies to ensure sustainability and to guard against raising consumption, but it represents a step forward.

Philosophically, UBI acknowledges the intrinsic worth of people regardless of productivity and growth. Austerity has created greater precarity through cuts to health and social welfare expenditure in a way sharply illuminated by the COVID-19 pandemic as we saw in Chapter 7. The need for investment in public services, health and social welfare is clear (Palmer, 2020). Stubbs (2020) sees investment alongside UBI as a way of building interlocking and interconnected welfare-oriented societies.

The idea of UBI not only diminishing economic insecurity but also contributing to an unleashing of a spirit of care, of reciprocity, of attentiveness to the needs of others, replacing the myth of individual responsibility with a sense of our mutual interconnectedness, may not be as utopian as it sounds and is a terrain of struggle that will be of immense importance in the future (Schulz, 2017; Stubbs, 2020). This is echoed by the World Basic Income (WBI) organisation's promotion of global UBI, which could be delivered through the United Nations or via other democratic processes (WBI, nd).

Palmer (2020) believes that one of the outcomes of the COVID-19 pandemic will be a deeper debate about the role of the state in social life – big state versus small state. He called on the government to be bold and to retain the enhanced sick pay and UC uplift, but also to move towards a minimum income guarantee that would be paid for by progressive taxation and closing the tax avoidance loopholes exploited by large global businesses and the very wealthy (see Stirling and Arnold, 2020). These measures have not been retained but the argument has begun. Severe global recession and increasing unemployment, acknowledged by the Office for Budget Responsibility on 14 April 2020, requires intervention through taxation and public spending. Currently, the UK has a weak employment safety net with unemployment benefits being one of the lowest Organisation for Economic Co-operation and Development (2022) rates, with payments now, especially since the austerity reductions since 2010, worth less than at any time since the creation of the welfare state (Brewer and Gardiner, 2020). Even the UC and working tax credit uplifts, representing a £7 billion injection, was just one-fifth of the cuts to welfare since 2010.

Similar to UBI, the New Economics Foundation call for a minimum income guarantee that would require a substantial overhaul of the social security system, although the intention is to cover the existing crisis (Stirling and Arnold, 2020). The minimum income guarantee value asked for is equivalent to that suggested by the Joseph Rowntree Foundation of £221 per week for each individual not covered by the job retention scheme or the self-employed income support scheme, and increasing those on UC or legacy benefits such as Job Seeker's Allowance or Employment Support Allowance to the same amount (HMRC, 2021). The minimum income guarantee would be administered through existing social security systems which are already in place and the costs funded through borrowing.

Somewhat akin to these arguments is Wistow's (2020) work suggesting that global politics and economics have been rendered so uncertain by COVID-19 that fundamental changes to the social contract are called for. He uses Rousseau's concept of the social contract to frame his own approach. While more guarded than others, Wistow suggests the current crisis provides an opportunity to review distributional justice and to question the current situation with a view to seeking greater equality as a normative rather than pragmatic goal. So, rather than offset the potential prospect of revolution as previous welfare reforms may have done, these changes towards equality would be done because it is a good thing in itself – akin to respecting the intrinsic worth of the individual as suggested in the arguments for UBI. Wistow recognises the complexity yet interconnectedness of personal, organisation and global systems and suggests that interactions between these systems can result in the emergence of transformational patterns to social welfare.

Wistow (2020) considers the multiple experiences of lockdown where the implicit assumption of government is that everyone is affected in the same way. There are questions of equity. Also, National Health Service policy has been greatly influenced by the pandemic at economic, social, political and organisational levels. The framing of health as the absence of disease and illness rather than as holistic well-being, following the World Health Organization, is important. The latter emphasises the importance of people's environments. All these factors represent conditions in which 'business as usual' can be questioned and greater equality can be pursued for all. Rebalancing the economy to work in the interests of society rather than the markets would be an important systemic move in the right direction to strengthen human ties across social systems and free people to achieve their potential (Wistow, 2020).

Conclusions

We have seen a call for a transformational approach in which the intrinsic worth of the person comes to the fore and the emphasis concerns universalism, unconditionality and equity. The search for simplification on welfare systems is often predicated upon matters of cost and the inherent logic of reducing costs to save public expenditure. Both UC and the various concepts of UBI provide a means of reducing bureaucracy and administration and thus may contribute to cutting costs. However, the former is based on means-testing, the application of eligibility criteria and increasing sanctions and conditions which in turn increase stigma and distress. UBI, however, is non-means-tested, designed to obviate the need for conditionality and to reduce stigma. Our ambivalence towards welfare and our suspicion of certain groups that do not engage in paid labour are such that the current status quo remains and UBI continues in pilot projects or ideals.

9

Containing the radicals and regulating the 'other': a history of the strange case of social work

Ambivalence towards social workers was illustrated clearly at the end of the year 2021 in the trial of the father and step-mother of six-year-old Arthur Labinjo-Hughes and the conviction of the step-mother and mother of murdered 16-month-old Star Hobson. Calls for a review of children's social work and blame of social workers for not protecting children populated the press and social media (Change.org, 2021; Townsend, 2021) while others pointed to systemic underfunding, complexities resulting from school closures and actions to curb the COVID-19 pandemic and the centrality of human relationships in safeguarding work (Ferguson, 2021). Contemporary ambivalences echoed the 1987 cartoon by Kal depicting the (spot-the-difference) lynching of one social worker for taking a child into care and another for leaving a child in an abusive family (Doel, 2017).

This chapter considers formalised welfare illustrated through the development of social work as an accepted and, indeed, necessary function of capitalist societies, but also as a potential societal irritant challenging the status quo and systemic inequities. The history of social work is explored through its diverse beginnings in bolstering the social system while advocating radical political and community change (Payne, 2005; Bamford and Bilton, 2020; Burt, 2020; Jones, 2020). The development of social work practice, and education, within the personal social services is interlinked with changes and developments in social policy. As Pinker notes, since 1970 social services have seen the radical restructuring of the organisation and functioning of statutory and non-statutory social work agencies and in professional social work education (see Offer and Pinker, 2017). In this context, we present the idea of social work as an ambiguous state regulated and promoted profession that seeks, in a Foucauldian sense, to 'discipline' its subjects whether those subjects are social workers themselves or the citizens they work with (Foucault, 1991). Somewhat differently, social work is also considered as offering a critique of the existing system, showing its flaws and lobbying for social reform and change. We draw on earlier work on ambivalence and historical shifts and turns in social work (Parker, 2020; Parker and Frampton, 2020).

A number of commentators adopt a Foucauldian approach to social work history and identify a range of discourses operating to define social work, and what underlying assumptions influenced its development (Parton, 1991; Cree, 1995; Skehill, 2007; Chambon, 2011; McGregor, 2015). We add a layer of complexity in terms of the ambivalent standing social work enjoys within society, also seeing those discourses as practices that constantly reshape their objects (Foucault, 1972; Parker, 2020).

Sociologically speaking, most histories of social work tend to locate the phenomenon within the functionalist aspects of those histories, the fixing of society (Burrell and Morgan, 1979). The elements of social work history that adhere to a more critical tradition, while celebrated, are less common (see Parker and Frampton, 2020). They are there, however, especially when critiquing the 19th century as political calls for social reform grew. The importance of more critical histories is seen in part in the social surveys of Charles Booth, in London, from 1886 to 1903 (Mangan and Sinclair, 2019), and Seebohm Rowntree in York in 1902, in developments within the Labour Party, and advances in sociological thinking that identified the structural roots to social ills. Critical thinking and practice came to the fore in the 1960s within Marxist-based radical social work and the growth of community development initiatives (Bailey and Brake, 1975; Corrigan and Leonard, 1978). It is not surprising, however, that social work's history is mainly located in the functional as social workers are employees whether or not they are considered to be professionals – a contested debate throughout this history – and whether or not political motivations for social work are considered fundamental (Parker and Doel, 2013). The complex and nuanced development begins to show the psychosocial ambivalence that underpins social work as much as it does other aspects of social welfare and highlights the dominant discourses at play within its policies and practices.

To discuss social work and its place within the context of welfare history demands that we first consider the contested question 'what is social work?' At first glance this may appear straightforward but it is something that warps and wefts with changing political and social mores, that has no single definition and must, necessarily, develop and act within its historical time and place. After exploring social work's character, we identify the threads of continuity with earlier historical practices and changes and increased constraints as a function of New Public Management, the discourses of self-responsibility and regulatory functions of safeguarding will be shown again to be altering our understanding of social work and diverging, at the macro level, from social work elsewhere in the world. However, the concept of a linear progression towards the construction of a formal, professionalised service is challenged and a more nuanced, multi-layered and complex view of social work's history is needed (Payne, 2005; Lorenz, 2008). As Lorenz

(2007, p 608) comments, social work history is 'a dynamic weaving of a multiplicity of different strands of identity'.

What is social work?

It is difficult to pinpoint the exact beginnings of social work for the reasons set out in the previous section (Payne, 2005; Parker and Frampton, 2020). However we determine the origins reflects a particular political and philosophical standpoint. If we consider the state functions of the personal social services as the beginnings of social work we might start back in the days of Poor Law, the overseers and assessors. For instance, Buzducea (2018) and Cree (2016) locate social administrative beginnings of social work in the Elizabethan Poor Law of 1601, providing relief for the needy of local parishes and the legislation relating to the care and treatment of mentally ill persons throughout the 18th and 19th centuries. The latter imposed a duty of care and/or control or regulation on local authorities that is echoed in contemporary mental health legislation (McGregor, 2015; Burt, 2020). However, this also needs to take into account the development of casework principles in charitable and more politically oriented yet independent services such as the Settlement Movement, the Charity Organisation Society (COS) and the Hospital Almoners in the 19th century. Douglas and Philpott describe the development of the notion of personal social services as a phenomenon emerging

> fitfully, from the tide of nineteenth century philanthropy and largely as a voluntary activity, often undertaken by women. Social work is a product of industrialised, urban societies, dealing with the personal consequences of social dislocation. And while Britain is one of the societies in which it can earliest be identified as a discrete activity, its forms differ from society to society according to the political and social culture and historical traditions. (Douglas and Philpott, 1998, p 7)

Perspectives on the development of social work's history differ. Burt (2020) sees a mixed chronological development that intertwines social administrative and regulatory functions alongside charitable and non-state beginnings, whereas Payne (2005), Rogowski (2010), Pierson (2011) and Bamford (2015) locate it more within 19th-century voluntary society provision. We might even restrict our study to the more modern development of social services departments in the creation of the welfare state in 1948, or even through the creation of generic social workers and centralised training post-Seebohm in the early 1970s. Indeed, Jones (2014, 2020) sees the crowning glory of social work represented by the introduction of the personal social services. Many commentators, however, chart the development of social work practice in its modern professionalised form not from its historical roots in the Poor Law, or even the charitable organisations, philanthropic and political movements of the 19th century but from a more familiar vantage point: the creation and development of the welfare state in 1948. Jones (2020) acknowledges the long and diverse history of social work but sees the development of three social welfare departments in 1948 as setting the scene for the birth of a modern unified social work service.

Confusion remains in Britain between social services departments, social work, and social security or the welfare benefit system. This, according to Adams (1996), reflects the low standing of social work in the minds of the general public. The topic is a difficult one to tackle because of the many conceptions and constructions of social work and the lack of agreed consensus on roles, tasks and meaning in social work. Adams summarises this well:

> Social work has a rather weak professional identity partly because social workers deal with a large proportion of the less powerful, less influential and low status members of society; social workers practise in diverse agencies, roles and settings and, unlike lawyers, doctors and engineers for example, do not draw upon a body of knowledge and expertise agreed and held in common to all in the profession. There are often uncertainties about what course of action would be most productive and there may be no agreement about this among social workers themselves, let alone among other professionals and ... the mass media. (Adams, 1996, p 6)

Defining social work is also complicated by the distinction between England and Wales, Scotland and Northern Ireland, which have different social work systems. It is an ambivalent entity. On the one hand it represents an administrative, legislative function for regulating and ordering social relations and families, and, on the other, as a campaign for enhanced social justice and human rights (IFSW, 2014). In Britain, social work developed from multiple influences including the Tudor Poor Law legislation and 19th-century religiosity, voluntarism and philanthropy.

The beginnings of state social administration: the Poor Laws

The social administrative and state functionary aspects of social work developed within and from the Poor Laws (Burt, 2020). The 1572 Act introduced the role of the overseer which replaced the parish officer role of collector, part of the 1552 Act. Overseers were selected by parish officers and confirmed by Justices of the Peace. Their roles concerned assessment, distribution of monies and supervision of poorhouses. In 1601, guidance was issued to overseers in *An Ease for Overseers*, which described their role with the impotent poor and demanded they acted sympathetically. However, there remained many complaints about the overseers and many demands for change. For instance, in Thomas Gilbert's 1782 Relief of the Poor Act, a system for hearing complaints was presented.

19th-century beginnings

The complexities of the Poor Law meant that by the time of the Royal Commission in 1832 the employment of paid overseers had become common, so much so that they were written into the Poor Law Amendment Act 1834. Section 46 states:

> [I]t shall be lawful for the said commissioners ... to direct the Overseers or Guardians of any Parish or Union ... to appoint such paid Officers with such qualifications as the said Commissioners shall think necessary for superintending or assisting in the Administration of the Relief and Employment of the Poor.

These centralised, managed and paid local government officers represented a precursor to contemporary social work roles and responsibilities (Burt, 2020). Their roles and duties were set out in Shaw's Manual (1865). A relieving officer had to be at least 21 years old, live in the district in which he worked, keep accounts of expenditure and commit full time to their office. Their role included visiting young persons who had been apprenticed, to check for payments in bastardy cases, to undertake foster care visits later in the 19th century, to proceed against the wilful neglect of children and to ensure school attendance, which were responsibilities associated with poor relief. From the implementation of Forster's Elementary Education Act 1870, relieving officers began to be appointed to enforce school attendance. The Education Act 1880 made the appointment of school attendance officers mandatory although there were regional differences in its enforcement. Residential care for children, physically and mentally disabled persons and older people derived from successive Poor Laws.

In the mid-19th century, social work concerned the relief of poverty and destitution and 'rescue' of prostitutes. It was, generally, a middle-class activity often underpinned by Christian ideals undertaken by women as a practical expression of religious devotion (Burt, 2020). Moral deficiencies were emphasised and 'rescue' formed the goal of work – to develop character and employability. The work was individually based and formed the beginnings of casework. The COS and Mrs Ellen Ranyard's Bible and Female Mission (1857) worked by gathering facts about client and situation, making plans and providing help according to perceived needs. Social work also had roots in other Victorian charities such as Dr Barnardo's, National Children's

Homes and the National Society for the Prevention of Cruelty to Children (NSPCC). The first almoner, Mary Stewart, was appointed at the Royal Free Hospital in London in 1895. Her work focused on preventing abuse of the system by those who could afford to pay by making assessments of circumstances and undertaking home visits. The COS concepts of self-reliance and deservingness underpinned the work.

Social work methods developed primarily through casework with children and the poor (Dr Barnardo's, Rudolf's Church of England Central Home for Waifs and Strays – now the Children's Society – Stephenson's, National Children's Homes). The COS was established in 1869 in the midst of increasing chaos in the numbers, remit and responsibilities of charitable bodies. The COS worked to introduce regulation into charitable distributions by assessment of claims made by deserving individuals. Their work was designed to provide the administrative means needed to prevent pauperism, to eliminate hand-outs and to encourage thrift. Using concepts derived from Poor Law they separated clients into two groups, the helpable (those with moral fibre to become industrious and law-abiding) and unhelpable (the feckless or ill, disabled). Those deemed undeserving were directed to the Poor Law (Skinner and Thomas, 2012).

The founders of the COS (Octavia Hill, Helen Bosanquet and Charles Loch) and the Toynbee Hall Settlement Movement (Canon and Mrs Barrett) began keeping systematic records of their casework, which introduced methodical approaches to social work practice that have been refined ever since; it was the beginnings of tightly organised assessment, bureaucratic case management and the regulation of those coming within the purview of social workers. Casework developed later from their systematic approaches and, in the following century, from psychoanalytic thinking. There was little concern with structural and external factors at this point.

Religious visiting and other visiting societies also grew throughout the 18th century and into the 19th century, which Burt (2020) considered particularly important for the development of social work. For instance, Methodism was overtly concerned with the morals of the poor and visiting became an established woman's role. In the late 19th century women were active as 'friendly visitors', a system of personal moral influence which originated in Boston in the US. The COS and religious friendly visiting movement ignored social conditions and was subject to increasing criticism by the burgeoning social reform movement which assumed that state provision was a necessary defence against the arguments of moral culpability promulgated by the COS (Burnham, 2011, 2012). However, the influence on nascent social work is marked in respect of casework, the emphasis on training and education, and friendly visiting for the parents of children with learning disabilities was suggested in the 1908 Royal Commission on the Care and

Control of the Feeble-minded as a means of supporting families as the basic unit of society and also reducing reliance on institutional care.

Political approaches that recognised the impact of social and economic conditions had an ally in the Settlement Movement. In 1884 the Reverend Samuel Barnett founded the Toynbee Hall settlement, which offered support, teaching and arts for poor people often provided by young men attending university but living among people in poverty, but women were also involved (Oakley, 2019). The emphasis was on small group discussion, activities and assistance within the group. Bowman Stephenson and Barnardo also favoured this way of working with children.

Towards the end of the 19th century other voluntary agencies important for the development of social work came into being; the Salvation Army founded in 1879, and the Police Court Missionaries of the Church of England Temperance Society in 1876 (later probation officers). In 1907 the Probation Officers Act appointed probation officers, who had become popular with magistrates for women, men and children to have a friendly influence on offenders.

The late 19th century witnessed an increased interest in mental ill-health. From 1845, under the Lunatic Asylums Act, union guardians and the Lunacy Commission became responsible for pauper lunatics. The Lunatics Asylum Act 1853 required a relieving officer to give three days' notice to a Justice of the Peace that a pauper was deemed to be a lunatic but also assumed responsibility, under section 68, for non-pauper lunatics in the area. In 1879, the Aftercare Association for Poor and Friendless Female Convalescents on Leaving Asylums provided patients with a few weeks' stay in ordinary family homes while helping them find employment. The Lunacy Act 1890 appointed relieving officers or others to report on lunatics and, where appropriate, to convey people to an institution.

The first child protection legislation in 1889 and 1898 allowed the NSPCC to take a child to a place of safety but also emphasised family responsibilities. The Acts also gave guardians the power to have children in workhouses adopted. The focus on child protection was continued in the Children Act 1908, section 12(1). To help families the legislation also made provision for child-care liaison across agencies, school meals, medical inspections and visiting in foster care. Health visiting was associated with social work and concerned itself with sanitary conditions. Statutory responsibilities grew with the Infant Life Protection Act 1897 and in the appointment of school attendance officers.

Between 1890 and 1914 the term social worker was increasingly used although it remained undefined. The development of proto-social work services was characterised by fragmentation but it covered core areas that became recognised fields of practice. Social work was associated with the work of women, protection and social regulation enshrined in legislation: the

Lunacy Act 1890; Prevention of Cruelty to Children Act 1889 and 1898; Infant Protection Act 1897; Children Act 1908; and Mental Deficiency Act 1913 (Burt, 2020).

The outset of the 20th century

Beatrice Webb's dissenting note to the Royal Commission on Poor Laws in 1909 was diametrically opposed to the COS (Hill and Loch) in suggesting that the deterrent effect of the Poor Law was ineffective and that charity would not overcome low wages, sweat shops, long working hours, slum landlords and complacent authorities. She demanded collective action to achieve optimum minimum conditions of life. She was backed in this by the statistical evidence form the social surveys of Charles Booth and Seebohm Rowntree. At the turn of the century, the Labour Party were represented in parliament and the Liberal government of 1906 saw great shifts in social welfare influencing the future direction of social work.

The first half of the 20th century witnessed the development and growth of social work in probation, mental health, learning disability, hospitals, child protection and adoption (Burt, 2020). Legislation offered more opportunities for social work to develop as a profession and integral part of state welfare provision in mental health and learning disability, although different nomenclature was employed, through the Mental Deficiency Act of 1913; Mental Deficiency (Amendment) Act 1927; and Mental Treatment Act 1930; in education through the Education Act 1918; and child care and protection through the Adoption Act 1926 and Children and Young Persons Act 1933.

There was an increased emphasis on training and publications in social work that further developed methods of visiting, an explicit family focus and assessment as a key task (Foss and West, 1914; McAdam, 1925; Lewis, 1929; Clement Brown, 1939). The assumption of poor relief functions by local authorities reinforced the statutory development of social work, while the establishment of Child Guidance Clinics and expansion of psychiatric social work furthered the professionalisation of social work (Goldberg, 1957–1958; Timms, 1964; Stewart, 2013). The sense of profession was enhanced by the development of professional associations: the Association of Psychiatric Social Workers in 1930; Association of Mental Health Workers in 1935; and the umbrella group, the British Federation of Social Workers, in 1934. Social work was beginning to combine a concern for social reform and environment alongside a sympathetic relational approach to individuals in contrast to its earlier moral focus (Foss and West, 1914; Atlee, 1920; McAdam, 1925).

In 1907 the Probation of Offenders Act permitted, and required under the 1925 Criminal Justice Act, that probation officers 'advise, assist and befriend' those on probation. Almoners were employed in voluntary and municipal hospitals. Most social work, however, was still located in voluntary agencies and concerned a relief model developed by Octavia Hill and colleagues in the COS. This only changed after the Second World War.

'Moral welfare' continued as an integral feature of social work. Cree's (2016) work on 'khaki fever' and sexual risk-taking in the First World War represented class-based, gendered assumptions in social work. 'Khaki fever', for Cree, represented a moral panic concerning young girls excited by the presence of soldiers and having sex with them. Two groups of middle-class women took it upon themselves to police the morals of these girls – the National Union of Women Workers' Women Patrols' Committee and the Women Police Service. While some women were befriended and protected from sexual assault the sexual regulation and surveillance curtailed the freedom that the women's groups themselves sought while reinforcing the care and control aspects of social work's history. Cree argues that the number of young girls involved was greatly overestimated but built upon assumed middle-class discourses of morality and sexual regulation of the poor.

Dickens (2018) discusses Clement Attlee's pivotal influence in the development of modern social work in his linkage of both individual and collective responsibilities as someone steeped in practice reflected the individual-moral tradition of the COS and, as a Fabian social reformer, concerned with structural socio-economic conditions. Attlee trained as a lawyer but was inspired by voluntary work in a boys' club in Stepney to join the Labour Party in 1907 and to work in social work. He worked with Beatrice and Sidney Webb on the national Campaign for the Breakup of the Poor Law, 1909–1910, as secretary of Toynbee Hall settlement in 1910, and as an 'official explainer' for the 1911 National Insurance Act for the Liberal government before gaining a lecturing position in social service in 1913. Even when elected as Member of Parliament in 1922 he continued to take on social work positions on the Limehouse Board of Poor Law Guardians, chairing their children's home and acting as their representative on the Metropolitan Asylums Board. His main contribution to the development of social work was his 1920 book, *The Social Worker*.

Dickens cogently argues that the dualistic separation of COS individualism and social reform's collectivism is simplistic and that Attlee's work demonstrates this through his teaching of the original COS curriculum at the London School of Economics (LSE), his adaptation of that approach to include more collectivist principles, and his support for a mix of voluntary agency and local authority provision: '[Attlee's] concept of social service replaces the ideas of generosity with justice, benevolence with duty, condescension with respect. Attlee argues that social workers and "service users" … are "fellow workers" in creating a better society' (Dickens, 2018, p 14). He maintained the concept of 'social service', influencing Beveridge's appreciation of it, and, indeed, being something that continued in the wording of the Seebohm report in 1968, which ushered in the concept of personal social services departments.

Second World War

If the role of social workers was not taken sufficiently seriously in preparations for the war then it was during the Blitz. Writing after the war, Titmuss stated that social workers:

> were needed because they knew about people and distress, because they could help to bring the wide array of statutory and voluntary agencies to bear on the several needs of a particular individual at a particularly urgent point in time, and because they were qualified to report in practical terms on the way in which one service reacted on another and on the people needing help. (Titmuss, 1950, pp 289–290)

Almoners, psychiatric social workers and those working with children and families were employed throughout, securing their place in post-war reconstruction, training and development (Younghusband, 1947; Goldberg, 1957–1958). Social work was writ large in the changes wrought by the welfare state.

Social work since the Second World War

In 1948 a tripartite system of personal social services was established under local government administration that reflected Beveridge's concern for universalism financed through social insurance. This system replaced the unwieldy number of independent and government agencies providing social services (Sullivan, 1996). The three new departments were specialised as opposed to generic. There was a department for children, physically and mentally ill people, and older and disabled people.

Children's services gained a boost from the general public seeing the extent of suffering and destitution in many evacuated children which led for demands, most notably by Lady Allen of Hurtwood, to change residential care (Allen, 1945). After the inquest into the death of Dennis O'Neill, a 12-year-old who was starved and beaten to death in a remote Shropshire farmhouse by his foster father after being placed by Newport Borough Council, Miss Myra Curtis was appointed to lead a committee of inquiry into the care of deprived children. The committee interpreted their brief widely and reported:

> [A] widespread and deplorable shortage of the right kind of staff, personally qualified and trained to provide the child with a substitute home background. The result in many (residential) homes was a lack

of personal interest and affection for the children. ... The child in these homes was not recognised as an individual with his rights and possessions, his own life to live and his own contribution to offer. (Hansard, 1946)

The report called for a wholesale reform of children's services and resulted in the passing of the Children Act 1948 which created a separate children's department and boosted emphasis on fostering and adoption.

The statutory position of social work was consolidated following the introduction of the welfare state in family policy through the Ingleby Committee (Home Office, 1960), in mental health through the Mackintosh Committee (Ministry of Health, 1951), in adoption (Hurst Report, Home Office and Scottish Home Department, 1954), the Boulder report into older people (Ministry of Health, 1957), and in juvenile delinquency (Home Office, 1960). The trajectory towards unified training and service was emphasised in Younghusband's 1959 report (Ministry of Health and Department of Health for Scotland, 1959). Social work was rapidly becoming an integral element of state provision and function.

Developments also occurred in social work practices. The role of enquiry and investigation gradually evolved into assessment of needs, building on expertise in taking social histories and assessing the whole environment of the person. This was written into legislation in the Children and Young Persons (Amendment) Act 1952, the Adoption Act 1950 and 1958, and the Streatfeild Committee (Home Office, 1961) concerning court reports. Preventive casework to support families was encouraged, as was monitoring and visiting children who were boarded out with a view to returning them to their families as soon as possible. These developments signposted the move towards a unified profession.

Until the 1960s attitudes reflecting the Poor Law remained that blamed or pathologised those in need and there was a grave problem of lack of resources to provide planned services. The prevailing theoretical paradigm for social work also had its roots in client treatment and the diagnosis and prescription of intervention. This, coupled with the Conservative government's alarm at the rising numbers of youngsters involved in and being convicted of criminal offences and the growing numbers of older people occupying hospital beds rather than receiving other more appropriate services, led to calls for change. In 1962 the Minister for Health, Enoch Powell, produced plans to develop care in the community. Alongside this, social workers campaigned for greater resources to tackle issues before they became a problem. The Probation Service called for a local authority controlled preventive family service to prevent juvenile offending.

The 1960s represented a time of development in sociological thinking, a growth in social work research and literature, an expanded university system and the formation of non-governmental social campaigning groups such as the Child Poverty Action Group, Gingerbread and Shelter (Jones, 2020). The push towards a unified profession was given impetus in this context and was supported by the Standing Conference of Social Work Organisations, which wanted a local authority base for social work. Scotland took the lead in dealing with troubled children and juvenile delinquency through the 1964 Kilbrandon Committee, which led to unified social work departments through the implementation of the Social Work (Scotland) Act 1968.

Towards unified social services departments

In 1965, with support from social policy advisor Richard Titmuss, the incoming Labour government established a committee to review local authority social services departments and family services. The appointment of the Seebohm Committee in 1965, reporting in 1968 (Secretary of State for the Home Department, 1968), addressed the fragmentation of services, inadequacies in provision, poor coordination and a lack of public knowledge about social work. Almost immediately upon receiving their brief they decided to exceed it (para 32), seeking to consolidate services in a single social services department and key social workers:

> [A] family or individual in need of social care should, as far as is possible, be served by a single social worker ... it is essential that the family or individual should be the concern of one social worker with a comprehensive approach to the social problem of his clients ... and through him the social service department as a whole can be held accountable for the standard of care the family receives. (Secretary of State for the Home Department, 1968, pp 160–162)

While the origins of contemporary statutory social work had begun with the creation of the welfare state it is at this point that local authority social work was formally born in England and Wales (Adams, 1996; Jones, 2020). The Seebohm Committee made three recommendations:

1. social services departments should be unified, bringing together the three separate departments;
2. social services departments should be headed by a director appointed by the Secretary of State for Health and Social Security;
3. social workers should have generic training and further research should be conducted into social work.

Unified social services departments were instituted in most authorities in 1972 under the Local Authority and Social Services Act 1970. The formation of the British Association of Social Work in 1970 further confirmed its professionalisation. The development of the Central Council for the Education and Training of Social Workers (CCETSW) in the following year allowed for development of a generic qualification for social work. Following local government reorganisation in 1974 the boundaries of the authorities were changed but generic departments remained. However, eligibility criteria were not considered or set, neither were priorities determined, nor the spiralling costs of a universalist service calculated. Furthermore, public confidence in social work began to wane after the death of Maria Colwell in 1973 and following many subsequent inquiries.

Seebohm changed the conceptualisation of social work practice. Until the development of generic departments, traditional models of social casework held sway. Seebohm indicated that personal problems were often a reflection of wider structural problems in society. There was a shift in emphasis from psychodynamic to more sociological and political perspectives. Common roles developed in assessment and planning, and the need for greater theoretical understanding and assessment criteria was recognised. Interdisciplinary assessments and comprehensive family assessments were developed. This period is generally considered a golden era in social work or its zenith, consolidating developments since the Second World War (Burt, 2020), soon after which it began to fall out of favour with governments and the general public (Rogowski, 2010; Pierson, 2011; Jones, 2020). However, research into training and into roles and remits continued (BASW, 1977; DHSS, 1976, 1978; Goldberg and Warburton, 1979; NISW, 1982; Fisher et al, 1984).

Sullivan (1996) believes generic social work reflects a misunderstanding of Seebohm's intentions. Seebohm called for the creation of generic departments comprising all services under one roof but not for workers who could perform all tasks. Prior to the 1960s, according to Pinker (1983), the majority of social work courses were specialised. The first generic course was offered at LSE in 1954. Following the implementation of Seebohm, however, the CCETSW introduced the Certificate of Qualification in Social Work (CQSW) that set out the content and methods of a course based on generic principles which led to a decline in expertise in specialisms in social work and was considered by some diluted training.

A theoretical shift took place from psychodynamic models to systems thinking which diverted attention from an individualised pathological paradigm towards a collectivist view (see Parker, 2021b for an overview of Pincus and Minhan, 1973; Goldstein, 1973; Specht and Vickery, 1977). Personal problems resulted from dissonance between different elements of an individual's or family's social system, their community, wider society and societal policies. Social workers became 'change agents' who worked towards engineering change in various sub-systems in the client-system's wider social world, although conflict remained between those who promoted social casework and those who took a structural and political view. There was also a growing emphasis on the legislative base of social work and increasing managerialism in practice.

Turn to the right

Throughout the first ten years of the Conservative government from 1979 to 1989, social work developed more refined systems of assessment, and established multidisciplinary work practices (Butrym, 1976; Davies and Challis, 1986). However, social work also entered a difficult period as child abuse assumed greater recognition in society and inquiries into child deaths positioned social work as a useful scapegoat (Parker, 2020; Parker and Frampton, 2020), leaving social work less secure, prone to continuous calls for improvement (DHSS Social Work Service, 1986) and legislative change such as the Children Act 1989.

With social, political and economic changes, continued high public spending, and increased demand for resources, Margaret Thatcher's government appointed Peter Barclay to review the roles and tasks of social work. This culminated in the Barclay report of 1982. Intent on 'rolling back the frontiers of the welfare state' (Mack and Lansley, 1985, p 5), the government believed that social services should be of a residual nature, addressing the needs of those who would not otherwise receive care. The Barclay report, however, emphasised the need for community action and voluntarism, and for the role of social workers to be transformed from agents of change to community enablers, rather than service providers. While it is generally considered to have had minimal impact, the Barclay report reaffirmed the importance of social work but set the course for a change in role and direction.

At the same time, the government was committed to reducing reliance on state provision and encouraging greater self-reliance. As such it was highly suspicious of social work as an arm of state-provided welfare and instituted a range of reports designed to evoke change (DHSS, 1981; Audit Commission 1985, 1986). Sir Roy Griffiths, a supermarket chairperson, was appointed to look into the reasons why community care development had been as slow as indicated in the 1986 Audit Commission report. His report recommended that the local authorities should be responsible for coordinating community care policy to the surprise and disapproval of the government. He did, however, promote welfare pluralism, or a mixed economy of care, which envisaged that local authority service provision would diminish and that there would be a significant increase in voluntary and private sector providers. Social workers became care managers who were responsible for assessment, the design and purchase of packages of care. These proposals gained all-party backing for a wide variety of disparate reasons and the National Health Service and Community Care Act 1990 was fully implemented in 1993.

The growing complexities of social work, and the desire to improve practice through regulation, led to increased emphasis on procedures and management (Webb, 2006; Jones, 2014; McGregor, 2015), which contained social work through professionalisation (Parker and Doel, 2013). The Children Act 1989 and NHS and Community Care Act 1990 reinforced the regulation through increased guidance, but developed prescribed roles that were entrenched in the social policy fabric. While the rise of managerialism in social work has been criticised, the positive elements of procedural and bureaucratic approaches have largely been ignored (Jones, 2014; McGregor, 2015; Burt, 2020).

The radical political changes in organisational structure that have occurred and the change to a market-dominated purchaser-provider split happened at the same time CCETSW reviewed its training and education. The Diploma in Social Work (DipSW) emphasised the competences needed for practice based on the rules and requirements for the qualification. The teaching input demanded by the DipSW was higher and employer-partnerships grew. This coincided with a change in funding for higher education in which universities demanded a greater degree of research activity and output.

'Things can only get better'?

This situation was inherited by New Labour who combined commitment to reducing public spending with stopping the drift towards residualism. New Labour adopted many of the social policy themes of the previous two decades on coming to power in 1997. Improving the quality of public services, including social work, formed the heart of their intent and to that end they introduced a modernising agenda. A major review of CCETSW determined that its regulatory and professional body functions could be carried out effectively by a Care Council in each devolved administration.

Since 1997, social and health care, alongside other public sector organisations, was subject to significant change under the auspices of the modernising agenda. Choice became a political mantra at both ends of the political spectrum and often associated unquestioningly with positive outcomes for those using services and agencies. Modernisation and change, which emphasised partnership, characterised New Labour (Cabinet Office, 1999), and was seen as a means of improving services while eliminating waste and maximising the use of public funds. The White Paper *Modernising Social Services* (Department of Health, 1998) set out the priorities for adult services in promoting independence, consistency and user involvement and for children's services as protection, quality of care and improving life chances.

The emphasis placed on increased regulation as a means of better protecting service users was articulated and workforce issues were considered in the context of increased control. The Health Act 1999 established a statutory duty of partnership between the NHS and local authorities (section 27), using the 'flexibilities' (section 31) which allowed for pooled budgets, delegation of responsibilities for commissioning services to a lead organisation, and an integration of health and social services (Department of Health, 2000).

The Care Standards Act 2000 made social work a protected title, brought in care councils, focused on continuing professional development and training, and reformed the qualification to a minimum of degree level. The 2003 *Every Child Matters* agenda dismantled social services departments and separated children and families social work from adult services which was increasingly encouraged to work more closely with health. The Care Standards Act emphasised standards as a way of improving social work and social care through regulation. The National Care Standards Commission, former Social Services Inspectorate and Audit Commission team were replaced by the Commission for Social Care Inspection, which combined regulation with an inspection function. The Social Care Councils established Codes of Practice to regulate the workforce, protect the social work title and create professional social work registration for the first time.

One unintended consequence of such scrutiny was the construction of a discourse of control within a climate of fear and vulnerability fuelled by popular interpretations of inquiries into tragedies such as the Bichard (2004) or Climbié inquiries (Laming, 2003). Indeed, the processes of 'quality control' and rigidification of practice appear located in a managerial discourse that stems from this modernising agenda. Humphrey (2003) questions whether or not the modernisation agenda led to improvements in service delivery or increased restriction and control, however, it was broadly welcomed, although it created a picture of care service structures in a state of flux.

In England, the General Social Care Council (GSCC) devolved award-giving powers to the universities, operating a system of accreditation of universities to grant degrees in social work (GSCC, 2002). A degree of control was maintained through a regional inspectorate function and education and training brief which places extra requirements for external examiners and reporting and monitoring requirements set out within accreditation criteria (GSCC, 2002). Changes in social work education were long awaited and the move to a graduate profession was welcome. However, while the degree award carried academic weight, the influence of professional body regulation grew.

Alongside the development of a professional regulatory body for social care, the creation of a training organisation in England, first as a National Training Organisation, for personal social services (TOPSS), acknowledged the often-ignored body of social care workers (TOPSS, 2002). TOPSS becoming a sector skills council with responsibility for a continuum of social care workforce needs, which assimilated social work practice learning into its purview. The Practice Learning Taskforce, set up by the Department of Health in 2003, was extended and placed within Topss England. The development of learning resource centres were initiated to support the learning needs of the social care workforce (Topss England/Taskforce, 2004). A homogenising tendency transmogrified social work and social care training and education into an amorphous concoction of competences and quality or indicative standards with little evidence of the potential benefits for improving services and practice.

Concepts of collaboration and partnership have become central to contemporary social care philosophy. Whittington (2003) describes partnership as a state of relationship between organisations, groups or individuals while collaboration represents the active process of working together or interacting at a strategic planning level, in joint or lead commissioning of services and management of pooled budgets and integrated services, or operationally within multidisciplinary team settings such as special projects and integrated services. The concept of personalisation has been much vaunted from both right-wing perspectives, that emphasise choice, to relational elements that focus on individually and culturally appropriate services in a changing world (Gardner, 2011; Braye and Preston-Shoot, 2020; Parker, 2021b).

Ambivalence, scapegoats and a sacrificial profession

The deaths of children, and adults, have led to public and political calls for reform, change and blame of social workers (Parker, 2020). The trend has grown since the Monckton inquiry report into the death of foster child Dennis O'Neill in 1945 (Home Office, 1945). Subsequent reform, regulation and registration, however, has led to increased political control and reduced capacity for political social work on behalf of human rights and social justice. This is demonstrated in the calls for reform following the publication of the inquiry into the death of Peter Connelly (Balls, 2008) and more recently relating to Arthur Labinjo-Hughes and Star Hobson (Change.org, 2021; Townsend, 2021). The death of Peter Connelly resulted in sweeping reform throughout social work (Social Work Reform Board, 2010), which, alongside a change of government in 2010 which ushered in austerity measures, bureaucratised and regulated practice, and concomitantly deflected blame from its own failings (Jones, 2014; Warner, 2015; Shoesmith, 2016; Parker, 2020).

Alongside wholesale reform, there was increasing recognition that monitoring and regulation alone would not improve practice and that social workers needed to be able to exert professional judgements (Munro, 2011).

Social workers were seen ambivalently as part of the problem to be managed and contained but also part of the solution to society's problems (Social Work Reform Board, 2012). These reforms corralled social work as part of the technologies of government, something echoed within recent English legislation for adults in the Care Act 2014 and in respect of children and families in the Children and Social Work Act 2017. Increased prescription and regulation has redefined social work, to an extent, as a safeguarding force. These changes further prevent social work's capacity for promoting change, while reinforcing a culture of blame and generating distrust within the general public. In tragedies, governments tend to respond to accusations of public distrust by shifting the blame from the child's actual killers to the services that were involved, arguing there were missed opportunities, poor practice and poor education of social workers that led to this tragedy occurring.

In February 2018, a consultation was held on the development of a separate regulatory framework for social work in England. From 2001 the GSCC held responsibility for registration and regulation of social workers and approval of qualifying courses but, in 2012, this was transferred to the Health and Care Professions Council. This transfer of role overtly aligned social work with the health professions, suggesting its practice focused on individualised social work as treatment of pathologies rather than consider the harmful effects of structural policy decisions such as austerity, or fighting for poverty reduction and equality opportunities. This reinforced the unspoken, tacitly approved governmental redefinition of social work. The government's political sense of social work is shown within the ministerial foreword to the consultation:

> Social Work England's primary objective will be protection of the public. It will achieve its objective through setting professional, education and training standards for social workers, and providing assurance that those registered meet the standards, are qualified and remain fit to practise. Not only will this help to better protect the public, but by promoting public confidence and trust, it will also bring real benefits to the social workers up and down the country who work to support vulnerable children, adults and families. (DfE/DHSC, 2018, p 4)

These words are not new; they refresh the idea that political control will prevent unruly and ill-educated social workers from doing harm and it reinforces a norm of regulation, control and anti-professionalism. We argue elsewhere that, in the minds of politicians and the general public, social work is there to fix and mend society's ills, but also functions to carry society's sins away as a scapegoat, a vessel in which to pour hatred, loathing and blame (Parker, 2020). It is both loved and hated at the same time; an ambivalent object in psychoanalytic terms (Freud, 1937). Because it arouses such strong emotions, in a paradoxical way, it keeps it in the public agenda.

Ambivalence: the public's love/hate relationship with social work

When child abuse investigations and inquiries come to the attention of the public, generally through the media, ambivalence is clear. For instance, social workers involved in the Cleveland Inquiry (Butler-Sloss, 1988) and in Orkney's ritual abuse allegations (Jenkins, 1992) became the objects of public hatred and disgust for removing children from their families, and no doubt exposing the public to practices they would rather not see and thus increasing that disgust as a way of coping with it (see Douglas, 1966). In the case of Maria Colwell, Jasmine Beckford, Kimberley Carlisle, Peter Connelly and Arthur Labinjo-Hughes social workers form the object of disgust and hatred because they did not remove and protect the child. In the case of Peter Connelly, the public display of 'bloodlust' deflected attention from growing austerity measures, and also focused the blame on social workers rather than the health and police services who had also been involved (although all three services were criticised in the inquiry report) (Balls, 2008; *The Sun*, 2008; LSCB Haringey, 2009). However, an alternative public relationship was also portrayed at the meeting of the Social Work Taskforce in December 2009, when the positive side of social work was promoted by the singer Goldie, who had spent time in local authority care as a youngster and spoke passionately at the meeting about the social workers who helped him.

The ambivalence is seen in the public wanting social work services to be available where there is need but, believing this to attract stigma, would prefer to avoid personal connections with them. This is understandable given that social workers practice in abusive, dangerous situations that reflect the dark side of human life. A love and hate relationship has developed which results in underfunding and blame as well as desire to control and direct so that the political gains can be made for the government in supporting its citizens.

Ambivalence about social work

Social work is a necessary part of the apparatus of modern government. It helps to regulate society, ensure the well-being of the workforce (potential, actual and past), and to safeguard members of the public from harm. It also acts as a buffer to deflect blame from government (in)actions. As such it can be demonised and scapegoated because of its cost, its rebellious, uncontained nature which criticises government, and because it 'fails' to protect and safeguard all citizens all of the time. Ambivalence, in a psychoanalytic sense, offers an explanatory framework for the two-sided face that society presents towards social work. Social work is both loved and hated. It is blamed for tragedies yet sought out when there are social and intrapersonal needs.

Social workers may also feel ambivalent about their position as part of the political infrastructure as local government employees, while continuing to actively campaign for social justice and human rights against their employers and organisations. The statutory safeguarding role of social workers in child protection, mental health and adult safeguarding grants their status and position as part of the human service professions. However, the increased prescription and regulation in practice that has resulted from this has turned much of social work into a state function. Social workers often find themselves in a liminal position betwixt and between the state and those people marginalised by the state (Parker, 2020).

It is in 'sacrifice' that social work maintains its public face – carrying away the transgressions of society and being loaded with guilt by society (displacement) (Parker, 2018). Sacrifice also presents a means of maintaining professional integrity by walking in solidarity with marginalised, disadvantaged and stigmatised people – social work offering itself as an expiation on behalf of the people with whom social workers practise. Alongside being sacrificial victims for government when things go wrong such as in the case of Peter Connelly and Eli Cox (Turner, 2018), social workers may also be seen as martyrs in solidarity with the dispossessed.

Social workers promote the social justice, well-being and human rights of those oppressed groups with whom they work and with people in emotional, social and spiritual distress by standing beside people and through this being associated with them. As a profession focused on human rights and social justice, however, social work concerns resistance, resilience and hope, which challenges the assumed uncleanness of those people who are marginalised and oppressed.

The rituals performed by social workers, including the sacrifices made, resonate with ambivalence. They represent both an abuse of a 'consumed object' and active technologies of resistance. If social workers remain part of the system their rituals simply assuage the guilt of those with power. If social workers resist the status quo and stand alongside marginalised people they have a chance to transform society and the lives of those with whom they practise.

Conclusions

Regulating the other has been part of social work's chequered and complex history from many sides and positions. Latterly there has been a development in social work towards containment of those who undertake these roles through the development of proceduralism, managerialism and scapegoating.

Reflecting on 50 years of the implementation of the recommendations of the Seebohm report, Jones (2020) identifies a number of key themes arising. Notably the increased professionalisation of social work, although it was not until 2002 that social work became a protected title following the implementation of the Care Standards Act. A number of shifts in ideology and practice also took place during that time from radical social work influenced by Marxist ideology, to anti-psychiatry, community action and anti-discriminatory and anti-oppressive approaches. The influence of New Right individualism, perpetuated by New Labour's Third Way, has led to a focus on personalisation of services and increased participation. There have been continued struggles over the period in respect of social work's remit and organisational context, whether it should remain a generic practice or fragment once again into a variety of specialisms, which has concomitant consequences for training and education. Social work has also moved into the public eye as a scapegoat given the inquiries of the period (Parker, 2020). It has shifted from a respected part of the welfare state from an earlier, more positive move away from the hated Poor Law guardians. Since New Labour, but originating beforehand, growth in managerial cultures and audit have also moulded social work's development and through austerity a focus on cost-cutting in local authorities has influenced thinking about privatisation and commercialisation of services (Burt, 2020; Jones, 2020).

Burt (2020) recognises that, throughout its history, social work has not been able to capture its common or unifying elements. He also highlights that its history stems from both public administration and voluntary effort and that sometimes commentators may be tempted to 'cherry-pick' history according to preferences. Given its mixed historical roots, the legislative and regulatory base is clear and continuities with the Poor Laws are evident. However, there is also a development of a clear value base that focuses on relationships and social justice, recognising that it has a humane and compassionate substrate as well.

10

W(h)ither welfare after Brexit and COVID-19?

This chapter will explore the complex current position of UK social welfare and consider where welfare might go if, indeed, it survives into the future as a formal citizen entitlement post-Brexit, the 2020–2021 COVID-19 pandemic and in a tense new socio-economic political global context following the war in Ukraine. This might appear to be alarmist. However, given the October 2021 withdrawal of the Universal Credit uplift introduced during the pandemic, a March 2022 budget that failed to address spiralling fuel and food costs, and a September 2022 emergency 'fiscal event' that offered tax reductions to business and high earners with little mention of public services, it appears that the needs of people requiring social protection continue to be misunderstood and unsupported. The chapter considers a variety of futures and draws upon Merton's theory of unanticipated, or unintended, consequences and Urry's (2016) anticipation of multiple futures. Predicting futures is difficult and can leave the one prognosticating, potentially promoting embarrassingly dated positions. However, if we consider such predictions to represent 'wicked' or at least complex problems we see possibilities that require us to analyse them from as many angles as one can (Rittel and Webber, 1973). This helps us explore what might be and what conceivable consequences might result, noting that it is not possible to identify causes and outcomes with complete confidence in 'wicked' problems. Connecting positions on Brexit, the pandemic and changing world events with prior historical understandings of the reasons why we provide welfare draws our excursus on its histories, interlinkages and differences to a close.

Theorising, anticipating and the future(s) of social welfare

In 1936 the American sociologist Robert K. Merton discussed the concept of unanticipated consequences of purposive actions. In later discussion, the term has often been altered to 'unintended' consequences. However, the two are different and need to be considered as distinct. Zwart (2015) distinguishes between consequences that are unintended – outcomes which are not explicitly desired but which may have, potentially, been anticipated – and those actions that are both unanticipated and unintended – that were not acknowledged or foreseen as potential outcomes and were also not explicitly desired. Precision is important here, and an introduction to Merton's thinking is warranted.

It must be remembered that unintended and/or unanticipated consequences do not automatically carry negative evaluations, indeed they may be positive or agonistic. The point is that they were either not explicitly considered or not explicitly promoted and desired as outcomes. Merton's (1936) original paper dealt with isolated purposive acts rather than coherent systems of action such as social welfare, although both can be considered under his schemata. He explains unforeseen consequences as not necessarily undesirable ones, while recognising that anticipated and intended ones may usually be desirable to the actor.

Merton was concerned that the terms were clearly defined in order to explore the phenomenon of social actions. Consequences are limited to elements that would not occur had the action not taken place. However, in practice there is also an interaction between the action and the context in which it occurs and the sum total of these may produce a range of consequences not always foreseen. Purposive action may be both unorganised and organised actions that are based on a range of possibilities. There are problems arising in these definitions to which he also drew attention. Causal imputation in the study of consequences is problematic as are *post facto* declarations of intent. Organised group actions will reduce the problem somewhat although not obviate it, but Merton suggests we always ask whether the consequences emanating from the actions 'make sense'.

While past experiences often represent a guide to anticipated outcomes, as do patterns of similarity, the anticipation of outcomes as discussed by Merton is limited by our current state of knowledge across a range of factors important to analysing social consequences. First, we must recognise that social and purposive actions are often based on opinion and estimate, which, to an extent, involves *ignorance* of what we do not know. There are also factors of *error* as our inferences may lead us to adopt the wrong choices for our intended or anticipated outcomes. Error may be the result of a lack of rigour in our preparatory thinking or be related to 'wish fulfilment' resulting from an over-emotional investment in the anticipated consequences. A third factor is the *'imperious immediacy of interest'* (Merton, 1936, p 901, emphasis added). This occurs when the overriding concerns of the actor lie with the foreseen immediate consequences to the exclusion of other consequences. These could be physiological, psychological or socio-cultural outcomes. For instance, in the rush to secure Brexit, the government of the day blithely accepted the Northern Ireland protocol to prevent the re-establishment of a hard border between Ireland and Northern Ireland, while being fully aware that in the longer term problems would arise (Barnier, 2021; Frost, 2022). Related to this is the factor of *basic values* in which no further consequences are considered because it is the actions designed to produce these basic values and the values themselves that are deemed necessary rather than anything else. An example being the assumed principle of Tory fiscal prudence over meeting the needs of people on low incomes or unemployed. The fifth factor in Merton's thesis is that the *prediction* or anticipation of consequences alters the course of action because it becomes an integral element to it.

Urry (2016) took forward this thinking, moving it from its functionalist beginnings into the realm of complex systems thinking. Urry starts from the premise that 'futures are unpredictable, uncertain and often unknowable, the outcome of many known and especially "unknown unknowns"' (2016, p 1). In order to negotiate this messy path towards actions for the future, he suggests it is '[n]ecessary to avoid the Scylla of technological determinism of the future, but also the Charybdis of completely open futures. The future is neither fully determined, nor empty and open' (Urry, 2016, p 12). Thinking about different futures is important for social science in anticipating and working towards change, to distinguish between the probable, the possible and the preferable futures that we want to see (Warden, 2021). Futures have been seen as either dystopian or utopian but increasingly the importance of the interplay between various systems introduces the core element of complexity (Urry, 2016).

Urry (2016) states that imagining futures requires embedding within complex analyses of multiple social structures. Complex structures such as social protection and welfare systems are unstable, interdependent and adaptive. They require constant analysis to deal continuously with wicked problems that often result in unanticipated or unintended consequences of social actions within them or the conditions surrounding them (Rittel and Webber, 1973). While Peters (2017) considers wicked problems to be rarer than thought and somewhat of a contemporary academic fad, he does recognise that all social policy problems share elements of wicked problems in terms of there being no obvious solutions to them and the potential for unintended and irreversible consequences. Social welfare policy post-Brexit and COVID-19 is certainly complex and interconnected (Pierson, 2021), but maybe not a 'super wicked problem' in the same sense as climate change (Levin et al, 2012). However, it seems to share Rittel and Webber's ten original characteristics of wicked problems:

1. difficult to define;
2. no stopping rule;
3. solutions are not true or false but axiological and political as good or bad;
4. there is no immediate or final test for proposed solutions;
5. all solutions may have irreversible consequences;
6. no clear solutions;
7. unique situations;
8. possibly symptoms of other problems;

9. multiple explanations;
10. those setting the policies have no right to be wrong.

Perhaps, allied with the intricacies of global financial precarity and socio-political tensions resulting from Russia's invasion of the Ukraine, there are elements of interactive complexity that can be described as a super-wicked problem. This makes social policy formulation necessary to address concomitant increasing need but also renders it impossible to determine with certainty.

Brexit and its consequences

A referendum vote on the UK's continued membership of the European Union took place on 23 June 2016. A referendum had been promised by the then Prime Minister, David Cameron, in the Conservative Party manifesto for the 2015 election (Conservative Party, 2015). It was suggested that this promise was included to assuage the Eurosceptics in the Conservative Party and a cynical attempt to derail the growing popularity of anti-European Union parties such as the United Kingdom Independence Party (UKIP; Smith, 2018). David Cameron did not want the UK to leave the European Union and does not seem to believe that this outcome was a possibility. The result, announced on Friday 24 June, that the UK had voted to leave the EU shocked and divided the people, countries and administrations of the UK.

We will explore what this vote might mean for social care and welfare in a post-Brexit UK. Brexit has significant consequences for social welfare. There have been increased moves towards homogenisation in statutory tasks, safeguarding or protection in the personal social services, and social and behavioural regulation of social protection or welfare benefits. The process of change is likely to be long and drawn out. However, whatever the end result, these moves towards insularity, restriction and regulation will have potentially long-lasting effects on UK social policy and welfare.

Why did the UK vote to leave the EU?

In earlier work we set out some of the reasons for the UK vote in favour of leaving the EU (Parker, 2019). Understanding Brexit itself is a complex state of affairs and cannot be reduced to Theresa May's incomprehensible and circuitous statement, 'Brexit means Brexit', which she made at her leadership campaign launch in July 2016, perhaps reinforcing the notion of politics by sound-bite. The ramifications and consequences of leaving the EU have been debated in depth and will continue to be so as the world reacts to unforeseen changes and challenges and the place of Britain and the UK within that world becomes clearer. The impact that Brexit has on social and public policy, institutions and practices remains unclear yet grounded within political and ideological futures.

The turnout for the referendum vote in 2016 was high, at 72.2 per cent of those eligible to vote and over 33 million votes. Results indicated that the vote was very close: 51.9 per cent (17,410,742) of voters voted Leave and 48.1 per cent (16,141,241) voted Remain (Electoral Commission, 2022). The results can be broken down further showing that Scotland, Northern Ireland and London clearly voted to Remain, while England, other than London, and Wales reflected the Leave vote. Despite the equivocal nature of the results by nation and region, the mantra 'the will of the people' was promoted while reflecting only the 17.4 million Leave votes while the 16.1 million people voting to Remain appeared to be ignored or dismissed (Seidler, 2018). When they did find a voice they were labelled 'remoaners' or castigated as 'undemocratic' (Price, 2016), which allowed the development of stigma and a hierarchical division in the UK between the Brexiters working for the 'will of the people' and those who wanted to overturn it. Despite the rhetoric of 'healing', these divisions ensured no healing could take place, as what was meant was simply acceptance and submission.

There was political turmoil in the aftermath of the vote. The prime minister at the time, David Cameron, resigned, the Labour Party were accused of a lacklustre campaign and having a Eurosceptic leader in Jeremy Corbyn. UKIP had secured its aim to leave the European Union. The Liberal Democrats, still confused and discredited after their involvement in the Coalition from 2010 to 2015, alongside the Greens, united behind a desire to hold a second referendum and to reverse the decision to leave the EU. The Scottish Nationalist Party took the result as a mandate for considering a second referendum on independence from the UK. While these political rumblings still continue, there is no clear view of what the UK post-Brexit future will look like over time; ideologues ply the hackneyed adage of 'taking back control' of borders, immigration, legislation and trade. Yet, daily reports abound of business, industry, public body anxieties and individual feelings of loss and being unwelcome, and concerns grow for the failure to take into account ramifications for the Good Friday Agreement and peace in Northern Ireland.

Victor Seidler's (2018) powerful (auto)ethnographic account captures the confusion in the UK when the referendum results were announced. Seidler, himself a refugee via the Kindertransport, highlighted the dangers of populism presented by the anger, rage and resistance to neoliberal globalisation lying behind the vote. Hate crime increased rapidly after the referendum. Home Office statistics indicated a 29 per cent increase on reported hate crimes to over 80,000 in 2016/2017 with over 60,000 having a racial element (O'Neill, 2017). The unleashed hatred seemed intimately bound to the discourses of 'controlling our borders' and the dangerous 'other' who is here 'taking our jobs', 'coming to do harm' or 'destroying our way of life', which, in turn, exerted an impact on the perceptions of health and social care workers (Seidler, 2018; Parker, 2019).

Powell (2017) argues that raw political and social divisions had been intensified by the austerity measures adopted after the 2008 financial crisis and this, in part, led to the Leave vote. As seen in Chapter 7, austerity has most effect on the working class, those disadvantaged and excluded from society, and immigrants. For Powell, austerity and its child, Brexit, have lent credence to far right ideologies that fuel blame, hostility and grievances against the political elite. Agonistically, Powell considers this may result in renewed left-wing thinking and political action, although there is no evidence of such. In a similar vein, McKenzie (2017) explored the anger and apathy of working-class people feeling excluded and left behind and believing they no longer 'existed' in the minds of political parties and society, something beginning in the Thatcher years. She describes the Brexit vote powerfully as a 'howl of anger' (McKenzie, 2017, p S278), something visceral not political. Although this focus presents dangers in legitimising White people's marginalisation and feeling as though they are 'strangers in their own lands' (Hochschild, 2016; Bhambra, 2017), such analyses may also occlude voting behaviours in which White, middle-class, South of England voters predominated in voting Leave (Dorling, 2016; Swales, 2016; Becker et al, 2017).

Hantrais (2019) suggested that the global financial crisis of 2007/2008 created a range of problems for the EU which was exacerbated by the crisis in the Eurozone and the refugee crisis. While these issues also affected the UK, she believes that the UK was never fully committed to the EU as a social and political project and that these combined factors added fuel to the desire to leave among the political classes and the public.

The impacts of Brexit on social welfare and care

European life has been influenced profoundly by the EU and this is the case for the UK. Living and working conditions, education, family and gender issues, old age, social inclusion and responses to migration are policy areas in which the European project has been concerned (Hantrais, 2019).

Since 1992 and the signing of the Maastricht Treaty there had been an increasing European approach to the social implications of population ageing, the refugees crisis and other areas of policy (Gomez-Jimenez and Parker, 2014; Hantrais, 2019). This had also led to shared welfare and social protection concerns (Martinelli et al, 2017). However, social policy has been diverse and complex throughout the history of the EU.

Harmonisations of social provisions required free movement of workers between member states and increased social union. The UK did not see EU involvement in domestic issues as appropriate and supported the widening of the union rather than deepening relationships across member states. However, the 2000 Charter of Fundamental Rights of the European Union provided a range of social and worker rights that many wanted to see adopted into UK domestic law after leaving. There is little impact yet because of the adoption of EU law into UK domestic law and the longer-term impact depends on the relationship between the UK and the EU over time. Potentially, UK social rights in respect of employment, anti-discrimination legislation, freedom of movement, regional developments, health and social care, gender equality and migrant rights will be affected. Before the referendum, Stalford (2016) reflected on the impact that Brexit might have on social welfare and family law, especially in respect of cross-national families and EU migration to the UK. These questions continue to unfurl, although the 2021 fuel shortages and supply-chain problems began to bite in areas of social spending.

In the EU Brexit has spurred on a more active social rights policy through the European Pillar of Social Rights adopted in 2017, whereas:

> [T]he implications of Brexit for UK social policy in the longer term will depend to a large extent on how governments manage a 'new' partnership with EU institutions and member states from the outside. Future social policy is also likely to be determined by the trading relationships that the UK negotiates with the rest of the world. (Hantrais, 2019, p 129)

Hantrais (2020) notes that Boris Johnson's Withdrawal Act left out section 4 on the Protection of Workers' Rights of Theresa May's Act, and removed references to 'level playing fields', replacing them with a commitment to upholding common high standards.

The referendum vote immediately wiped over three trillion dollars from the value of financial markets (Goodwin and Heath, 2016). Cost implications ever since, while contested, remain considerable. Farnsworth (2017) points out the precarity of the UK's funding base for social welfare since lost-cost EU markets are made inaccessible and complex. Taylor-Gooby (2017) agrees, suggesting that the only certainties from Brexit are a fall in the pound against the euro, and continued economic difficulties. In an earlier paper, he drew attention to a discernible shift in UK social policy from seeing social cohesion and social protection at the core of the welfare state to a social policy direction that seeks to exacerbate social decisions and to reduce the expenditure and reach of the welfare state still further (Taylor-Gooby, 2016). With a focus on creating a regressive tax policy and, prior to COVID-19, making it harder and more conditional to claim welfare benefits, while at the same time increasing stigma on those in receipt of benefits, social policy after the referendum has set an agenda of significant roll-back of the welfare state. Gingrich and King (2019) see this shift clearly within the promotion of welfare conditionality and workfare and the adoption of an increasingly harsh, restrictive social protection or welfare benefit system that has grown in the UK from the late 20th century onwards.

Austerity was continued until the 2019 election, and since then in all but name, social divisions have risen, and inflation post-Brexit and post-COVID rose sharply in the first half of 2022, leading to a fall in living standards, especially for those in more disadvantaged positions – a trajectory into poverty and social need (Mendoza, 2015; Varoufakis, 2017).

EU workers in social care and the National Health Service

Before the EU referendum took place, social care managers expressed concern about the potentially damaging repercussions of a vote to leave (Stalford, 2016). James Churchill, chief executive officer of Social Care Training Ltd, indicated rather presciently that the impact of leaving the EU would be profound, especially for those who were less well off. He argued that savings from EU payments were exaggerated and the resulting costs to the economy of leaving were far greater (Churchill, 2016). The winter National Health Service (NHS) crisis in early 2018 offered initial evidence of problems resulting from leaving the EU (Ham, 2018). The numbers of workers migrating to work in health and social care, about one in five of the workforce, comprised of 28 per cent from the EU with the rest born outside, fell and led to a much reduced workforce unable to cope with increased demands. This situation continued and following the removal of pandemic restrictions the growth in waiting lists for routine operations and health care became apparent, with the NHS reaching its lowest approval rating for many years in 2022 (Wellings et al, 2022). From a human resources perspective, Churchill also surmised that working conditions could well be less attractive if the UK left the EU and damaging the workforce even further. Concerns grew that a UK no longer tethered to EU work directives might lead to employer organisations reducing workers' rights and conditions, creating profound difficulties for an area of employment already fraught with low wages and difficult conditions (Montero, 2017).

Manthorpe et al (2018) undertook an examination of pre-Brexit secondary data concerning the perceptions of social and home care managers on decision-making when recruiting and employing staff. They noted great stress in maintaining an adequate workforce while remaining within the guidance and legislation, especially when employing people from overseas. Writing after the referendum, they concluded that these concerns would be greatly amplified post-Brexit, having a potentially catastrophic effect of care provision. Whereas in Read and Fenge's (2019) research conducted after the referendum, greater restrictions on the employment of EU and non-EU workers were believed to significantly increase the challenges of creating a sustainable workforce in the high-care-need region in which their research was conducted.

The debate concerning the social care workforce debate was overshadowed, however, by pejorative claims made about immigration (Montero, 2017). Before the referendum, EU citizens contributed about a 0.6 per cent growth in the UK economy each year while one in five social care workers were non-UK nationals and many of these from the EU. Indeed, Mulholland (2017), using official national statistics, revealed that there were 209,000 EU nationals in health and social care in 2016, a rise of 72 per cent from 2009. Indeed, in 2016, 4.95 per cent NHS staff and 5 per cent of the social care and social work workforce were EU nationals (House of Lords, 2016). The future at that point for the workforce was unclear and the House of Lords Library note called for clarity on rights to work and remain for EU nationals, something that emerged fitfully towards the end of the second decade. This was further confirmed and demanded within a House of Commons Health Report (2017), which indicated there were over 90,000 people in social care from the EU and that such numbers would continue to be necessary. Central questions remained concerning the future rights and entitlements of non-UK staff, professional education and regulation, EU work time directives and conditions which had a significant bearing on the future of heath and social care delivery.

Glasper (2018) drew attention to the National Audit Office report noting social care staff shortages. In part this had resulted from pre-Brexit population dynamics but has been compounded by high staff turnover, increasing demand, vacancy management, low wages and poor working conditions. Brexit has compounded these problems and the COVID-19 pandemic has exacerbated these. M. Morris (2019) adds that the cuts to social and health care prior to Brexit and the pandemic have increased the impact on the most disadvantaged communities. This is something that the updated Marmot report has also highlighted (Marmot et al, 2020).

By 2020, ten years of austerity and benefit reform had deleteriously affected people's well-being, social care and the workforce delivering it had been delivered a broadside by Brexit fallout and the future for social welfare in Britain seemed bleak. It was in this context that the pandemic took hold.

The impacts of COVID-19

At the December 2019 election and into January 2020 it was Brexit and withdrawal from the EU that continued to dominate people's thinking. However, in the space of two months the focus had altered rapidly and the UK was preparing to enter its first period of lockdown owing to the developing pandemic and Europe had been declared the epicentre of the pandemic on 13 March 2020 (Hantrais, 2020).

The increased complexity of social care and social welfare resulting from COVID-19 and governmental reactions to it, including the marginalisation of social care in the early stages of the first wave of the pandemic, adds significantly to the exploration of potential futures for social welfare (Bambra et al, 2021; Parker and Veasey, 2021; Pierson, 2021). The ways in which Universal Credit was applied, alongside the Coronavirus Job Retention Scheme and assistance for employees and self-employed citizens, offers insight into the ways in which welfare and support was understood by the government at the time (HMRC, 2021).

The impact on the economy of shutting down businesses had immediate and prolonged effects on the UK's economy. However, the ability to fund business and employment based projects, alongside an uplift in Universal Credit, highlighted that previous government thinking on austerity had been a political strategy rather than a necessity, which was the way it was sold to the general public. The impact on social welfare was such that the government claimed there would be no more austerity measures, and billions were poured into supporting business. While this uplift moved 400,000 children out of poverty, its removal in September 2021 suggests a misunderstanding, deliberate or otherwise, of people in poverty remained (National Statistics, 2022).

Hantrais and Letablier (2021) compare and contrast the impact of and response to the COVID-19 pandemic in the EU. The UK had already left by this time and was no longer subject to the policy-making machinery of the EU, although similar pressures remained on policy making. The Maastricht Treaty 1992 had adopted public health concerns as a legitimate aspect of EU policy making, however, the Lisbon Treaty 2007 had reinforced the idea that each member state could determine its own health policy. This has caused some difficulties in forming an adequate policy response across the EU to the pandemic and begs the question whether closer social union could have helped in saving lives and offset the divisions aggravated by the uncertain policy position. The UK had to adopt its own approach to social and health policy and welfare during the pandemic.

The HM Revenue and Customs Coronavirus Job Retention Scheme allowed employers to claim some of the wages of their employees if they had been furloughed or put on flexible furlough. The Universal Credit system has played a major role in supporting people on low income or out of work during the pandemic. However, Baumberg Geiger et al (2021) estimated that around half a million people were eligible for Universal Credit at the start of the pandemic but did not claim it. There are varied and, no doubt, interacting reasons for the non-take-up, including the perceived stigma associated with benefit claims, the assumed complexity and difficulty of completing an application and/or experiencing the future threat of sanctions. Also, around half those people not making a claim believed they were eligible but did not want to claim because they felt they did not need benefits. Also, it was estimated that between 280,000 and 390,000 people wrongly assumed they were not eligible for Universal Credit or other benefits. Before the pandemic incomes had fallen, borrowing from friends and banks had increased, some were using food banks. These findings indicated a range of changes to the benefit system were necessary. The project suggested that the Department for Work and Pensions (DWP) publish take-up estimates so that non-take-up does not remain hidden. It was accepted that clearer information had been developed but recommended that still greater clarity be published concerning benefits and the application process; perhaps also developing a single application gateway. This would assist in correcting misconceptions about the system and facilitate applications. The research team recognised that addressing benefit stigma was, to an extent, out of the hands of the DWP and that discourses concerning claimants have improved during the pandemic. However, they recommended that claimants should be treated with dignity and that the DWP and government ministers consistently speak respectfully about those people claiming benefits.

Welfare practices have been significantly affected by the pandemic where community nursing and social work interpersonal relationships have had to change and adapt and where care home staff have had to adopt new practices. These different relational techniques are practised with those people made vulnerable by societal practices and structures and therefore it results in deeper consequences (Bowers et al, 2021; Parker, 2021a, 2021b). Social distancing requirements and changed health and social care practices also affected support provided for breastfeeding mothers, although this seemed to differ between different geographical areas (Brown and Shenker, 2021). Given women's experiences often as carers for older people the pandemic has also highlighted the inadequacies of UK care provision and support for those involved in informal care (Baxter, 2020).

The impact on school children and those working in educational settings has also been affected, whether that is in respect of children's mental health, teachers' susceptibility to infection or socio-educational attainments (COVID-19 Advisory Sub-groups on Education and Children's Issues, 2020; Hantrais and Letablier, 2021). Indeed, the implications from COVID-19 have exposed the depth of social divisions in the UK. For instance, the risks of infection and death among some ethnicities became clear (Otu et al, 2020; PHE et al, 2020). Also, questions have been raised concerning how people fare according to their household composition, especially in respect of psychological and physical health (Okabe-Miyamoto et al, 2021). Rose et al (2021) explored the impact of school closures across society, and critiqued the development of plans for reintroducing students – something that was patchy at best and ad hoc in the main. The availability and necessity of free school meals, resources and connections with social welfare and (digital) poverty have also highlighted socio-economic disparities that have been exacerbated by the pandemic.

The Covid Realities research project, conducted by the Universities of York and Birmingham and the Child Poverty Action Group, has compiled the stories, experiences and perspectives of families on low incomes during the pandemic (Covid Realities, 2021; Patrick et al, 2022a, 2022b). This project has highlighted the challenges faced and shown how the social security system is in need of reform if it is to adequately meet the needs of people on low incomes drawing on the £20 per week uplift to Universal Credit. Baumberg Geiger et al (2021), however, stress that the uplift has performed well for people during this time, even if future reform is necessary. The project has heard from people who are homeless, women affected by the pandemic, and children and young people. Women have, as we have seen in Chapter 6, experienced deeper hardship in the pandemic, indeed domestic violence and abuse appeared to rise significantly during that time alongside cuts to refuges and draconian penalties for breaking lockdowns which may have prevented women seeking external help or safety (Women's Aid, 2020; Parker and Veasey, 2021).

UK social policy took an interventionist approach during the pandemic in setting up the Job Retention Scheme, extending Universal Credit to the self-employed, introducing the £20 per week uplift and finding unprecedented funds to support health and welfare schemes. However, this was replicated in other EU countries as well. The EU recovery plan set out on 27 May 2020, in *Next Generation EU* – was built around a Green Deal and supported fair and inclusive recovery programmes, although this was rejected by the frugal four. The impact is still, however, uncertain: 'What the combined impact of Brexit and COVID-19 will mean for EU and UK social policy in the longer term, and ultimately for European social integration, are questions that are likely to remain open for some time to come' (Hantrais, 2020, p 12).

Post-Brexit and post-pandemic restriction British society displays a contested fomentation of opinion, practice and potential for policy development. The precarious relationship between the British public and the NHS has come into sharp relief, as shown in the British Social Attitudes Survey (Wellings et al, 2022). Adult social care and health care jobs remain unfilled and attract low status, pay and conditions, despite some relaxation of visa conditions for overseas workers. Social work remains a harried and harassed profession in the face of public reaction to care tragedies, although its status as a useful governmental scapegoat is being challenged by other public services also attracting such opprobrium (Preston and Samuel, 2021). In future social welfare contexts we may question whether health will be rationed, based on behavioural conditions or eligibility criteria, whether social services become a residual service and deal predominantly with safeguarding and social regulation, whether education becomes more about training for economic productivity or learning and well-being, whether social security remains focused on bolstering paid employment, and unpaid caregiving remains hidden and gendered. Indeed, Pierson (2021) argues for a fundamental shift in our conception and ways of doing welfare, and that political responses to COVID-19 illustrate clearly the necessity of continued state intervention in welfare, a call echoed by Spicker (2022).

The redistribution of wealth, as a means of fulfilling some of the promise of the welfare state, requires now a sharp focus on ownership, property and taxation (Pierson, 2021). Whether governments in Britain in the immediate future will have the appetite for such is unclear and this, in turn, makes the future of state-organised social welfare uncertain, although the either cynical or ignorant UK Spring budget of 2022 entrenched the more residual, austerity-based politics of early 21st-century Conservatism (Alston, 2018; Partington and Elgot, 2022).

Conclusions

Predicting the future, as we have noted, leaves the predictor a hostage to fortune. The twists and turns of history are complex and small perturbations in one sector can have profound effects in another. However, the ways in which social welfare is developing in the UK post-Brexit and after the initial years of the COVID-19 pandemic to some extent represent the unintended consequences of austerity and complacency, alongside 'wicked' problems resulting from these events. The war in Ukraine in 2022 added a further set of consequences that could not have been predicated or anticipated. It demonstrated clearly, however, that global interconnections in political, economic and social domains are central to any future developments. To identify the impacts of such events may lead to accusations of playing 'Captain Hindsight', as former Prime Minister Boris Johnson retorted to Keir Starmer in respect of Brexit and the pandemic (Sleigh, 2020). However, post-Brexit welfare planning shows a serious lack of prior planning, and perhaps underlies a lack of political concern for those made vulnerable by society's operations and structures. Indeed, this is something that is lent credence by the failure to implement recommendations from prior pandemic modelling and planning, the continued policy of austerity, and the 2021 attempts at debunking structural causes and factors implicated in social divisions (see Sewell, 2021). The impact of COVID-19 magnified the inequalities in society and exposed the significant social needs of many people. The ways these have been addressed demonstrate ambivalence – having to help those who are vulnerable but laying the responsibility for that vulnerability at the feet of individuals rather than locating it within the structures and responses of society as a whole.

Merton's thoughts on unintended consequences ring true, especially when overlaid with understandings from complex systems thinking that recognise the interconnections of all things. As we move into unknown futures and uncharted territories in social welfare and human support we need to consider all eventualities, to consider the insignificant alongside the seemingly obvious if we are to support people adequately and appropriately.

Looking back to the beginnings of our journey in social welfare we recognised that welfare and human support were part of the human condition from the earliest times. It seems that such compassion remains. Despite the structural failings of government in supporting refugees and those fleeing from war (Besana, 2022), within hours of the 'Homes for Ukraine' scheme being launched on 18 March, approximately 150,000 people in Britain had signed up to offer homes to people (*Independent*, 2022). This bifurcated response reflects the twin drivers of economy and compassion in welfare.

Alongside these distinctions in approaches to social welfare and between care and control, we have seen a number of other interconnecting themes throughout its history. These include binary distinctions designed to produce stigma and control and hegemonic normativity in the system, which allows the reproduction of power relations, and provides those in power with a useful scapegoat or deflection from their own failings. Often this creates systems that promote limited eligibility and behavioural conditionality or, sometimes, universality. The administrative control that results from this controlling system, and the bureaucracy of people-regulation, reflects a tendency towards centralisation and simplification, which creates unintended and unanticipated consequences.

Belief, political ideology, will and agency have driven welfare history as relational compassion has become codified. The question of whether or not we want a state welfare system, a marketised, individual responsibility system, a 'Third Way', an anarchic system of compassion or something else demands that we draw on psychosocial understandings of the compassionate selves we may be, alongside political will. Nothing is clear-cut. The histories of social welfare that we have explored have been underpinned by division and distinction between the 'deserving' and 'undeserving', the 'givers' and the 'receivers', the 'haves' and the 'have nots'. These are influenced and performed according to discourse relations that maintain these divisions; they keep people beholden and under obligation. These discourses and our ambivalence towards social welfare reflect the status quo that allows inequalities, over-consumption and feeds the climate crisis. However, as the climate crisis consumes our social lives as well as our ecology it is imperative that we move towards a greener social welfare that acknowledges the importance of sustainability, equity and mutual interdependence and compassion, which can only be achieved through universal, unconditional and individual rights or entitlements as human citizens of the planet. The beginnings of such a green approach may in part be seen in the advancement of a UBI, but a more fundamental shift still is needed as suspicion, ambivalence and vested interests remain.

References

Abel-Smith, B. and Townsend, P. (1965) *The Poor and the Poorest: A New Analysis of the Ministry of Labour's Family Expenditure Surveys of 1953–54 and 1960*, LSE Occasional Papers on Social Administration No 17, G, London: Bell and Sons.

Abraham, K. (1927/1988) 'A short history of the development of the libido', in D. Bryan and A. Strachey (eds), *Selected Papers of Karl Abraham*, New York: Karnac, pp 218–301.

Abrams, P. (1963) 'The failure of social reform 1918–20', *Past and Present*, 24: 43–64.

Adams, R. (1996) *Social Work and Empowerment*, Birmingham: BASW.

Allen, M. (Lady Allen of Hurtwood) (1945) *Whose Children?* London: The Favil Press.

Alston, P. (2018) 'Report of the Special Rapporteur on extreme poverty and human rights on his visit to the United Kingdom of Great Britain and Northern Ireland, Human Rights Council', *A/HRC/41/39/Add.1, United Nations General Assembly*, available from: https://documents-dds-ny.un.org/doc/UNDOC/GEN/G19/112/13/PDF/G1911213.pdf?Open Element [Accessed 29 May 2019].

Alzobaidee, H.L.K. (2015) 'Social protection and safety nets in Iraq', *Institute of Development Studies, Centre for Social Protection, United Nations World Food Programme*, available from: https://www.ids.ac.uk/download.php?file=files/dmfile/SocialprotectionandsafetynetsinIraq.pdf [Accessed 1 June 2018].

Andrzejewski, S. (1954) *Military Organisation and Society*, London: Routledge and Kegan Paul.

Arai, L. (2009) *Teenage Pregnancy: The Making and Unmaking of a Problem*, Bristol: Policy Press.

Aschwanden, C. (2020) 'The false promise of herd immunity for COVID-19', *Nature*, 21 October, available from: https://www.nature.com/articles/d41586-020-02948-4 [Accessed 23 November 2021].

Ashencaen Crabtree, S., Parker, J., Crabtree Parker, I. and Crabtree Parker, M. (2018) 'Development as eradication: The pillage of the Jakun "people's bank" of Tasik Chini, Pahang', *South East Asian Research*, 26(3): 283–298.

Ashencaen Crabtree, S., Esteves, L. and Hemingway, A. (2021) 'A "new (ab) normal"?: Scrutinising the work-life balance of academics under lockdown', *Journal of Further and Higher Education*, 45(9): 1177–1191.

Ashworth, W. (1968) *The Genesis of Modern British Town Planning: A Study in Economic and Social History of the Nineteenth and Twentieth Centuries*, London: Routledge and Kegan Paul.

Aspalter, C. (2021a) 'The importance of distinguishing between ideal-typical and real-typical models', in C. Aspalter (ed), *Ideal Types in Comparative Social Policy*, London: Routledge, pp 60–89.

Aspalter, C. (2021b) 'Ten worlds of welfare regimes', in C. Aspalter (ed), *Ideal Types in Comparative Social Policy*, London: Routledge, pp 107–168.

Atkinson, K., Oerton, S. and Burns, D. (1998) 'Happy families? Single mothers, the press and the politicians', *Capital and Class*, 64: 1–11.

Atlee, C. (1920) *The Social Worker*, London: G. Bell and Sons.

Audit Commission (1985) *Managing Social Services for the Elderly More Effectively*, London: HMSO.

Audit Commission (1986) *Making a Reality of Community Care*, London: HMSO.

Bailey, A.R. and Bryson, J.R. (2006) 'A Quaker experiment in town planning: George Cadbury and the construction of Bournville model village', *Quaker Studies*, 11(1): 89–114.

Bailey, R. and Brake, M. (eds) (1975) *Radical Social Work*, London: Edwin Arnold.

Balls, E. (2008) 'Baby P.: Ed Ball's statement in full', *The Guardian*, 1 December, available from: https://www.theguardian.com/society/2008/dec/01/baby-p-ed-balls-statement [Accessed 20 September 2017].

Bambra, C. and Smith, K. (2010) 'No longer deserving? Sickness benefit reform and the politics of (ill) health', *Critical Public Health*, 20(1): 71–83.

Bambra, C., Lynch, J. and Smith, K.E. (2021) *The Unequal Pandemic: COVID-19 and Health Inequalities*, Bristol: Policy Press.

Bamford, T. (2015) *A Contemporary History of Social Work: Learning From the Past*, Bristol: Policy Press.

Bamford, T. and Bilton, K. (2020) *Social Work: Past, Present and Future*, Bristol: Policy Press.

Barnett, C. (1986) *The Audit of War: The Illusion and Reality of Britain as a Great Nation*, London: Macmillan.

Barnett, C. (1995) *The Lost Victory: British Dreams, British Reality, 1945–1950*, London: Macmillan.

Barnier, M. (2021) *My Secret Brexit Diary*, Cambridge: Polity.

Bartley, P. (1998) 'Preventing prostitution: The ladies' association for the care and protection of young girls in Birmingham, 1887–1914', *Women's History Review*, 7(1): 37–60.

BASW (British Association of Social Workers) (1977) *The Social Work Task*, Birmingham: BASW.

Batkalova, K. (2018) 'Binary oppositions in traditional culture of Japanese and Kazakh people', *Astra Salvensis*, 6(11): 463–480.

Bauer, M.W. and Knill, C. (2012) 'Understanding policy dismantling: An analytical framework', in M.W. Bauer, A. Jordan, C. Green-Pedersen and A. Hértier (eds), *Dismantling Public Policy: Preferences, Strategies, and Effects*, Oxford Scholarship Online, doi: 10.1093/acprof:oso/9780199655646.003.0002

Baumberg, B. (2013) 'Benefits and the cost of living', *British Social Attitudes Survey, 31, NatCen Social Research*, available from: https://www.bsa.natcen.ac.uk/media/38191/bsa31_benefits_and_the_cost_of_living.pdf [Accessed 3 August 2022].

Baumberg, B. (2016) 'The stigma of claiming benefits: A quantitative study', *Journal of Social Policy*, 45(2): 181–199.

Baumberg, B., Bell, K. and Gaffney, D. (2012) *Benefits Stigma in Britain*, London: Turn2Us.

Baumberg Geiger, B., Scullion, L., Summers, K., Martin, P., Lawler, C., Edmiston, D., Gibbons, A., Ingold, J., Roberthaw, D. and de Vries, R. (2021) 'Non-take-up of benefits at the start of the COVID-19 pandemic', *Welfare at a (Social) Distance*, Project Report, Health Foundation, available from: https://62608d89-fc73-4896-861c-0e03416f9922.usrfiles.com/ugd/62608d_c06b922f6c94473f89f95ecd0bca328d.pdf [Accessed 21 April 2021].

Baxter, L. (2020) 'A hitchhiker's guide to caring for an older person before and during coronavirus-19', *Gender, Work and Organization*, 27(5): 763–773.

BBC (2006) 'UK settles WWII debt to allies', available from: http://news.bbc.co.uk/1/hi/uk/6215847.stm [Accessed 12 October 2015].

Beatty, C. and Fothergill, S. (2018) 'Welfare reform in the United Kingdom 2010–16: Expectations, outcomes and local impacts', *Social Policy and Administration*, 52(5): 950–968.

Beck, G. and Thane, P. (eds) (1991) *Maternity and Gender Politics: Women and the Rise of the European Welfare States, 1880s–1950s*, London: Routledge.

Becker, S.O., Fetzer, T. and Novy, D. (2017) 'Who voted for Brexit? A comprehensive district-level analysis', *Centre for Economic Performance Discussion Paper No 1480*, April, available from: http://cep.lse.ac.uk/pubs/download/dp1480.pdf [Accessed 20 September 2017].

Bekkers, R. and Wiepking, P. (2011) 'A literature review of empirical studies of philanthropy: Eight mechanisms that drive charitable giving', *Nonprofit and Voluntary Sector Quarterly*, 40(5): 924–973.

Bellamy, E. (1888) *Looking Backward, 2000–1887*, Boston: Ticknor and Co.

Bentham, J. (1789/2007) *An Introduction to the Principles of Morals and Legislation*, Mineola: Dover Publications.

Berger, P.L. and Luckmann, T. (1966) *The Social Construction of Reality*, Garden City: Doubleday.

Berg-Weger, M. (2016) *Social Work and Social Welfare* (4th edn), New York: Routledge.

Bernades, J. (1997) *Family Studies: An Introduction*, London: Routledge.

Besana, M. (2022) 'We need to reject the UK government's bespoke approach to refugees', *BMJ*, 376, doi: 10.1136/bmj.o569

Beveridge, W. (1942) *Social Insurance and Allied Services*, Cmnd 6404, London: HMSO.

Beveridge, W. (1948) *Voluntary Action: A Report on Methods of Social Advance*, London: George Allen and Unwin.

Bhambra, G.K. (2017) 'Brexit, Trump, and "methodological whiteness": On the misrecognition of race and class', *The British Journal of Sociology*, 68(S1): S214–S232.

Bhattacharyya, G. (2015) *Crisis, Austerity and Everyday Life*, Basingstoke: Palgrave Macmillan.

Bichard, M. (2004) *The Bichard Inquiry Report*, HM653, London: The Stationery Office.

BIEN (Basic Income Earth Network) (2022) Basic Income Earth Network, available from: https://basicincome.org [Accessed 6 December 2022].

Black, D. (1980) *Inequalities in Health: Report of a Research Working Group*, London: DHSS.

Blakemore, K. and Warwick-Booth, L. (2013) *Social Policy: An Introduction* (4th edn), Maidenhead: Open University Press.

Blond, P. (2010) *Red Tory: How Left and Right Have Broken Britain and How We Can Fix It*, London: Faber & Faber.

Bochel, H. (2011) 'Conservative approaches to social policy since 1997', in H. Bochel (ed), *The Conservative Party and Social Policy*, Bristol: Policy Press, pp 1–22.

Bochel, H. (2020) 'Liberal welfare states', in B. Greve (ed), *Routledge Handbook of the Welfare State* (2nd edn), London: Routledge, pp 176–186.

Booth, R. (2019) 'Computer says no: the people trapped in Universal Credit's black hole', *The Guardian*, 14 October, available from: https://www.theguardian.com/society/2019/oct/14/computer-says-no-the-peo ple-trapped-in-universal-credits-black-hole?CMP=Share_iOSApp_Other [Accessed 14 October 2019].

Bourdieu, P. (1977) *Outline of a Theory of Practice*, Cambridge: Cambridge University Press.

Bourdieu P. (1994) *In Other Words*, Cambridge: Polity.

Bourdieu, P. (1996) 'On the family as a realized category', *Theory, Culture and Society*, 13(3): 19–26.

Bourdieu, P. (1998) *Practical Reason*, Cambridge: Polity.

Bourdieu, P. and Wacquant, L.J.D. (1992) *An Invitation to Reflexive Sociology*, Chicago: University of Chicago Press.

Bowers, B., Pollock, K, Oldman, C. and Barclay, S. (2021) 'End-of-life care during COVID-19: Opportunities and challenges for community nursing', *British Journal of Community Nursing*, 26(1): 44–46.

Bowman, S. (2014) 'The negative income tax and basic wage are pretty much the same thing', *Adam Smith Institute*, available from: https://www.adamsm ith.org/blog/welfare-pensions/the-negative-income-tax-and-basic-inc ome-are-pretty-much-the-same-thing [Accessed 4 July 2020].

Braye, S. and Preston-Shoot, M. (eds) (2020) *The Care Act 2014*, London: SAGE.

Breeze, B. (2005) 'The return of philanthropy', *Prospect*, 16 January, available from: https://www.prospectmagazine.co.uk/magazine/thereturnofphilanthropy [Accessed 25 January 2022].

Bregman, R. (2018) *Utopia for Realists and How We Get There*, London: Bloomsbury.

Brewer, M. and Gardiner, L. (2020) 'Key take-aways from the Chancellor's package of measures to support workers in the coronavirus crisis', *Resolution Foundation*, available from: https://www.resolutionfoundation.org/comment/key-take-aways-chancellors-package-of-measures-to-support-workers-coronavirus-crisis/ [Accessed 12 October 2021].

Brewer, M., Corlett, A., Handscomb, K. and Tomlinson, D. (2021) 'The living standards outlook, 2021', *Resolution Foundation*, available from: https://www.resolutionfoundation.org/app/uploads/2021/01/Living-standards-outlook-2021.pdf [Accessed 25 August 2022].

Briar, C. (1997) *Working for Women? Gendered Work and Welfare Policies in Twentieth-century Britain*, London: UCL Press.

Briggs, S. and Foord, M. (2017) 'Food banks and the transformation of British social welfare', *Czech and Slovak Social Work*, 17(4): 72–86.

Brown, A. and Shenker, N. (2021) 'Experiences of breastfeeding during COVID-19: Lessons for future practical and emotional support', *Maternal and Child Nutrition*, 17(1): 1–15.

Brundage, A. (2002) *The English Poor Laws, 1700–1930*, Basingstoke: Palgrave Macmillan.

Buchholtz, A.K. and Brown, J.A. (2012) 'Corporate philanthropy research', *Proceedings of the International Association for Business and Society*, 17: 70–71.

Bull, H.W. (1991) 'Learning for life: Educational provision at Cadbury, 1831–1981', PhD thesis, Aston University, available from: https://ethos.bl.uk/OrderDetails.do?uin==uk.bl.ethos.305181 [Accessed 25 April 2020].

Burchardt, T. (2001) 'The "welfare state"', in P. Alcock, H. Glennerster, A. Oakley and A. Sinfield (eds), *Welfare and Wellbeing: Richard Titmuss's Contribution to Social Policy*, Bristol: Policy Press, pp 41–48.

Burnette, J. (2004) 'The wages and employment of female day-labourers in English agriculture, 1740–1850', *Economic History Review*, 57(4): 664–690.

Burnham, D. (2011) 'Selective memory: A note of social work historiography', *British Journal of Social Work*, 41(1): 5–21.

Burnham, D. (2012) *The Social Worker Speaks: A History of Social Work Through the Twentieth Century*, Farnham: Ashgate.

Burrell, G. and Morgan, G. (1979) *Sociological Paradigms and Organizational Analysis*, London: Heinemann.

Burt, M. (2020) *A History of the Roles and Responsibilities of Social Workers*, London: Routledge.

Butler-Sloss, E. (1988) *Report of the Inquiry into Child Abuse in Cleveland 1987*, Cmd 412, London: HMSO.

Butrym, Z. (1976) *The Nature of Social Work*, London: Macmillan.

Button, D. and Coote, A. (2021) 'A social guarantee: The case for universal services', *New Economics Foundation*, available from: https://neweconomics.org/uploads/files/Universal-services-paper.pdf [Accessed 22 August 2022].

Buzducea, D. (2018) *Social Work: History, Recent Debates and High-risk Groups*, Bucharest: Tritanic.

Cabinet Office (1999) *Modernising Government*, Cm 4310, London: The Stationery Office.

Calnitsky, D. (2016) '"More normal than welfare": The Mincome experiment, stigma, and community experience', *Canadian Review of Sociology*, 53(1): 26–71.

Cameron, D. (2009) 'The Big Society', *Hugo Young Memorial Lecture*, 10 November, available from: http://www.conservatives.com/News/Speeches/2009/11/David_Cameron_The_Big_Society.aspx [Accessed 12 June 2015].

Canci, A., Minozzi, S. and Tarli, S.M.B. (1996) 'New evidence of tuberculosis spondylitis from Neolithic Liguria (Italy)', *International Journal of Osteoarchaeology*, 6(3): 497–501.

Care of Children Committee (1946) *Report of the Care of Children Committee*, Cmd 6922, London: His Majesty's Stationery Office.

Carroll, N. (2017) 'Lone mothers experiences of stigma: A comparative study', unpublished PhD, University of Huddersfield, available from: https://eprints.hud.ac.uk/id/eprint/34358 [Accessed 15 May 2021].

Cassidy, L.M., Maoldúin, R.Ó., Kador, T., Lynch, A., Jones, C., Woodman, P.C., Murphy, E., et al (2020) 'A dynastic elite in monumental Neolithic society', *Nature*, 582: 384–388.

Centre for Social Justice (2009) 'Dynamic benefits: Towards welfare that works', *Centre for Social Justice*, available from: https://www.centreforsocialjustice.org.uk/core/wp-content/uploads/2016/08/CSJ-dynamic-benefits.pdf [Accessed 24 August 2016].

Ceolta-Smith, J., Salway, S. and Tod, A.M. (2018) 'Experiences from the frontline: An exploration of personal advisers' practice with claimants who have health-related needs within UK welfare-to-work provision', *Health and Social Care in the Community*, 26(4): 598–608.

Chadwick, H. (1993) *The Early Church*, London: Penguin.

Chambon, A. (2011) 'The material presence of early social work: The practice of the archive', *British Journal of Social Work*, 44(4): 625–644.

Change.org (2021) 'A law dedicated to Arthur to ensure that no other child suffering abuse is left to die', available from: https://www.change.org/p/10downingstreet-a-law-dedicated-to-arthur-to-ensure-that-no-other-child-suffering-abuse-is-left-to-die/sign?cs_tk=AsuYAljcwCjoAwJsw2EAAXicyyvNyQEABF8BvEaHLY3U7nIXNocGgxBywu4%3D&pt=AVBldGl0aW9uAJ3e4QEAAAAAYboxf6%252B5S3VkYzIyODcyNg%253D%253D&source_location=aa_sign_ask&utm_campaign=dff08a38255341b2bc9c7e9f94c16e0d&utm_content=exp_var_1_v0_2_0&utm_medium=email&utm_source=aa_sign_ask&utm_term=cs [Accessed 15 December 2021].

Charlesworth, L. (2010a) *Welfare's Forgotten Past: A Socio-legal History of the Poor Law*, London: Routledge.

Charlesworth, L. (2010b) 'England's early "Big Society": Parish welfare under old Poor Law', *History and Policy*, available from: https://www.historyandpolicy.org/policy-papers/papers/englands-early-big-society-parish-welfare-under-old-poor-law [Accessed 2 June 2020].

Chauhan, A. and Foster, J. (2014) 'Representations of poverty in British newspapers: A case of "othering" the threat', *Journal of Community and Applied Social Psychology*, 24(5): 390–405.

Cheetham, M., Moffatt, S., Addison, M. and Wiseman, A. (2019) 'Impact of Universal Credit in North East England: A qualitative study of claimants and support staff', *BMJ Open* [online] 9(7): 1–9, https://bmjopen.bmj.com/content/9/7/e029611

Chenoweth, J.M. (2019) 'Reconstructing a changing religious landscape: The material traces of Barbados Quakers, 1655–1800', *International Journal of Historical Archaeology*, 23(2): 462–495.

Child, J. (1690) *A Discourse about Trade*, London: A Towle – the Text Creation Partnership, available from: https://quod.lib.umich.edu/cgi/t/text/text-idx?c=eebo;idno=A32827.0001.001 [Accessed 16 February 2021].

Churchill, J. (2016) 'Brexit and social care: Bad news all round', *Association for Real Change*, available from: http://arcuk.org.uk/blog/brexit-and-social-care-bad-news-all-round/ [Accessed 12 March 2018].

Claeys, G. (ed) (2001) *The Chartist Movement in Britain, 1838–1850*, London: Pickering and Chatto.

Clarke, S. (1978) 'The origins of Lévi-Strauss's structuralism', *Sociology*, 12(3): 405–439.

Clement Brown, S. (1939) 'The methods of social case workers', in F.C. Bartlett, M. Ginsburg, E.J. Lindgren and R.H. Thouless (eds), *The Study of Society: Methods and Problems*, London: Kegan Paul, Trench, Trubner and Co., pp 381–383.

Clifford, D. (2017) 'Charitable organisations, the great recession and the age of austerity: Longitudinal evidence for England and Wales', *Journal of Social Policy*, 46(1): 1–30.

Cobbett, W. (1830/2001) *Rural Rides*, Harmondsworth: Penguin Classics.

Coe, S.D. and Coe, M.D. (2013) *The True History of Chocolate* (3rd edn), London: Thames and Hudson.

Coffman, E. (2006) 'Sweet charity', *Christian History and Biography*, 89: 11.

Communities and Local Government (2006) *Getting Connected: Guidelines for Operating Reconnections Policies for Rough Sleepers – Outline Framework*, London: CLG.

Conservative Party (2010a) *Invitation to Join the Government of Britain: The Conservative Manifesto 2010*, London: Conservative Party.

Conservative Party (2010b) *Building the Big Society*, available from: https://assets.publishing.service.gov.uk/government/uploads/system/uploads/attachment_data/file/78979/building-big-society_0.pdf [Accessed 6 December 2022].

Conservative Party (2015) *The Conservative Party Manifesto 2015: Strong Leadership. A Clear Economic Plan. A Brighter, More Secure Future*, available from: https://www.conservatives.com/manifesto2015 [Accessed 21 March 2018].

The Conservative and Unionist Party (2019) *Get Brexit Done Unleash Britain's Potential*, available from: https://www.conservatives.com/our-plan/conservative-part-manifesto-2019 [Accessed 5 December 2022].

Conway, S. (2010) 'The British army, "military Europe", and the American War of Independence', *The William and Mary Quarterly*, 67(1): 69–100.

Corrigan, O. (2009) 'Migrants, welfare systems and social citizenship in Ireland and Britain: users or abusers?' *Journal of Social Policy*, 39(2): 415–437.

Corrigan, P. and Leonard, P. (1978) *Social Work Practice under Capitalism: A Marxist Approach*, London: Macmillan.

Covid Realities (2021) 'Covid realities', available from: https://covidrealities.org [Accessed 15 April 2021].

COVID-19 Advisory Sub-group on Education and Children's Issues (2020) 'Education setting and COVID-19 transmission', *Education Journal*, 433: 30–35.

Cree, V.E. (1995) *From Public Streets to Private Lives: The Changing Task of Social Work*, Aldershot: Avebury.

Cree, V.E. (2016) '"Khaki fever" during the First World War: A historical case study of social work's approach towards young women, sex and moral danger', *British Journal of Social Work*, 46(7): 1839–1854.

Crowther, M.A. (1981) *The Workhouse System, 1834–1929: The History of an English Social Institution*, London: Batsford.

Curry, R. (2019) 'More than 3,500 homeless veterans slipping through the net each year, new campaign claims', *Inside Housing*, 24 September, available from: https://www.insidehousing.co.uk/news/news/more-than-3500-homeless-veterans-are-slipping-through-the-net-each-year-new-campaign-claims-63401 [Accessed 19 October 2019].

Dagilyte, E. and Greenfields, M. (2015) 'United Kingdom welfare benefit reforms in 2013–2014: Roma between the pillory, the precipice and the slippery slope', *Journal of Social Welfare and Family Law*, 37(4): 476–495.

Daly, A. (2018) 'Embodied austerity: Narratives of early austerity from a homelessness and resettlement service', *Ethics and Social Welfare*, 12(1): 65–77.

Daly, M. (1994) 'Comparing welfare states: Towards a gender friendly approach', in D. Sainsbury (ed), *Gendering Welfare States*, London: SAGE, pp 101–117.

Daly, M. (2000) *The Gender Division of Welfare: The Impact of the British and German Welfare States*, Cambridge: Cambridge University Press.

Daly, M. and Rake, K. (2003) *Gender and the Welfare State*, Cambridge: Polity.

Daunton, M. (ed) (1996) *Charity, Self-interest and Welfare in the English Past*, New York: St Martin's Press.

Daunton, M. (2008) *State and Market in Victorian Britain: War, Welfare, and Capitalism*, Woodbridge: The Boydell Press.

Davies, B. and Challis, D. (1986) *Matching Resources to Needs in Community Care*, Aldershot: Gower.

Deacon, T.W. (1990) 'Rethinking mammalian brain evolution', *American Zoology*, 30(4): 629–705.

Dean, H. (2002) *Welfare Rights and Social Policy*, Harlow: Pearson Education.

Dean, H. (2020) *Understanding Human Need* (2nd edn), Bristol: Policy Press.

Defoe, D. (1704) *Giving Alms No Charity*, London: Booksellers of London and Westminster, available from: https://socialsciences.mcmaster.ca/~econ/ugcm/3ll3/defoe/alms [Accessed 16 February 2021].

Dench, G. (2010) *What Women Want: Evidence from British Social Attitudes* (2nd edn), London: Hera.

Department for Education (2020) *Guidance: Providing Free School Meals During the Coronavirus (COVID-19) Outbreak*, available from: https://www.gov.uk/government/publications/covid-19-free-school-meals-guidance [Accessed 17 March 2021].

Department of Health (1998) *Modernising Social Services: Promoting Independence, Improving Protection, Raising Standards*, Cmd 4169, London: The Stationery Office.

Department of Health (2000) *No Secrets: The Development of Multi-agency Responses to the Abuse of Vulnerable Adults*, London: The Stationery Office.

Department of Health (2012) 'The new public health role of local authorities', *Department of Health*, available from: https://assets.publishing.service.gov.uk/government/uploads/system/uploads/attachment_data/file/213009/Public-health-role-of-local-authorities-factsheet.pdf [Accessed 2 April 2019].

Derrida, J. (1976) *Of Grammatology*, Baltimore: Johns Hopkins University Press.

de Tocqueville, A. (1835/1997) *Memoir on Pauperism*, Chicago: Ivan R. Dee.

Devereux, E. and Power, M.J. (2019) 'Fake news? A critical analysis of the "Welfare Cheats, *Cheat Us All*" campaign in Ireland', *Critical Discourse Studies*, 16(3): 347–362.

DfE/DHSC (Department for Education/Department of Health and Social Care) (2018) *Social Work England: Consultation on Secondary Legislative Framework*, available from: https://consult.education.gov.uk/social-work-england-implementation-team/social-work-england-consultation-on-secondary-legi/ [Accessed 3 July 2018].

DHSS (Department of Health and Social Services) (1976) *Manpower and Training for the Social Services*, London: HMSO.

DHSS (Department of Health and Social Services) (1978) *Social Services Teams: The Practitioner's View*, London: HMSO.

DHSS (Department of Health and Social Services) (1981) *Care in the Community: A Consultative Document on Moving Resources for Care in England*, London: HMSO.

DHSS Social Work Service (1986) *Inspection of the Supervision of Social Workers in the Assessment and Monitoring of Cases of Child Abuse when Children Subject to a Care Order Have Been Returned Home*, London: HMSO.

Dickens, C. (1837–1839/1994) *Oliver Twist*, London: Penguin.

Dickens, J. (2018) 'Clement Atlee and the social service idea: Modern messages for social work in England', *British Journal of Social Work*, 48(1): 5–20.

Digby, A. (1998) 'Poverty, health, and the politics of gender in Britain, 1970–1948', in A. Digby and J. Stewart (eds), *Gender, Health and Welfare*, London: Routledge, pp 67–90.

DiMaggio, P.J. and Powell, W.W. (1983) 'The iron cage revisited: Institutional isomorphism and collective rationality in organizational fields', *American Sociological Review*, 48(2): 147–160.

Dinstein, Y. (2017) *War, Aggression and Self Defence* (6th edn), Cambridge: Cambridge University Press.

Doel, M. (2017) *Social Work in 42 Objects (and More)*, Lichfield: Kirwin Maclean Associates.

Dorling, D. (2016) 'Brexit: The decision of a divided country', *Danny Dorling website*, available from: http://www.dannydorling.org/?p55568 [Accessed 20 September 2017].

Douglas, A. and Philpott, T. (1998) *Caring and Coping: A Guide to Social Services*, London: Routledge.

Douglas, M. (1966) *Purity and Danger: An Analysis of the Concept of Pollution and Taboo*, London: Routledge and Kegan Paul.

Downes, A. and Lansley, S. (2018) 'Introduction', in A. Downes and S. Lansley (eds), *It's Basic Income: The Global Debate*, Bristol: Policy Press, pp 1–11.

Dunkerley, D. and Glasner, P. (1998) 'Empowering the public? Citizen's juries and the new genetic technologies', *Critical Public Health*, 8(3): 181–192.

Durkheim, E. (1912/2001) *The Elementary Forms of Religious Life*, Oxford: Oxford University Press.

Dwyer, P. (2004) *Understanding Social Citizenship: Themes and Perspectives for Policy and Practice* (2nd edn), Bristol: Policy Press.

Dwyer, P. and Wright, S. (2014) 'Universal Credit, ubiquitous conditionality and its implications for social citizenship', *Journal of Poverty & Social Justice*, 22(1): 27–35.

Dwyer, P., Scullion, L., Jones, K., McNeill, J. and Stewart, A.B.R. (2020) 'Work, welfare and wellbeing: The impacts of welfare conditionality on people with mental health impairments on the UK', *Social Policy & Administration*, 54(2): 311–326.

Eckersley, P. and Tobin, P. (2019) 'The impact of austerity on policy capacity in local government', *Policy and Politics*, 47(3): 455–472.

Eden, F.M. (1797) *The State of the Poor: Or, An History of the Labouring Classes in England*, vol III, London: Various.

Electoral Commission (2022) 'Results and turnout at the EU referendum', available from: https://www.electoralcommission.org.uk/who-we-are-and-what-we-do/elections-and-referendums/past-elections-and-referendums/eu-referendum/results-and-turnout-eu-referendum [Accessed 20 February 2022].

Elfleet, H. (2019) 'Gender responsive governance: From Elizabeth Fry to Baroness Jean Corston', *Prison Service Journal*, 246: 41–46.

Ellison, N. (2014) 'The socio-economic context of social policy', in H. Bochel and G. Daly (eds), *Social Policy*, London: Routledge, pp 13–38.

Englander, D. (1998) *Poverty and Poor Law Reform in 19th Century Britain, 1834–1914: From Chadwick to Booth*, London: Longman.

Erikson, P.A. and Murphy, L.D. (2017) *A History of Anthropological Theory* (5th edn), Ontario: University of Toronto Press.

Esmark, A. and Schoop, S.R. (2017) 'Deserving social benefits? Political framing and media framing of "undeservingness" in two welfare reforms in Denmark', *Journal of European Social Policy*, 27(5): 417–432.

Esping-Andersen, G. (1990) *The Three Worlds of Welfare Capitalism*, Cambridge: Polity.

Esping-Andersen, G. (2009) *The Incomplete Revolution: Adapting to Women's New Roles*, Cambridge: Polity.

Esquivel, V. and Kaufmann, A. (2017) *Innovations in Care: New Concepts, New Actions, New Policies*, Berlin: Friedrich-Ebert-Stiftung.

Etzioni, A. (2003) 'Communitarianism', in K. Christensen and D. Levinson (eds), *Encyclopedia of Community: From the Village to the Virtual World*, vol.1, A–D, Thousand Oaks: SAGE, pp 224–228.

Eurydice (2020) 'How is Covid-19 affecting schools in Europe?', available from: https://eacea.ec.europa.eu/national-policies/eurydice/content/how-covid-19-affecting-schools-europe_en [Accessed 17 March 2021].

Faherty, V. (2006) 'Social welfare before the Elizabethan Poor Laws: The early Christian tradition, AD 33 to 313', *Journal of Sociology and Social Welfare*, 33(2): 107–122.

Falls, C.B. (1941) *The Nature of Modern Warfare*, London: Methuen.

Fareshare (2022) 'Marcus Rashford's work with Fareshare', available from: https://fareshare.org.uk/marcus-rashford/ [Accessed 12 February 2022].

Farnsworth, K. (2017) 'Taking back control or empowering big business? New risks to the welfare state in the post-Brexit competition for investment', *Journal of Social Policy*, 46(4): 699–718.

Fasing, A.E., Aisenbrey, S. and Schömann, K. (2013) 'Women's retirement income in Germany and Britain', *European Sociological Review*, 29(5): 968–980.

Faulks, K. (1998) *Citizenship in Modern Britain*, Edinburgh: Edinburgh University Press.

Ferguson, H. (2021) 'The death of Arthur Labinjo-Hughes raises hard questions: We must address them all', *The Guardian*, 3 December, available from: https://www.theguardian.com/commentisfree/2021/dec/03/the-death-of-arthur-labinjo-hughes-raises-difficult-questions-we-must-address-them-all [Accessed 3 December 2021].

Finkel, A. (2019) *Compassion: A Global History of Social Policy*, London: Red Globe Press.

Finlayson, G. (1990) 'A moving frontier: Voluntarism and the state in British social welfare, 1911–49', *Twentieth Century British History*, 1(2): 183–206.

Fisher, M., Newton, C. and Sainsbury, E. (1984) *Mental Health Social Work Observed*, London: George Allen and Unwin.

Fitzpatrick, T. (2001) *Welfare Theory: An Introduction*, Basingstoke: Palgrave.

Fitzroy, A. (1904) *Report for the Inter-Departmental Committee on Physical Deterioration*, Cmnd 2175, London: HMSO.

Fitzroy, F. and Jin, J. (2018) 'Basic income and a public job offer: Complementary policies to reduce poverty and unemployment', *Journal of Poverty and Social Justice*, 26(2): 191–206.

Fletcher, D. and Wright, S. (2018) 'A hand up or a slap down? Criminalising benefit claimants in Britain via strategies of surveillance, sanctions and deterrence', *Critical Social Policy*, 38(2): 324–344.

Folsom, J.K. (1945) 'British family welfare', *Marriage and Family Living*, 7(2): 25–38.

Ford, P. (1934/2018) *Work and Wealth in a Modern Port: An Economic Survey of Southampton*, London: Routledge.

Forman-Cody, L. (2000) 'The politics of illegitimacy in an age of reform: Women, reproduction and political economy in England's New Poor Law of 1834', *Journal of Women's History*, 11(4): 131–156.

Forster, J. (1974) *Class Struggle in the Industrial Revolution: Early Industrial Capitalism Three English Towns*, London: Methuen.

Foss, W. and West, J. (1914) *The Social Worker and Modern Charity*, London: Adam and Charles Black.

Foucault, M. (1972) *The Archaeology of Knowledge*, London: Tavistock.

Foucault, M. (1981) 'The order of discourse', in R. Young (ed), *Untying the Text: A Post-Structural Anthology*, Boston: Routledge & Kegan Paul, pp 48–78.

Foucault, M. (1984) *A History of Sexuality*, vol 1, New York: Pantheon.

Foucault, M. (1991) *Discipline and Punish: The Birth of the Prison*, London: Penguin.

Fourier, C. (1836/2017) *La Fausse Industrie*, Miami: HardPress.

Fox Bourne, H.B. (1876) *The Life of John Locke, Vol.2*, London: Henry S. King.

Frampton, M. (2019) *European and International Social Work*, Weinheim: Beltz Juventa.

Fraser, D. (2009) *The Evolution of the British Welfare State* (4th edn), Basingstoke: Palgrave.

Fraser, D. (2017) *The Evolution of the British Welfare State* (5th edn), London: Palgrave.

Frayer, D.W., Horton, W.A., Macchiarelli, R. and Mussi, M. (1987) 'Dwarfism in an adolescent from the Italian late Upper Palaeolithic', *Nature*, 330: 60–62.

Freud, A. (1937) *The Ego and the Mechanisms of Defence*, London: Hogarth Press and Institute of Psychoanalysis.

Freud, S. (1962) *Totem and Taboo*, New York: W.W. Norton.

Frost, D.G.H. (2022) 'What is seen and what is not seen: The UK, Europe and beyond', *Churchill Lecture, University of Zurich*, available from: https://login01.myfactory.cloud/EIZ/CustomUpload/374O357O340O370O356O369O350O324O372O369O366O367O352O328O365O370O371O360O371O372O371O352O365O355O356O369O340O365O360O/Frost_Zurich_speech_2.pdf?dp=1&DocumentID=717066&DocMail=-1 [Accessed 30 March 2022].

Frost, L. and Hoggett, P. (2008) 'Human agency and social suffering', *Critical Social Policy*, 28(4): 438–460.

Fry, E. (1827) *Observations on the Siting, Superintendence, and Government of Female Prisoners*, London: John and Arthur Arch. Cornhill, Hatchard and Son, and S. Wilkin.

Fukagai, Y. (2005) 'Minimum wage regulation bill and the political arithmetic, 1795–1796', *The History of Economic Thought*, 47(2): 75–91.

Furgal, M.T. (1987) 'Thomas Chalmers' poor relief theories and their implementation in the early nineteenth century', unpublished PhD thesis, University of Edinburgh, available from: https://era.ed.ac.uk/handle/1842/9426 [Accessed 6 June 2021].

Gardiner, A.G. (1923) *Life of George Cadbury*, London: Cassell and Co.

Gardner, A. (2011) *Personalisation in Social Work*, London: SAGE.

Garrett, P.M. (2018) *Welfare Words: Critical Social Work and Social Policy*, London: SAGE.

Garthwaite, K. (2011) 'The language of shirkers and scroungers: Talking about illness, disability and coalition welfare reform', *Disability and Society*, 26(3): 369–372.

Gentleman, A. (2019) *The Windrush Betrayal: Exposing the Hostile Environment*, London: Guardian Faber Publishing.

Gibson, K. (2018) 'Who's in a family? Changing views of illegitimate children raise both moral and economic issues', *History Today*, 68(12), available from: https://www.historytoday.com/archive/history-matters/whos-family [Accessed 23 March 2019].

Giddens, A. (1994) *Beyond Left and Right: The Future of Radical Politics*, Cambridge: Polity.

Giddens, A. (1998) *The Third Way: The Renewal of Social Democracy*, Cambridge: Polity.

Gingrich, J. and King, D. (2019) 'Americanising Brexit Britain's welfare state?', *Political Quarterly*, 90(1): 89–98.

Girard, R. (1972) *La Violence et le Sacré*, Paris: Grasset.

Girard, R. (1986) *The Scapegoat*, Baltimore: The Johns Hopkins University Press.

Glasper, A. (2018) 'Strategies to alleviate shortages of nurses in adult social care', *British Journal of Nursing*, 27(6): 334–335.

Gleadle, K. (2001) *British Women in the Nineteenth Century*, Basingstoke: Macmillan.

Glucksmann, M. (2000) *Cottons and Casuals: The Gendered Organisation of Labour in Time and Space*, London: Routledge.

Godwin, W. (1793/1985) *An Enquiry Concerning Political Justice, and its Influence on General Virtue and Happiness*, London: Penguin.

Goffman, E. (1963) *Stigma: Notes on the Management of Spoiled Identity*, Englewood Cliffs: Prentice Hall.

Goldberg, E.M. (1957–1958) 'The psychiatric social worker in the community', *British Journal of Social Work*, 4(2): 4.

Goldberg, E.M. and Warburton, R.W. (1979) *Ends and Means in Social Work: The Development and Outcome of a Case Review System for Social Workers*, London: George Allen and Unwin.

Goldstein, H. (1973) *Social Work Practice: A Unitary Approach*, Columbia: University of South Carolina Press.

Gomez-Jimenez, M.-L. and Parker, J. (eds) (2014) *Active Ageing? Perspectives from Europe on a Vaunted Topic*, London: Whiting and Birch.

Goodwin, M.J. and Heath, O. (2016) 'The 2016 referendum, Brexit and the left behind: An aggregate level analysis of the result', *The Political Quarterly*, 87(3): 323–332.

Gorsky, M. (1999) *Patterns of Philanthropy: Charity and Society in Nineteenth Century Bristol*, Woodbridge: Boydell Press.

Gov.UK (nd) 'Universal Credit', available from: https://www.gov.uk/universal-credit [Accessed 20 November 2020].

Gov.UK (2014) 'David Cameron on families', available from: https://www.gov.uk/government/speeches/david-cameron-on-families [Accessed 21 January 2021].

Gray, P. (2014) *An Independent Review of the Personal Independence Payment Assessment*, London: HMSO, available from: https://www.gov.uk/government/publications/personal-independencepayment-pip-assessments-first-independent-review [Accessed 11 May 2020].

Gray, P. (2017) *The Second Independent Review of the Personal Independence Payment Assessment*, London: HMSO, available from: https://www.gov.uk/government/uploads/system/uploads/attachment_data/file/604097/pip-assessment-second-independent-review.pdf [Accessed 11 May 2020].

Green, G. (1893) *The History of the Poor Law*, London: Greenwich and Deptford Labour Guardians Committee.

Green, G., Emslie, C., O'Neill, D., Hunt, K. and Walker, S. (2010) 'Exploring the ambiguities of masculinity in accounts of emotional distress in the military among young ex-servicemen', *Social Science & Medicine*, 71(8): 1480–1488.

Greenberg, N., Jones, E., Fear, T.F. and Wessely, S. (2011) 'The injured mind in the UK Armed Forces', *Philosophical Transactions of the Royal Society B*, 366(1562): 261–267.

Gregory, L. (2017) 'Workers on tap but income drying up? The potential implications for incomes and social protection of the "gig economy"', in J. Hudson, C. Needham and E. Heins (eds), *Social Policy Review 29: Analysis in Debates and Policy*, Bristol: Policy Press, pp 23–41.

Gregory, L. (2018) *Exploring Welfare Debates: Key Concepts and Questions*, Bristol: Policy Press.

Greve, B. (2008) 'What is welfare?', *Central European Journal of Public Policy*, 2(1): 50–73.

Greve, B. (2015) *Welfare and the Welfare State: Present and Future*, London: Routledge.

Greve, B. (2019) 'What is welfare and public welfare?', in B. Greve (ed), *Routledge Handbook of the Welfare State* (2nd edn), London: Routledge, pp 5–12.

Grier, J (2001) 'A spirit of friendly rivalry? Voluntary societies and the formation of post-war child welfare legislation in Britain', in J. Lawrence and P. Starkey (eds), *Welfare and Social Action in the Nineteenth and Twentieth Centuries*, Liverpool: Liverpool University Press.

Griffin, E. (2013) 'Sex, illegitimacy and social change in industrializing Britain', *Social History*, 38(1): 139–161.

Griffin, E. (2018) *A Short History of the British Industrial Revolution* (2nd edn), London: Palgrave.

Griffin, E. (2020) *Bread Winner: An Intimate History of the Victorian Economy*, New Haven and London: Yale University Press.

Griffiths, R. (1988) *Community Care: Agenda for Action*, London: HMSO.

Griffiths, R. (2021) 'Complexities for claimants: The reality of the £20 weekly uplift to Universal Credit', *Institute for Policy Research*, available from: https://www.bath.ac.uk/publications/complexities-for-claimants-the-reality-of-the-20-weekly-uplift-to-universal-credit/attachments/Complexities-for-claimants-october-2021.pdf [Accessed 4 February 2022].

GSCC (2002) *Accreditation of Universities to Grant Degrees in Social Work*, London: General Social Care Council.

Haagh, L. (2019) *The Case for Universal Basic Income*, Cambridge: Polity.

Hagist, D.N. (2012) *British Soldiers, American War: Voices of the American Revolution*, Yardley: Westholme Publishing.

Hall, C.A. (2017) 'A family for nation and empire', in G. Lewis (ed), *Forming Nation, Framing Welfare*, London: Routledge, pp 9–54.

Hall, R.G. (2009) 'Hearts and minds: The politics of everyday life and Chartism, 1832–1840', *Labour History Review*, 74(1): 27–43.

Halliday, E. (2017) 'Useful work for idle hands or a brightening and elevating influence? The introduction of the Brabazon Employment Scheme to Glasgow's public institutions in the late 19th century', *Family and Community History*, 20(2): 145–156.

Ham, C. (2018) 'Preventing a recurrence of this winter's crisis', *The King's Fund*, 22 January, available from: https://www.kingsfund.org.uk/blog/2018/01/preventing-recurrence-winter-crisis#funding-and-staffing [Accessed 28 September 2018].

Hansard (1946) *Child Care*, Vol 430, debated 19 November 1946, available from: https://hansard.parliament.uk/Commons/1946-11-19/debates/7e0b9a90-3202-48c8-8aaf-99f9a920c1b3/ChildCare [Accessed 3 March 2020].

Hansard (1976) *House of Lords Debate (Lord Wallace of Coslany)*, 24 November 1976, 378 cc7–22, available from: https://hansard.parliament.uk/Lords/1976-11-24/debates/a5409e18-9c37-4eae-bb0c-80e8a37039b5/LordsChamber [Accessed 3 March 2020].

Hantrais, L. (2019) *What Brexit Means for EU and UK Social Policy*, Bristol: Policy Press.

Hantrais, L. (2020) *Afterword: What Brexit Means for EU and UK Social Policy*, Bristol: Policy Press.

Hantrais, L. and Letablier, M.-T. (2021) *Comparing and Contrasting the Impact of the COVID-19 Pandemic in the European Union*, London: Routledge.

Harding, S. and Libal, K. (2012) 'Iraqi refugees and the humanitarian costs of the Iraq War: What role for social work?' *International Journal of Social Welfare*, 21(1): 94–104.

Hardman, P. (2007) 'The origins of late eighteenth-century prison reform in England', unpublished PhD thesis, University of Sheffield, available from: https://etheses.whiterose.ac.uk/3037/ [Accessed 19 May 2019].

Hardy, T. (1874/2012) *Far From the Madding Crowd*, London: Penguin.

Harkness, S. (2016) 'The effect of employment on the mental health of lone mothers in the UK before and after New Labour's welfare reforms', *Social Indicators Research*, 128(2): 763–791.

Harmitz, W. (2013) 'The impact of welfare reform on Newham, east London', *Journal of Poverty and Social Justice*, 21(3): 265–268.

Harris, B. (2004) *The Origins of the Welfare State: Social Welfare in England and Wales, 1800–1945*, Basingstoke: Palgrave Macmillan.

Harris, J. (2021) 'How will post-Covid Britain look? For many, like it did in the brutal 19th century', *The Guardian*, 28 November, available from: https://www.theguardian.com/commentisfree/2021/nov/28/covid-britain-boris-johnson-poverty-hunger [Accessed 6 January 2022].

Harris, N. (2014) 'Welfare reform and the shifting threshold of support for disabled people', *Modern Law Review*, 77(6): 888–927.

Hart, A.M. (2015) *Where the UK Went Wrong 1945–2015: A Personal Journey*, London: Xlibris UK.

Hasian, M. (2008) 'Critical memories of crafted virtues: The Cadbury chocolate scandals, mediated reputations, and modern globalized slavery', *Journal of Communication Inquiry*, 32(3): 249–270.

Hayashi, N. (2010) 'Defoe and the principle of trade', *The Kyoto Economic Review*, 79(1): 66–76.

Heard, D. and Lake, B. (1997) *The Challenge of Attachment for Caregiving*, London: Routledge.

Heasman, K. (1965) *Christians and Social Work*, London: SPCK.

Herdin, T. (2012) 'Deconstructing typologies: Overcoming the limitations of the binary opposition paradigm', *International Communication Gazette*, 74(1): 603–618.

Higgs, C. (2012) *Chocolate Islands: Cocoa, Slavery and Colonial Africa*, Athens, OH: Ohio University Press.

Hill, M. and Irving, Z. (2020) *Exploring the World of Social Policy: An International Approach*, Bristol: Policy Press.

Hindle, S. (2004) *On the Parish?: The Micro-Politics of Poor Relief in Rural England 1550–1750*, Oxford: Oxford University Press.

Hinrichs, K. (2021) 'Recent pension reforms in Europe: More challenges, new directions. An overview', *Social Policy and Administration*, 55(3): 409–422.

Hirst, P. (1993) *Associative Democracy: New Forms of Economic and Social Governance*, Cambridge: Polity.

HMRC (2021) 'Claims for wages through the Coronavirus Job Retention Scheme', available from: https://www.gov.uk/guidance/claim-for-wages-through-the-coronavirus-job-retention-scheme [Accessed 23 April 2021].

Hobsbawm, E.J. (1973) *The Age of Revolution*, London: Cardinal.

Hobsbawm, E. and Rudé, G. (2001) *Captain Swing*, London: Phoenix.

Hochschild, A.R. (2016) *Strangers in Their Own Land: Anger and Mourning on the American Right*, New York: The New Press.

Hollis, P. (1989) *Ladies Elect: Women in English Local Government, 1865–1914*, Oxford: Oxford University Press.

Holman, R. (1996) 'Fifty years ago: The Curtis and Clyde reports', *Children and Society*, 10(3): 197–209.

Home Office (1945) *Report by Sir William Monckton KCMG KCVO MC KC on the Circumstances which Led to the Boarding Out of Dennis and Terence O'Neill at Bank Farm, Minsterly and the Steps Taken to Supervise Their Welfare*, Cmd 6636, London: Home Office.

Home Office (1961) *Report of the Interdepartmental Committee on the Business of the Criminal Courts*, London: HMSO.

Home Office (Ingleby Committee) (1960) *Report of the Committee on Children and Young Persons*, London: HMSO.

Home Office and Scottish Home Department (1954) *Report of the Departmental Committee on the Adoption of Children*, London: HMSO.

House of Commons (1834) *Report from His Majesty's Commissioners for Inquiring into the Administration and Practical Operation of the Poor Laws*, London: UK Parliamentary Papers, available from: https://parlipapers.proquest.com/parlipapers/result/pqpdocumentview?accountid=9679&groupid=107802&pgId=790075cd-c066-419c-afa8-73491157fabc&rsId=17D1DF8AA43#0 [Accessed 12 June 2021].

House of Commons Health Committee (2017) *Brexit and Health and Social Care: People and Process*, eighth report of session 2016–17, HC 640, London: House of Commons.

House of Commons Library (2022) *Support for UK Veterans*, Research Briefing, 13 June, available from: https://researchbriefings.files.parliament.uk/documents/CBP-7693/CBP-7693.pdf [Accessed 18 August 2022].

House of Lords (2016) *Library Note – NHS and Social Care Workforce: Implications of Leaving the European Union*, House of Lords, LLN 2016/039.

Howard, J. (1777) *The State of the Prisons in England and Wales*, Warrington: William Eyres.

Howells, G. (2003) '"On account of their disreputable characters": Parish-assisted emigration from rural England, 1834–1860', *History*, 88(292): 587–605.

Hubble, N., Taylor, J and Tew, P. (eds) (2019) *Growing Old with the Welfare State*, London: Bloomsbury.

Huck, C. (2014) 'Barriers and facilitators in the pathway to care in military veterans', unpublished DClinPsych thesis, University College London, available from: https://discovery.ucl.ac.uk/id/eprint/1449254/ [Accessed 4 March 2020].

Hudson, J., Lunt, N., Hamilton, C., Mackinder, S., Meers, J. and Swift, C. (2017) 'Nostalgia narratives? Pejorative attitudes to welfare in historical perspective: survey evidence from Beveridge to the British Social Attitudes Survey', *Journal of Poverty and Social Justice*, 24(3): 227–243.

Humphrey, J.C. (2003) 'New Labour and the regulatory reform of social care', *Critical Social Policy*, 23(1): 5–24.

IFSW (International Federation of Social Workers) (2014) *Global Definition of Social Work*, available from: http://ifsw.org/get-involved/global-definit ion-of-social-work/ [Accessed 6 June 2016].

Independent (2022) 'Tens of thousands register interest as Homes for Ukraine scheme launches', *The Independent*, 18 March, available from: https://www. independent.co.uk/news/uk/government-ukraine-homes-priti-patel-prime-minister-b2038603.html [Accessed 25 March 2022].

Jacobs, K. and Manzi, T. (2013) 'New localism, old retrenchment: The "Big Society", housing policy and the politics of reform', *Housing, Theory and Society*, 30(1): 29–45.

James, J. (2018) 'Sophia Heathfield of Hawnes, Bedfordshire: Punishment victim or victor? A study of power and control in the workhouse under the New Poor Law (1853–1856)', *Family and Community History*, 21(3): 202–229.

Jawad, R. (2012) 'Thinking about religious welfare and rethinking social policy in the British context', *Social Policy and Society*, 11(4): 613–624.

Jeanpierre, L. (2010) 'Les structures d'une pensée d'exil: La formation du structuralisme de Claude Lévi-Strauss', *French Politics, Culture and Society*, 28(1): 58–76.

Jeffries, T. (2021) 'Is the state pension triple lock doomed? Failure of Lords' last-ditch battle sparks warnings of future "tweaks" and more broken promises', *This is Money*, 14 November, available from: https://www.this ismoney.co.uk/money/pensions/article-10208055/Is-state-pension-tri ple-lock-doomed-ditch-battle-lost.html [Accessed 16 November 2021].

Jenkins, D. (1992) *Intimate Enemies: Moral Panics in Contemporary Great Britain*, Piscataway: Aldine Transaction.

Jensen, T. and Tyler, I. (2015) '"Benefits broods": The cultural and political crafting of anti-welfare commonsense', *Critical Social Policy*, 35(4): 470–491.

Jeremy, D.J. (1991) 'The enlightened paternalist in action: William Lever at Port Sunlight before 1914', *Business History*, 33(1): 58–81.

Jones, C. and Novak, T. (1999) *Poverty, Welfare and the Disciplinary State*, Abingdon: Routledge.

Jones, O. (2012) *Chavs: The Demonization of the Working Class*, London: Verso.

Jones, P. and King, S. (2020) *Pauper Voices, Public Opinion and Workhouse Reform in Mid-Victorian England: Bearing Witness*, Basingstoke: Palgrave.

Jones, R. (2014) 'The best of times, the worst of times: Social work and its moment', *British Journal of Social Work*, 44(3): 485–502.

Jones, R. (2020) '1970–2020: A fifty year history of the personal social services and social work in England and across the UK', *Social Work and Social Sciences Review*, 21(3): 8–44.

Jordan, B. (2008) *Welfare and Well-being: Social Value in Public Policy*, Bristol: Policy Press.

Jordan, B. (2012) 'The low road to basic income? Tax-benefit integration in the UK', *Journal of Social Policy*, 41(1): 1–17.

Jordan, B. and Drakeford, M. (2012) *Social Work and Social Policy under Austerity*, Basingstoke: Palgrave Macmillan.

Jordan, W.K. (1959) *Philanthropy in England, 1480–1660*, London: George Allen and Unwin.

Jordan, W.K. (1960) *The Charities of London 1480–1660*, London: Allen and Unwin.

Joy, M. and Shields, J. (2018) 'Austerity in the making: Reconfiguring social policy through social impact bonds', *Policy and Politics*, 46(4): 681–695.

Katz, M. (2013) 'The biological inferiority of the undeserving poor', *Social Work and Society, International Online Journal*, 11(1): 1–17.

Kelly, M. and Ó Gráda, C. (2011) 'The Poor Law of Old England: Institutional innovation and demographic regimes', *Journal of Interdisciplinary History*, 41(3): 339–360.

Kiely, R., McCrone, D., Bechhofer, F. and Stewart, R. (2000) 'Debatable land: National and local identity in a border town', *Sociological Research Online*, 5(2): 66–79.

Kim, J.W. and Choi, Y.J. (2013) 'Feminisation of poverty in 12 welfare states: Consolidating cross regime variations', *European Journal of Social Welfare*, 22(4): 347–359.

King, S. (2000) *Poverty and Welfare in England, 1700–1850: A Regional Perspective*, Manchester: Manchester University Press.

King, S. (2004) ' "We might be trusted": Female Poor Law Guardians and the development of the New Poor Law: The case of Bolton, England, 1880–1906', *International Review of Social History*, 49(1): 31–32.

King, S. (2010) *Women, Welfare and Local Politics, 1880–1920*, Eastbourne: Sussex Academic Press.

King, S. (2019) *Writing the Lives of the English Poor 1750s–1830s*, Montreal and Kingston: McGill-Queens University Press.

Kingori, P. and Gerrets, R. (2019) 'Why the pseudo matters to global health', *Critical Global Health*, 29(4): 379–389.

Kirk-Wade, E. (2022) 'Reducing the Universal Credit taper rate and the effect in incomes', *House of Commons Library*, available from: https://com monslibrary.parliament.uk/reducing-the-universal-credit-taper-rate-and-the-effect-on-incomes/ [Accessed 21 February 2022].

Klausen, J. (1998) *War and Welfare: Europe and the United States, 1945 to the Present*, New York: St Martin's Press.

Kootstra, A. (2016) 'Deserving and undeserving welfare claimants in Britain and the Netherlands: Examining the role of ethnicity and migration status using a vignette experiment', *European Sociological Review*, 32(3): 325–328.

Korpi, W. (2010) 'Class and gender inequalities in different types of welfare states: The Social Citizenship Indicator Program', *International Journal of Social Welfare*, 19(s1): S14–S24.

Kropotkin, P. (1902/2021) *Mutual Aid: A Factor in Evolution*, Montreal: Black Rose Books.

Labour (2019) 'Universal basic services: The right to a good life', available from: https://labour.org.uk/wp-content/uploads/2019/09/12730_19-Universal-Basic-Services_v5.pdf [Accessed 22 August 2022].

Lambie-Mumford, H. and Green, M.A. (2017) 'Austerity, welfare reform and the rising use of food banks by children in England and Wales', *Area*, 49(3): 273–279.

Laming, H. (2003) *The Victoria Climbié Inquiry Report*, Cm 5730, London: The Stationery Office.

Lansley, S. (2022) *The Richer The Poorer: How Britain Enriched the Few and Failed the Poor. 200 Year History*, Bristol: Policy Press.

Laplanche, J. and Pontalis, J.B. (1973) *The Language of Psycho-Analysis*, New York: W.W. Norton.

Larkin, P.M. (2018) 'Universal Credit, "positive citizenship", and the working poor: Squaring the eternal circle', *Modern Law Review*, 81(1): 114–131.

Lawson, N. (1992) *The View from Number 11: Memoirs of a Tory Radical*, London: Bantam Press.

Layder, D. (2003) *Understanding Social Theory* (2nd edn), London: SAGE.

Leichsenring, K. (2021) 'Applying ideal types in long-term care analysis', in C. Aspalter (ed), *Ideal Types in Comparative Social Policy*, London: Routledge, pp 187–206.

Lemert, E. (1967) *Human Deviance: Social Problems and Social Control*, Englewood Cliffs: Prentice-Hall.

Levin, K.B., Cashore, S.B. and Auld, G. (2012) 'Overcoming the tragedy of super wicked problems: Constraining our future selves to ameliorate global climate change', *Policy Studies*, 45(2): 121–152.

Lévi-Strauss, C. (1958) *Anthropologie Structurale*, Paris: Plon.

Lévi-Strauss, C. (1971) *The Elementary Structures of Kinship*, Boston: Beacon Press.

Lévi-Strauss, C. (1973) 'Structuralism and ecology', *Interdisciplinary Research*, 12(1): 7–23.Lewis, E.O. (1929) 'The ascertainment and notification of mental defectives conference on mental welfare', *Mental Welfare*, 10(4): 4.

Lewis, J. (1983) 'Dealing with dependency: State practices and social realities, 1870–1945', in J. Lewis (ed), *Women's Welfare/Women's Rights*, London: Croom Helm, pp 17–37.

Lewis, J. (1993) *Women and Social Action in Victorian and Edwardian England*, London: Edward Elgar.

Lewis, J. (1994) 'Gender, the family and women's agency in the building of "welfare states": The British case', *Social History*, 19(1): 37–55.

Lister, R. (2004) 'The Third Way's social investment state', in J. Lewis and R. Surender (eds), *Welfare State Change: Towards a Third Way?* Oxford: Oxford University Press, pp 157–181.

Lizardo, O. (2010) 'Beyond the antimonies of structure: Lévi-Strauss, Giddens, Bourdieu and Sewell', *Theory and Society*, 39(2): 651–688.

Lomax, L. (2017) 'The health benefits of chocolate and recipes for National Chocolate week', *English Institute of Sport*, available from: https://www.eis2 win.co.uk/article/the-health-benefits-of-chocolate-and-recipes-for-natio nal-chocolate-week-part-2/ [Accessed 2 April 2021].

London, J. (1903) *The People of the Abyss*, London: Macmillan.

Lorenz, W. (2007) 'Practising history: Memory and professional contemporary practice', *International Social Work*, 50(5): 597–612.

Lorenz, W. (2008) 'Paradigms and politics: Understanding methods paradigms in an historical context: The case of social pedagogy', *British Journal of Social Work*, 38(4): 625–644.

Lowe, R. (1976) 'The erosion of state intervention 1917–24', *Economic History Review*, 31(2): 270–286.

LSCB Haringey (2009) 'Serious case review: Baby Peter', available from: http://www.haringeylscb.org/sites/haringeylscb/files/execut ive_summary_peter_final.pdf [Accessed 15 June 2018].

Lugo-Ocando, J. and Harkins, S. (2015) 'How Malthusian ideology crept into the newsroom: British tabloids and the coverage of the "underclass"', *Critical Discourse Studies*, 13(1): 78–93.

Lyne, M. and Parker, J. (2020) 'From Ovid to Covid: The metamorphosis of advanced decisions to refuse treatment into a safeguarding issue', *Journal of Adult Protection*, 22(6): 361–369.

Machin, R. (2017) 'Made to measure? An analysis of the transition from Disability Living Allowance to Personal Independence Payment', *Journal of Social Welfare and Family Law*, 39(4): 435–453.

Machin, R. (2020) 'Regressive and precarious: Analysing the UK social security system in the light of the findings on the UN Special rapporteur on poverty and human rights', *Social Work and Social Sciences Review*, 21(3): 70–85.

Mack, J. and Lansley, S. (1985) *Poor Britain*, London: Routledge.

Mackworth, H. (1704) *A Bill for the Better Relief, Employment and Settlement of the Poor*, London: House of Commons.

MacLean, P.D. (1990) *The Triune Brain in Evolution*, New York: Plenum Press.

Macleod, I. and Powell, E. (1952) *Social Services: Needs and Means*, London: Conservative Political Centre.

Macnicol, J. (1978) 'Family allowances and less eligibility', in P. Thane (ed), *The Origins of British Social Policy*, London: Croom Helm, pp 173–202.

Macqueen, A. (2005) *The King of Sunlight: How William Lever Cleaned the World*, London: Corgi.

Make Mine Chocolate (nd) 'Make mine chocolate', available from: https://twitter.com/mmc_rabbit [Accessed 10 January 2021].

Malinowski, B. (1984) *Argonauts of the Western Pacific*, Long Grove: Waveland Press.

Malpass, P. (2012) 'Book review: *Poverty: A Study of Town Life*', *Housing Studies*, 27(3): 398–404.

Malthus, T. (1798/2015) *An Essay on the Principle of Population and Other Writings*, London: Penguin Books.

Mangan, M. and Sinclair, I. (2019) *Charles Booth's London Poverty Maps*, London: Thames and Hudson.

Manthorpe, J., Harris, J., Stevens, M. and Moriarty, J. (2018) '"We're effectively becoming immigration officers": Social care managers' experiences of the risk work of employing migrant care workers', *Health, Risk and Society*, 20(3/4): 113–125.

Manzi, T. (2015) 'The Big Society and the conjunction of crises: Justifying welfare reform and undermining social housing', *Housing, Theory and Society*, 32(1): 9–24.

Manzi, T. and Richardson, J. (2017) 'Rethinking professional practice: The logic of competition and the crisis of identity in housing practice', *Housing Studies*, 32(2): 209–224.

Marcus (pseud.) (1838/2019) *On the Possibility of Limiting Populousness*, Miami: HardPress.

Marks, L. (1993) 'Medical care for pauper mothers and their infants: Poor law provision and local demand in east London, 1870–1929', *Economic History Review*, 46(3): 518–542.

Marmot, M. (2010) *Fair Society, Healthy Lives: The Marmot Review: Strategic Review of Health Inequalities in England post-2010*, London: The Marmot Review.

Marmot, M., Allen, J., Boyce, T., Goldbalt, P. and Morrison, J. (2020) *Health Equity: The Marmot Review Ten Year On*, London: Institute for Health Equity, available from: https://www.health.org.uk/publications/reports/the-marmot-review-10-years-on [Accessed 2 June 2022].

Marsh, D. (2015) 'Welcome to the election. But only if you're a hard working family', *The Guardian*, 20 March, available from: https://www.theguard ian.com/media/mind-your-language/2015/mar/20/welcome-to-the-elect ion-but-only-if-youre-a-hardworking-family [Accessed 15 February 2021].

Marshall, T.H. (1949/1992) 'Citizenship and social class', in T.H. Marshall and T. Bottomore (eds), *Citizenship and Social Class*, London: Pluto Press, pp 3–51.

Martin, C. (2011) 'Adam Smith and Liberal economics: Reading the minimum wage debate of 1795–1796', *Economic Journal Watch*, 8(2): 11–125.

Martin, S., Longo, F., Lomas, J. and Claxton, K. (2021) 'Causal impact of social care, public health and healthcare expenditure on mortality in England: Cross-sectional evidence for 2013/2014', *BMJ Open*, 11(10): e046417, doi: 10:1136/bmjopen-2020-0464417

Martineau, H. (1839/2021) *Deerbrook*, Maroussi: Alpha Editions.

Martinelli, F., Anttonen, A. and Mätze, M. (eds) (2017) *Social Services Disrupted: Changes, Challenges and Policy Implications for Europe in Times of Austerity*, Cheltenham: Edward Elgar.

Marwick, A. (ed) (1988) *Total War and Social Change*, Basingstoke: Palgrave.

Mason, T. (2014) NAO opens new investigation into Big Society Network Funding, available from: http://www.civilsociety.co.uk/finance/news/content/18358/nao_opens_new_investigation__into_big_society_netw ork_funding [Accessed 21 February 2015].

Mauss, M. (1967) *The Gift: The Form and the Reason for Exchange in Archaic Societies*, London: Taylor & Francis.

May, T. (2006) *Victorian and Edwardian Prisons*, Oxford: Shire Library.

Mayhew, H. (2005) *The London Underworld in the Victorian Period*, Mineola: Dover.

McAdam, E. (1925) *The Equipment of the Social Worker*, London: George Allen and Unwin.

McAllister, L., Callaghan, J. and Fellin, L.C. (2019) 'Masculinities and emotional expression in UK servicemen: "Big boys don't cry"?', *Journal of Gender Studies*, 28(3): 257–270.

McCaffery, J.F. (1981) 'Thomas Chalmers and social change', *The Scottish Historical Review*, 60(19): 32–60.

McCann, P. (ed) (1977) *Popular Education and Socialisation in the Nineteenth Century*, London: Methuen.

McConnell, A. (2010) 'Policy success, policy failure and grey areas in between', *Journal of Public Policy*, 30(3): 345–362.

McDonagh, B. and Bustillos Morales, J. (2020) *Universal Basic Income*, London: Routledge.

McDonald, K. (2013) *Our Violent World: Terrorism in Society*, London: Palgrave.

McGoey, L. (2016) *No Such Thing as a Free Gift: The Gates Foundation and the Price of Philanthropy*, London: Verso.

McGowen, R. (1995) 'The well-ordered prison: England, 1780–1865', in N. Morris and D.J. Rothman (eds), *The Oxford History of the Prison: The Practice of Punishment in Western Society*, Oxford: Oxford University Press, pp 79–109.

McGregor, C. (2015) 'History as a resource for the future: A response to "Best of times, worst of times: Social work and its moment"', *British Journal of Social Work*, 45(5): 1630–1644.

McIntosh, M.K. (2014) 'Poor relief in Elizabethan English communities: An analysis of collectors' accounts', *Economic History Review*, 67(2): 331–357.

McKenzie, L. (2017) 'The class politics of prejudice: Brexit and the land of no-hope and glory', *The British Journal of Sociology*, 68(S1): S266–S280.

Mead, L. (1997) *From Welfare to Work: Lessons from America*, London: IEA Health & Welfare Unit.

Mendoza, K.-A. (2015) *Austerity: The Demolition of the Welfare State and the Rise of the Zombie Economy*, Oxford: New Internationalist Publications.

Metropolitan and Central Committee (1820) *Report of the Metropolitan and Central Committee, Appointed for the Relief of the Manchester Sufferers*, Ludgate-Hill: William Hone.

Merton, R.K. (1936) 'The unanticipated consequences of purposive social action', *American Sociological Review*, 1(6): 894–904.

Mill, J.S. (1848/2004) *Principles of Political Economy*, London: Prometheus.

Ministry of Defence (2019) 'War pension scheme annual statistics 1 April 2009 to 31 March 2019', available from: https://assets.publishing.service. gov.uk/government/uploads/system/uploads/attachment_data/file/811 382/20190627_-_WPS_National_Statistics_Bulletin_-_O.pdf [Accessed 30 March 2021].

Ministry of Health (1951) *Report of the Committee on Social Workers in the Mental Health Services*, London: HMSO.

Ministry of Health (1957) *Survey of Services to the Chronic Sick and Elderly 1954–1955*, London: HMSO.

Ministry of Health and Department of Health for Scotland (1959) *Report of the Working Party on Social Workers in the Local Authority Health and Welfare Services*, London: HMSO.

Ministry of Housing, Communities and Local Government (2019) 'Statutory homelessness January to March (Q1) 2019: England', available from: https://assets.publishing.service.gov.uk/government/uploads/sys tem/uploads/attachment_data/file/831246/Statutory_Homelessness_ Statistical_Release_Jan_to_March_2019.pdf [Accessed 1 November 2019].

Minority Report of the Poor Law Commission (1909) *Royal Commission on the Poor Laws and Relief of Distress*, Wellcome Collection, available from: https://wellcomecollection.org/works/qyhjfw7n [Accessed 15 August 2021].

Mitton, L. (2012) 'The history and development of social policy', in J. Baldock, L. Mitton, N. Manning and S. Vickerstaff (eds), *Social Policy* (4th edn), Oxford: Oxford University Press, pp 27–51.

Monroe, J. (2022) 'The UK government is balancing its books on the backs of the poor', *The Guardian*, 13 March, available from: https://www.theg uardian.com/commentisfree/2022/mar/13/the-uk-government-is-balanc ing-its-books-on-the-backs-of-the-poor [Accessed 13 March 2022].

Montero, A. (2017) 'Brexit threatens social care jobs and funding', *The Guardian*, 21 February, available from: https://www.theguardian.com/soc ial-care-network/2017/feb/21/social-care-immigration-brexit-jobs-fund ing [Accesssed 12 March 2018].

Moore, D., Pienaar, K., Dilkes-Frayne, E. and Frazer, S. (2017) 'Challenging the addiction/health binary with assemblage thinking: An analysis of consumer accounts', *International Journal of Drug Policy*, 44(1): 155–163.

More, T. (1516/1910) *Utopia*, London: J.M. Dent and sons.

Morgan, D. (1996) *Family Connections*, Cambridge: Polity.

Morgan, D. (1999) 'Risk and family practices: Accounting for change and fluidity in family life', in E.B. Silva and C. Smart (eds), *The New Family*, London: SAGE, pp 179–209.

Morris, L.D. (2019) '"Moralising" welfare and migration in austerity Britain: A backdrop to Brexit', *European Societies*, 21(1): 76–100.

Morris, M. (2019) 'Silver linings amid the clouds', *British Journal of Nursing*, 28(3): 142.

Morris, W. (1890) *News from Nowhere*, London: Commonweal.

Mulholland, H. (2010) 'David Cameron, Ed Milliband and Vince Cable at the CBI', *The Guardian*, 25 October, available from: https://www. theguardian.com/politics/blog/2010/oct/25/cbi-economy, [Accessed 21 October 2015].

Mulholland, H. (2017) 'Brexit fears trigger exodus of crucial EU health and social care workforce', *The Guardian*, 5 July, available from: https://www. theguardian.com/society/2017/jul/05/brexit-fears-exodus-eu-health-soc ial-care-workforce [Accessed 12 March 2018].

Munro, E. (2011) *The Munro Review of Child Protection: Final Report: A Child-Centred System*, Cm 8062, London: TSO.

Murray, C. (1990) *The Emerging British Underclass*, London: Institute of Economic Affairs Health & Welfare Unit.

Murray, C. (2006) *In Our Hands: A Plan to Replace the Welfare State*, Washington: AEI Books.

Murray, C. (2013) *Coming Apart: The State of White America*, London: Random House.

National Institute for Social Work (NISW) (1982) *Social Workers: Their Role and Tasks*, London: Bedford Square Press.

National Statistics (2022) 'Households below average national income: An analysis of the income distribution FYE 1995 to FYE 2021', available from: https://www.gov.uk/government/statistics/households-below-aver age-income-for-financial-years-ending-1995-to-2021/households-below-average-income-an-analysis-of-the-income-distribution-fye-1995-to-fye-2021 [Accessed 31 March 2022].

Nicholls, G. (2016) *A History of the English Poor Law, Vol III*, London: Routledge.

No Homeless Veterans (nd) 'Need to know', available from: https://www.stoll.org.uk/no-homeless-veterans/need-to-know/ [Accessed 16 May 2021].

Norman, J. (2010) *The Big Society: The Anatomy of the New Politics*, Buckingham: University of Buckingham Press.

Northcutt, R.G. (2002) 'Understanding vertebrate brain evolution', *Integrative and Comparative Biology*, 42(4): 743–756.

Nussbaum, M. (2011) *Creating Capabilities: The Human Development Approach*, Cambridge, MA: Harvard University Press.

Oakley, A. (2019) *Women, Peace and Welfare: A Suppressed History of Social Reform, 1880–1920*, Bristol: Policy Press.

Oakley, A. (2001) 'The family, poverty and population: Commentary', in P. Alcock, H. Glennerster, A. Oakley and A. Sinfield (eds), *Welfare and Wellbeing: Richard Titmuss's Contribution to Social Policy*, Bristol: Policy Press, pp 11–16.

Obinger, H. and Petersen, K. (2017) 'Mass warfare and welfare state: Causal mechanisms and effects', *British Journal of Political Science*, 47(2): 203–227.

Obinger, H., Petersen, K. and Starke, P. (eds) (2018) *Warfare and Welfare: Military Conflict and Welfare State Development in Western Countries*, New York: Oxford University Press.

Odijie, M. (2020) 'Cocoa and child slavery in West Africa', *African History*, 38(4): 519–540.

Off, C. (2014) *Bitter Chocolate: Anatomy of an Industry*, New York and London: The New Press.

Offer, J. and Pinker, R. (2017) *Social Welfare and Welfare Pluralism: Selected Writings of Robert Pinker*, Bristol: Policy Press.

Office for Budget Responsibility (OBR) (2022) 'Welfare spending', *Office for Budget Responsibility*, available from: https://obr.uk/fiscal_categories/welfare-spending/ [Accessed 2 September 2022].

Office for National Statistics (ONS) (2017) 'How is the welfare budget spent?', available from: https://www.ons.gov.uk/economy/governmentp ublicsectorandtaxes/publicsectorfinance/articles/howisthewelfarebudgetsp ent/2016-03-16 [Accessed 12 December 2021].

ONS (2019) 'What is the difference between sex and gender?', available from: https://www.ons.gov.uk/economy/environmentalaccounts/artic les/whatisthedifferencebetweensexandgender/2019-02-21 [Accessed 31 January 2022].

ONS (2020a) 'Families and households in the UK: 2020', available from: https://www.ons.gov.uk/peoplepopulationandcommunity/birthsdea thsandmarriages/families/bulletins/familiesandhouseholds/2020 [Accessed 12 January 2022].

ONS (2020b) 'Domestic abuse during the coronavirus (COVID-19) pandemic, England and Wales: November 2020', available from: https://www.ons.gov.uk/peoplepopulationandcommunity/crimeandjustice/artic les/domesticabuseduringthecoronaviruscovid19pandemicenglandandwa les/november2020 [Accessed 21 February 2021].

O'Hara, M. (2020) *The Shame Game: Overturning the Toxic Poverty Narrative*, Bristol: Policy Press.

Okabe-Miyamoto, K., Folk, D., Lyubominsky, S. and Dunn, E.W. (2021) 'Changes in social connection during COVID-19 social distancing: It's not (household) size that matters, it's who you're with', *PLoS ONE*, 16(1): 1–16.

Okamura, T. (2004) 'Joseph Rowntree's garden village', *Annals for the Society for the History of Economic Thought*, 46(46): 31–51.

O'Neill, A. (2017) 'Hate crime, England and Wales, 2016/17', Statistical Bulletin 17/17, *Home Office*, available from: https://www.gov.uk/governm ent/uploads/system/uploads/attachment_data/file/652136/hate-crime-1617-hosb1717.pdf [Accessed 28 March 2018].

Oppenheim, L. (1912) *International Law: A Treatise. Vol. ii. War and Neutrality* (2nd edn), London, New York, Bombay and Calcutta: Longmans, Green and Co.

Opperman, A.D. (2015) *While It is Yet Day: The Story of Elizabeth Fry*, Hertfordshire: Orphans.

Organisation for Economic Co-operation and Development (OECD) (2019) 'Under pressure: The squeezed middle class', available from: https://www.oecd.org/social/under-pressure-the-squeezed-middle-class-689afed1-en.htm [Accessed 3 January 2022].

OECD (Organisation for Economic Co-operation and Development) (2022) 'Benefits in unemployment, share of previous income (indicator)', available from: https://data.oecd.org/benwage/benefits-in-unemployment-share-of-previous-income.htm [Accessed 21 February 2022].

Orloff, A.S. (1993) 'Gender and the social rights of citizenship: State policies and gender relations in comparative perspective', *American Sociological Review*, 58(3): 303–328.

Orloff, A.S. (2009) 'Tendering the comparative analysis of welfare states: An unfinished agenda', *Sociological Theory*, 27(3): 317–343.

Orme, J. (2001) *Gender and Community Care*, Basingstoke: Palgrave.

Oschmiansky, F., Kull, S. and Schmid, G. (2001) *Faule Arbeitslose? Politische Konjunkturen einer Debatte*, Discussion paper // Wissenschaftszentrum Berlin für Sozialforschung, Forschungsschwerpunkt: Arbeitsmarkt und Beschäftigung, Abteilung:Arbeitsmarktpolitik und Beschäftigung, No. FS I 01-206, available from: http://hdl.handle.net/10419/43929 [Accessed 15 June 2017].

Otu, A., Ahinkarah, B.O., Ameyaw, E.K., Seidu, A.-A. and Yaya, S. (2020) 'One country, two crises: What COVID-19 reveals about health inequalities among BAME communities in the United Kingdom and the sustainability of its health system', *International Journal for Equity in Health*, 19(1): 1–6.

Owen, D. (1964) *English Philanthropy*, Cambridge, MA: Belknap Press.

Page, R.M. (2011) 'The conservative party and the welfare state since 1945', in H. Bochel (ed), *The Conservative Party and Social Policy*, Bristol: Policy Press, pp 23–40.

Page, R.M. (2014) 'Conservative governments and the welfare state since 1945', in H. Bochel and G. Daly (eds), *Social Policy* (3rd edn), London: Routledge, pp 143–169.

Page, R.M. (2018) '"Good solid Conservatism": Theresa May's "doctrine" and her approach to the welfare state', in C. Needham, E. Heins and J. Rees (eds), *Social Policy Review 30: Analysis and Debate in Social Policy, 2018*, Bristol: Policy Press/SPA, pp 111–130.

Palmer, R. (2020) 'Never again – after this crisis fades we need to fix our threadbare safety net', *TaxJustice.UK*, available from: https://www.taxjustice.uk/blog/never-again-after-this-crisis-fades-we-need-to-fix-our-threadbare-social-safety-net [Accessed 1 June 2021].

Pankhurst, E. (1914) *My Own Story*, London: Eveleigh Nash.

Pareto, V. (1909) *Manuel d'Economie Politque*, Paris: Girard.

Parker, J. (2018) 'Social work, precarity and sacrifice as radical action for hope', *International Journal of Social Work and Human Services Practice*, 6(2): 46–55.

Parker, J. (2019) 'Descent or dissent? A future of social work education in the UK post-Brexit', *European Journal of Social Work*, 23(5): 837–848.

Parker, J. (2020) 'The establishment (and disestablishment) of social work in Britain: The ambivalence of public recognition', *Journal of Comparative Social Work*, 15(1): 108–130.

Parker, J. (2021a) 'Structural discrimination and abuse: COVID-19 and people in care homes in England and Wales', *Journal of Adult Protection*, 23(3): 169–180.

Parker, J. (2021b) *Social Work Practice* (6th edn), London: SAGE.

Parker, J. and Doel, M. (2013) 'Professional social work and the professional social work identity?', in J. Parker and M. Doel (eds), *Professional Social Work*, London: Learning Matters/SAGE, pp 1–18.

Parker, J. and Frampton, M. (2020) 'By dint of history: Ways in which social work is (re)defined by historical and social events', *Social Work and Society Online*, 18(3), https://ejournals.bib.uni-wuppertal.de/index.php/sws/article/view/688/1303

Parker, J. and Veasey, K. (2021) 'Universal Credit, gender and structural abuse', *Journal of Adult Protection*, 23(6): 358–369.

Parker, J., Ashencaen Crabtree, S., Crabtree Parker, M. and Crabtree Parker, I. (2019) '"Behaving like a Jakun!": A case study of conflict, "othering" and indigenous knowledge in the Orang Asli of Tasik Chini, Pahang, Malaysia', *Journal of Sociology and Development*, 3(1): 23–45.

Parker, J., Cutler, C. and Heaslip, V. (2020) 'Dementia as *Zeitgeist*: Social problem construction and the role of a contemporary distraction', *Sociological Research Online*, doi: 10.1177/1360780420929033

Partington, R. and Elgot, J. (2022) 'Spring statement 2022: Keypoints at a glance', *The Guardian*, 23 March, available from: https://www.theguardian.com/uk-news/2022/mar/23/spring-statement-2022-key-points-rishi-sunak-budget [Accessed 23 March 2022].

Parton, N. (1991) *Governing the Family: Child Care, Child Protection and the State*, London: Macmillan.

Pascall, G. (2012) *Gender Equality in the Welfare State*, Bristol: Policy Press.

Patrick, R., Garthwaite, K., Power, M., Kaufman, J., Page, G., Pybus, K., Warnock, R., et al (2022a) *Covid Realities: Documenting Life on a Low Income During the Pandemic*, available from: https://cdn.sanity.io/files/brhp578m/production/87675ee74d31a305f15c0d8de203e3dd21c50c38.pdf [Accessed 31 January 2022].

Patrick, R., Power, M., Garthwaite, K., Kaufman, J., Page, G. and Pybus, K. (2022b) *A Year Like No Other: Life on a Low Income During COVID-19*, Bristol: Policy Press.

Paul, G.O. (1784) *Thoughts on the Alarming Progress of Gaol Fever or Typhus*, Gloucester: Gloucester Journal.

Payne, M. (2005) *The Origins of Social Work: Continuity and Change*, Basingstoke: Palgrave Macmillan.

Peacock, A. and Wiseman, J. (1961) *The Growth of Public Expenditure in the United Kingdom*, Princeton: Princeton University Press.

Pearce, D.M. (1978) 'The feminization of poverty: Women, work and welfare', *Urban and Social Change Review*, 11(1): 28–36.

Pemberton, H. (2018) *The Fowler Inquiry into Provision for Retirement and the Pension Reforms of 1986: A Witness Seminar*, Bristol: University of Bristol Department of History.

Pennycock, M. and Whittaker, M. (2012) *Conditions Uncertain: Assessing the Implications of Universal Credit In-work Conditionality*, London: The Resolution Centre.

Persky, J. (1997) 'Classical family values: Ending the Poor Laws as they knew them', *Journal of Economic Perspectives*, 11(1): 179–189.

Peters, B.G. (2017) 'What is so wicked about wicked problems? A conceptual analysis and a research program', *Policy and Society*, 36(3): 385–396.

PHE, HSE and FOM (2020) 'COVID-19 risks and outcomes for ethnic minorities: Mitigation of risks of COVID-19 in occupational settings with a focus on ethnic minority groups – Consensus Statement from PHE, HSE and FOM, a consensus statement from Public Health England with the Health and Safety Executive and the Faculty of Occupational Medicine', *Education Journal*, 433: 38–40.

Phillipson, C. (2013) 'Commentary: The future of work and retirement', *Human Relations*, 66(1): 143–153.

Pierson, C. (2021) *The Next Welfare State? UK Welfare after COVID-19*, Bristol: Policy Press.

Pierson, J. (2011) *Understanding Social Work: History and Context*, London: McGraw-Hill.

Pierson, P. (1994) *Dismantling the Welfare State: Reagan, Thatcher and the Politics of Retrenchment*, Cambridge: Cambridge University Press.

Pietrusiak, J. (2004) 'The local philanthropy of the Reckitt family with particular reference to Hull Garden Village', *Quaker Studies*, 8(2): 141–171.

Pigou, A.C. (1920) *The Economics of Welfare*, London: Macmillan.

Pilgrim Trust (1938/2014) *Men Without Work*, Cambridge: Cambridge University Press.

Pincus, A. and Minahan, A. (1973) *Social Work Practice: Model and Method*, Itasca: Peacock.

Pinker, R. (1979/2021) *The Idea of Welfare*, London: Routledge.

Pinker, R. (1983) 'Social welfare and the education of social workers', in P. Bean and S. Macpherson (eds), *Approaches to Welfare*, London: Routledge, pp 150–166.

Piven, F.F. and Cloward, R.A. (1971) *Regulating the Poor: The Functions of Public Welfare* (1st edn), New York: Vintage Books.

Piven, F.F. and Cloward, R.A. (1993) *Regulating the Poor: The Functions of Public Welfare* (3rd edn), New York: Vintage Books.

Polanyi, K. (1944) *The Great Transformation*, New York: Farrar and Rinehart.

Porter, B.D. (1994) *War and the Rise of the State: The Military Foundations of Modern Politics*, New York: Free Press.

Powell, K. (2017) 'Brexit positions: Neoliberalism, austerity and immigration – the (im)possibilities? of political revolution', *Dialectical Anthropology*, 41(3): 225–240.

Preston, R. and Samuel, M. (2021) 'End "staggering misuse" of children's social workers to allow more direct work, says care review', *Community Care*, 17 June, available from: https://www.communitycare.co.uk/2021/06/17/end-staggering-misuse-childrens-social-workers-allow-direct-work-says-care-review/ [Accessed 3 March 2022].

Price, A. (2016) 'Shout loud, Remainers – democracy means giving the majority a hard time', *The Conversation*, available from: https://theconversation.com/shout-loud-remainers-democracy-means-giving-the-majority-a-hard-time-67020 [Accessed 17 April 2018].

Priestley, J.B. (1934) *English Journey*, London: William Heinemann Ltd. and Victor Gollancz.

Priestley, J.B. (2001) *An Inspector Calls and Other Plays*, London: Penguin.

Prochaska, F. (1980) *Women and Philanthropy in Nineteenth-Century England*, Oxford: Oxford University Press.

Prochaska, F. (2006) *Christianity and Social Service in Modern Britain: The Disinherited Spirit*, Oxford: Oxford University Press.

Proctor R. (2008) 'Agnotology: A missing term to describe the cultural production of ignorance (and its study)', in R. Proctor and L. Schiebinger (eds), *Agnotology: The Making and Unmaking of Ignorance*, Stanford: Stanford University Press, pp 1–33.

Putnam, R.D. (2000) *Bowling Alone: The Collapse and Revival of American Community*, New York: Simon & Schuster.

Puttick, K. (2012) '"21st century welfare" and Universal Credit: Reconstructing the wage-work-welfare bargain', *Industrial Law Journal*, 41(2): 236–249.

Raphael, D., Bryant, T. and Mendly-Zambo, Z. (2018) 'Canada considers a basic income guarantee: Can it achieve health for all?', *Health Promotion International*, 1–7, doi: 10.1093/heapro/day/058

Rathbone, E. (1924) *The Disinherited Family*, London: Edward Arnold & Co.

Rathbone, E. (1940) *The Case for Family Allowances*, London: Penguin.

Ray, L. (2018) *Violence and Society* (2nd edn), London: SAGE.

Read, R. and Fenge, L.-A. (2019) 'What does Brexit mean for the UK social care workforce? Perspectives from the recruitment and retention frontline', *Health and Social Care in the Community*, 27(3): 676–682.

The Reading Mercury (1795) 11 May, p 1, *British Newspaper Archive*, available from: https://www.britishnewspaperarchive.co.uk/viewer/BL/0000367/17950511/001/0001 [Accessed 8 September 2021].

Rediker, M. (2017) 'The cave-dwelling vegan who took on Quaker slavery and women: The nation's first radical abolitionist was one of the most dramatic outspoken figures of the 18th century. Yet few historians have even heard of the amazing Benjamin Lay', *Smithsonian*, 48(5): 34–41.

Rees, A. (2012) 'Nineteenth-century planned industrial communities and the role of aesthetics in spatial practices: The visual ideologies of Pullman and Port Sunlight', *Journal of Cultural Geography*, 29(2): 185–214.

Reeve, K. (2017) 'Welfare conditionality, benefit sanctions and homelessness in the UK: Ending the "something for nothing culture" or punishing the poor?' *Journal of Poverty and Social Justice*, 25(1): 65–78.

Reid, M. (2013) 'Social policy, "deservingness" and sociotemporal marginalization: Katrina survivors and FEMA', *Sociological Forum*, 28(4): 742–763.

Repo, K. (2004) 'Combining work and family in two welfare state contexts: A discourse analytic perspective', *Social Policy and Administration*, 38(6): 622–639.

Rhaphael, D., Bryant, T. and Mendly-Zanbo, Z. (2019) 'Canada considers a basic income guarantee: Can it achieve health for all?', *Health Promotion International*, 34(5): 1025–1031.

Rhys Williams, J. (1943) *Something to Look Forward To*, London: MacDonald and Co.

Ricardo, D. (1817) *On the Principles of Political Economy, and Taxation*, available from: http://www.gutenberg.org/ebooks/33310 [Accessed 20 February 2019].

Richardson, R. (2012) *Dickens and the Workhouse: Oliver Twist and the London Poor*, Oxford: Oxford University Press.

Rittel, H.W.J. and Webber, M.M. (1973) 'Dilemmas in a general theory of planning', *Policy Sciences*, 4(2): 155–169.

Robertson, E. (2009) *Chocolate, Women and Empire: A Social and Cultural History*, Manchester: Manchester University Press.

Robertson, E., Korczynski, M. and Pickering, M. (2007) 'Harmonious relations? Music at work on the Rowntree and Cadbury factories', *Business History*, 49(2): 211–234.

Robson, J.M. (ed) (1965) *The Collected Works of John Stuart Mill, Volume II – The Principles of Political Economy with Some of Their Applications to Social Philosophy (Books I–II)*, London: Routledge and Kegan Paul.

Rodríguez-Fernández, J.R. and Themelis, S. (2021) 'Guaranteed minimum income and universal income programs: Implications for adult education', *Australian Journal of Adult Learning*, 61(1): 63–85.

Rogowski, S. (2010) *Social Work: The Rise and Fall of a Profession*, Bristol: Policy Press.

Romano, S. (2015) 'Idle paupers, scroungers and shirkers: Past and new stereotypes of the undeserving welfare claimant in the UK', in L. Foster, A. Brinton, C. Deeming and T. Haux (eds), *In Defence of Welfare 2*, Bristol: Policy Press, pp 65–67.

Rose, S., Twist, L., Lloyd, P., Rutt, S., Badr, K., Hope, C. and Styles, B. (2021) *Impact of School Closures and Subsequent Support Strategies on Attainment and Socio-Emotional Wellbeing in Key Stage 1*, London: National Foundation for Educational Research.

Rosenzweig, S. (1938) 'The definition of ambivalence', *Psychology and Psychotherapy*, 17(2): 223–226.

Rowntree, B.S. (1901) *Poverty: A Study of Town Life*, London: Macmillan and Co.

Rowntree, B.S. (1941) *Poverty and Progress: A Second Study of York*, London: Longmans, Green.

Rowntree, B.S. and Lavers, G. (1951) *Poverty and the Welfare State: A Third Social Survey of York Dealing only with Economic Questions*, London: Longmans, Green and Co.

Ruckert, A., Huynh, C. and Labanté, R. (2017) 'Reducing health inequalities: Is universal basic income the way forward?', *Journal of Public Health*, 40(1): 3–7.

Ryan, R.M. and Deci, E.L. (2001) 'On happiness and human potentials: A review of research on hedonic and eudaimonic well-being', *Annual Review of Psychology*, 52(1): 141–166.

Sales, R. (2002) 'The deserving and the undeserving? Refugees, asylum seekers and welfare in Britain', *Critical Social Policy*, 22(3): 456–478.

Sameroff, A. (2019) *Universal Basic Income: For and Against*, Australia: Rational Rise Press.

Sanders, A. and Shorrocks, R. (2019) 'All in this together? Austerity and the gender-age gap in the 2015 and 2017 British general elections', *British Journal of Politics and International Relations*, 21(4): 667–688.

Sarangi, S. and Slembrouck, S. (1996) *Language, Bureaucracy and Social Control*, London: Longman.

Satre, L.J. (2005) *Chocolate on Trial: Slavery, Politics and the Ethics of Business*, Athens, OH: Ohio University Press.

Schulz, P. (2017) 'Universal basic income in a feminist perspective and gender analysis', *Global Social Policy*, 17(1): 89–92.

Scullion, L. and Curchin, K. (2022) 'Examining veterans' interactions with the UK social security system through a trauma-informed lens', *Journal of Social Policy*, 51(1): 96–113.

Scullion, L., Jones, K., Dwyer, P., Hynes, C. and Martin, P. (2021) 'Military veterans and welfare reform: Bridging two policy worlds through qualitative longitudinal research', *Social Policy and Society*, 20(4): 670–683.

Seabrook, J. (2013) *Pauperland: A Short History of Poverty in Britain*, London: C. Hurst & Co.

Sealey, C. (2015) *Social Policy Simplified: Connecting Theory with People's Lives*, London: Palgrave.

Secretary of State for the Home Department (1968) *Report of the Committee on Local Authority and Allied Personal Social Services*, London: HMSO.

Seidler, V. (2018) *Making Sense of Brexit: Democracy, Europe and Uncertain Futures*, Bristol: Policy Press.

Sen, A. (1983) 'Poor relatively speaking', *Oxford Economic Papers*, 35(2): 153–169.

Sen, A. (1999) *Development as Freedom*, Oxford: Oxford University Press.

Sewell, T. (2021) *Commission on Race and Ethnic Disparities: The Report*, available from: https://assets.publishing.service.gov.uk/government/uploads/system/uploads/attachment_data/file/974507/20210331_-_CRED_Report_-_FINAL_-_Web_Accessible.pdf [Accessed 9 November 2021].

Shaver, S. (2019) 'Gender issues in welfare states', in B. Greve (ed), *Routledge Handbook of the Welfare State* (2nd edn), London: Routledge, pp 81–91.

Shaw's Manual (1865) *Shaw's Union Officers' and Local Boards of Health Manual for 1865*, London: Shaw and Sons.

Sherwood, M.M. (1917) *Concerning the Relief of the Poor or Concerning Human Need, Studies in Social Work*, New York: New York School of Philanthropy.

Shoesmith, S. (2016) *Learning from Baby P*, London: Jessica Kingsley Publishers.

Sims-Schouten, W., Skinner, A. and Rivett, K. (2019) 'Child safeguarding practices in light of the deserving/undeserving paradigm: A historical and contemporary analysis', *Child Abuse and Neglect*, 94: 104025, doi: 10.1016/j.chiabu.2019.104025

Singer, A. (2005) 'Serving up charity: The Ottoman public kitchen', *Journal of Interdisciplinary History*, 35(3): 481–500.

Sircar, N.R. and Friedman, E.A. (2018) 'Financial security and public health: How basic income and cash transfers can promote health', *Global Public Health*, 13(12): 1878–1888.

Skeggs, B. (1997) *Formations of Class and Gender*, London: SAGE.

Skehill, C. (2007) 'Researching the history of social work: Exposition of a history of the present approach', *European Journal of Social Work*, 10(4): 449–463.

Skidmore, G. (2005) *Elizabeth Fry. A Quaker Life: Selected Letters and Writings*, Oxford: Altamira Press.

Skinner, A. and Thomas, N. (2012) '"A pest to society": The Charity Organisation Society's domiciliary assessments into the circumstances of poor families and children', *Children and Society*, 32(2): 135–140.

Slack, P. (1990) *The English Poor Law, 1531–1782*, Cambridge: Cambridge University Press.

Slater, T. (2012) 'The myth of "broken Britain": Welfare reform and the production of ignorance', *Antipode*, 46(4): 948–969.

Slave Free Chocolate (nd) 'Slave free chocolate', available from: https://www.slavefreechocolate.org/ethical-chocolate-companies [Accessed 6 January 2022].

Sleigh, S. (2020) 'Boris Johnson calls Keir Starmer "Captain Hindsight" during grilling over are comments during PMQs', *Evening Standard*, 8 July, available from: https://www.standard.co.uk/news/politics/boris-johnson-keir-starmer-captain-hindsight-pmqs-a4492341.html [Accessed 3 April 2021].

Slothus, R. (2007) 'Framing deservingness to win support for welfare state retrenchment', *Scandinavian Political Studies*, 30(3): 323–344.

Smith, A. (1776/1982) *The Wealth of Nations: Books I–III*, London: Penguin.

Smith, A. (2010) 'Discourses of morality and truth in social welfare: The surveillance of British widows of the First World War', *Social Semiotics*, 20(5): 519–535.

Smith, C., Child, J. and Rowlinson, M. (1990) *Reshaping Work: The Cadbury Experience*, Cambridge: Cambridge University Press.

Smith, D. (2013) 'Delinquency and welfare in London, 1939–1949', *London Journal*, 38(1): 67–87.

Smith, D.E. (1987) *The Everyday World as Problematic: A Feminist Sociology*, Boston: Northeastern University Press.

Smith, E.T. (2012) 'Elizabeth Taylor Cadbury (1858–1951): Religion, materialism and social reform in Birmingham, 1888–1914', PhD thesis, University of Birmingham, available from: https://ethos.bl.uk/OrderDetails.do?uin==uk.bl.ethos.549903 [Accessed 3 June 2021].

Smith, J. (2018) 'Gambling on Europe: David Cameron and the 2016 referendum', *British Politics*, 13(1): 1–16.

Social Work Reform Board (2010) *Building a Safe and Confident Future: One Year On*, London: Social Work Reform Board.

Social Work Reform Board (2012) *Building a Safe and Confident Future: Maintaining Momentum*, available from: https://assets.publishing.service.gov.uk/government/uploads/system/uploads/attachment_data/file/175947/SWRB_progress_report_-_June_2012.pdf [Accessed 15 June 2018].

Sparke, M. (2018) 'Welcome, its suppression, and the in-between spaces of refugee sub-citizenship: Commentary to Gill', *Fennia*, 196(2): 215–219.

Specht, H. and Vickery, A. (eds) (1977) *Integrating Social Work Methods*, Reading, MA: Allen and Unwin.

Spicker, P. (2022) *How to Fix the Welfare State: Some Ideas for Better Social Services*, Bristol: Policy Press

Spicker, P., Leguizamon, S.A. and Gordon, D. (eds) (2007) *Poverty: An International Glossary* (2nd edn), London: Zed Books.

Stalford, H. (2016) 'The UK referendum on membership of the EU: Whither social welfare and family law', *Journal of Social Welfare and Family Law*, 38(2): 115–117.

Standing, G. (2016) *The Precariat: The New Dangerous Class*, London: Bloomsbury.

Standing, G. (2017) *Basic Income and How We Can Make It Happen*, London: Penguin.

Steinmetz, G. (2006) 'Bourdieu's disavowal of Lacan: Psychoanalytic theory and the concepts of "habitus" and "symbolic capital"', *Constellations*, 13(4): 445–460.

Stephens, R. (2019) 'The Universal Basic Income: Should it replace the existing social security system?', *Policy Quarterly*, 15(1): 30–37.

Stewart, J. (2013) *Child Guidance in Britain 1918–55: The Dangerous Age of Childhood*, London: Pickering and Chatto.

Stillion Southard, B.F. (2016) 'The plain style in early anti-slavery discourse: Reassessing the rhetorical beginnings of Quaker and Puritan advocacy', *Quarterly Journal of Speech*, 102(3): 286–306.

Stirling, A. and Arnold, S. (2020) 'Building a minimum income guarantee for the UK: The UK economy needs a new safety net to survive recession', *The New Economics Foundation*, available from: https://neweconomics.org/2020/03/building-a-minimum-income-protection [Accessed 20 July 2022].

Stott, M. (ed) (2011) *The Big Society Challenge*, Cardiff: Keystone Development Trust Publications.

Stubbs, P. (2020) 'Time for a universal basic income?', *LeftEast*, available from: http://www.criticatac.ro/lefteast/time-for-a-universal-basic-income/ [Accessed 12 September 2021].

Sturdy, S. (2002) 'Alternative publics: The development of government policy on personal health care, 1905–2011', in S. Sturdy (ed), *Medicine, Health and the Public Sphere in Britain, 1600–2000*, London: Routledge, pp 241–259.

Sullivan, M. (1996) *The Development of the British Welfare State*, London: Prentice-Hall.

The Sun (2008) 'Baby P petition', *The Sun*, 13 November, p 9.

Sutcliffe, A. (1981) *British Town Planning: The Formative Years*, Leicester: Leicester University Press.

Swales, K. (2016) *Understanding the Leave Vote: UK in a Changing Europe*, London: NatCen, available from: http://natcen.ac.uk/media/1319222/natcen_brexplanationsreport-final-web2.pdf [Accessed 20 September 2017].

Tait, I.W. (1995) 'Voluntarism and the state in British social welfare 1914–1939', PhD thesis, University of Glasgow, available from: https://ethos.bl.uk/OrderDetails.do?uin==uk.bl.ethos.297456 [Accessed 3 June 2021].

Tarrant, A. (2021) *Fathering and Poverty: Uncovering Men's Participation in Low-income Family Life*, Bristol: Policy Press.

Taylor-Gooby, P. (2016) 'The divisive welfare state', *Social Policy and Administration*, 50(6): 712–733.

Taylor-Gooby, P. (2017) 'Re-doubling the crises of the welfare state: The impact of Brexit on UK welfare politics', *Journal of Social Policy*, 46(4): 815–835.

Taylor-Gooby, P. (2018) 'Participation and solidarity in a changing welfare state', in P. Beresford and S. Carr (eds), *Social Policy First Hand: An International Introduction to Participatory Social Welfare*, Bristol: Policy Press, pp 22–31.

Terpstra, N. (2004) 'Showing the poor a good time: Caring for body and spirit in Bologna's civic charities', *Journal of Religious History*, 28(1): 19–34.

Thane, P. (1978) 'Women and the Poor Law in Victorian and Edwardian England', *History Workshop Journal*, 6: 29–51.

Thane, P. (2000) *Old Age in English History: Past Experiences, Present Issues*, Oxford: Oxford University Press.

Thatcher, M. (1993) *The Downing Street Years*, London: HarperCollins.

Thompson, E.P. (1963) *The Making of the English Working Class*, London: Victor Gollancz Ltd.

Thompson, E.P. (1991) *Customs in Common*, London: Merlin Press.

Tihelková, A. (2015) 'Framing the "scroungers": The re-emergence of the stereotype of the undeserving poor and its reflection in the British press', *Brno Studies in English*, 41(2): 121–139.

Tilley, L. (2012) 'The bioarchaeology of care', *The Archaeological Record*, 12(3): 41–46.

Tilley, L. (2015) *Theory and Practice in the Bioarchaeology of Care*, New York: Springer International.

Tilley, L. and Oxenham, M.F. (2011) 'Survival against the odds: Modeling the social implications of care provision to seriously disabled individuals', *International Journal of Paleopathology*, 1(1): 35–42.

Tilley, L. and Nystrom, K. (2018) 'A "cold case" of care: Looking at old data from a new perspective in mummy research', *International Journal of Paleopathology*, 25(1): 72–81.

Timmins, N. (2017) *The Five Giants: A Biography of the Welfare State* (3rd edn), London: HarperCollins.

Timms, N. (1964) *Psychiatric Social Work in Great Britain 1939–1962*, London: Routledge and Kegan Paul.

Titley, C. (2013) *Joseph Rowntree*, Oxford: Shire Books.

Titmuss, R. (1950) *Problems of Social Policy*, London: HMSO.

Titmuss, R. (1974) *Social Policy*, London: Allen and Unwin.

Titmuss, R. (2001a) 'War and social policy', in P. Alcock, H. Glennerster, A. Oakley, and A. Sinfield (eds) *Welfare and Wellbeing: Richard Titmuss's Contribution to Social Policy*, Bristol: Policy Press, pp 71–80.

Titmuss, R. (2001b) 'The position of women', in P. Alcock, H. Glennerster, A. Oakley and A. Sinfield (eds), *Welfare and Wellbeing: Richard Titmuss's Contribution to Social Policy*, Bristol: Policy Press, pp 31–40.

Topple, S. (2020) 'DWP havoc as a Universal Credit deaths scandal emerges', *The Canary*, available from: https://www.thecanary.co/uk/analysis/2020/02/12/dwp-havoc-as-a-universal-credit-deaths-scandal-emerges/ [Accessed 3 March 2021].

TOPSS (2002) *National Occupational Standards for Social Workers in England*, London: TOPSS.

Topss England/Taskforce (2004) *The Future of the Practice Learning Taskforce, Consultation Paper*, Leeds: Topss England.

Torfs, L., Adrianssens, S., Lagaert, S. and Willens, S. (2021) 'The unequal effects of austerity measures between income-groups on the access to healthcare: A quasi-experimental approach', *International Journal for Equity on Health*, 20(79): 1–10.

Torry, M. (2016) *The Feasibility of Citizen's Income*, New York: Palgrave Macmillan.

Torry, M. (2018) 'History and the contemporary debate in the UK', in A. Downes and S. Lansley (eds), *It's Basic Income: The Global Debate*, Bristol: Policy Press, pp 123–127.

Tout, H. (1938) *The Standard of Living in Bristol: A Preliminary Report on the Work of the University of Bristol Social Survey*, Bristol: Bristol University Press.

Townsend, J. (1786/1817) *A Dissertation on the Poor Laws*, London: Ridgways.

Townsend, M. (2021) 'Don't be fooled by deceitful parents top child expert warns social workers', *The Observer*, 5 December, available from: https://www.theguardian.com/society/2021/dec/05/dont-be-foo led-by-deceitful-parents-top-child-expert-warns-social-workers [Accessed 5 December 2021].

Trinkaus, E. and Zimmerman, M.R. (1982) 'Trauma among the Shanidar Neandertals', *American Journal of Physical Anthropology*, 57(1): 61–76.

Turner, A. (2018) ' "Over-optimistic" social workers did too little to challenge neglect within family whose baby died, review finds', *Community Care*, available from: https://www.communitycare.co.uk/2018/06/11/ over-optimistic-social-workers-did-too-little-to-challenge-neglect-wit hin-family-whose-baby-died-review-finds/ [Accessed 14 June 2018].

Twining, L. (1898) *Workhouses and Pauperism and Women's Work in the Administration of the Poor Laws*, London: Methuen.

UK Government (2016) 'The United Kingdom government response to the report by the United Nations committee on the rights of persons with disabilities under article 6 of the optional protocol to the convention', available from: http://www.ohchr.org/Documents/HRBodies/CRPD/ CRPD.C.17.R.3-ENG.doc [Accessed 12 March 2018].

UK Parliament (2018) 'Personal Independence Payment, question for Department for Work and Pensions', available from: https://questions-sta tements.parliament.uk/written-questions/detail/2018-12-19/203812#, [Accessed 12 February 2019].

United Nations (2016) 'Committee on the Rights of Persons with Disabilities: Inquiry concerning the United Kingdom of Great Britain and Northern Ireland carried out by the Committee under article 6 of the Optional Protocol to the Convention', available from: http://www. ohchr.org/Documents/HRBodies/CRPD/CRPD.C.15.R.2.Rev.1-ENG. doc [Accessed 12 February 2019].

Urry, J. (2016) *What is the Future?* Cambridge: Polity.

Vallely, P. (2020) *Philanthropy: From Aristotle to Zuckerberg*, London: Bloomsbury.

Van der Waal, J., Achterberg, P., Houtman, D., de Koster, W. and Marevska, K. (2010) '"Some are more equal than others": Economic egalitarianism and welfare chauvinism in the Netherlands', *Journal of European Social Policy*, 20(4): 350–363.

Van de Velde, S., Boyd, A., Villagut, G., Alonso, J., Briffaerts R., de Graaf, R., Florescu, et al (2019) 'Gender differences in common mental disorders: A comparison of social risk factors across four European welfare regimes', *European Journal of Public Health*, 29(3): 481–487.

Van Parijs, P. and Vanderborght, Y. (2017) *Basic Income: A Radical Proposal for a Free Society and a Sane Economy*, Cambridge, MA: Harvard University Press.

Vantsos, M. and Kiroudi, M. (2007) 'An Orthodox view of philanthropy and Church diaconia', *Christian Bioethics*, 13(2): 251–268.

Varoufakis, Y. (2017) *And the Weak Suffer What They Must: Europe, Austerity and the Threat to Global Security*, London: Penguin.

Veasey, K. and Parker, J. (2021) 'Welfare conditionality, sanctions and homelessness: Meanings made by homeless support workers', *Journal of Humanities and Applied Social Science*, Early Cite, https://www.emerald.com/insight/2632-279X.htm

Verden, N. (2002) 'The rural labour market in the early nineteenth century: Women's and children's employment, family income, and the 1834 Poor Law Report', *Economic History Review*, 55(2): 299–323.

Vis, B., van Kersbergen, K. and Hylands, T. (2011) 'To what extent did the financial crisis intensify the pressure to reform the welfare state?' *Social Policy and Administration*, 45(4): 338–353.

Wacquant, L. (2009) *Punishing the Poor: The Neoliberal Government of Social Insecurity*, Durham, NC: Duke University Press.

Waldfogel, J. (2010) *Britain's War on Poverty*, New York: Russell Sage Foundation.

Walsh, D., Dundas, R., McCartney, G., Gibson M. and Seaman, R. (2022) 'Bearing the burden of austerity: how do changing mortality rates in the UK compare between men and women?', *Journal of Epidemiology and Community Health*, 76(12), doi: 10.1136/jech-2022-219645

Walton, E. (2018) 'A truth universally acknowledged: Moving to Universal Credit leads to large debt and poor mental health', *British Journal of General Practice*, 68(677): 577.

Walvin, J. (1997) *Fruits of Empire: Exotic Produce and British Taste, 1600–1800*, New York: New York University Press.

Warden, J. (2021) 'Regenerative futures: From sustaining to thriving together', *The RSA*, available from: https://www.thersa.org/globalassets/pdfs/reports/from-sustaining-to-thriving-together-final.pdf [Accessed 22 February 2022].

Warner, J. (2015) *The Emotional Politics of Social Work and Child Protection*, Bristol: Policy Press.

Warwick-Booth, L. (2019) *Social Inequality* (2nd edn), London: SAGE.

WBI (World Basic Income) (nd) 'How a world basic income could work', available from: https://www.worldbasicincome.org.uk/how-wbi-could-work.html, [Accessed 29 September 2021].

Weaver, J.D. (2001) *The Non-Violent Atonement*, Grand Rapids: Eerdmans.

Webb, S. (2006) *Social Work in a Risk Society: Social and Political Perspectives*, Basingstoke: Palgrave Macmillan.

Webb, S. and Webb, B. (1927–1929) *English Poor Law History Vols. I-III*, London: Longmans, Green and Co.

Webster, F. and Robins, K. (1993) '"I'll be watching you": Comment on Sewell and Wilkinson', *Sociology*, 27(2): 243–252.

Webster, I. (2015) 'The Public Works Loan Board 1817–76 and the financing of public infrastructure', unpublished PhD thesis, Sheffield Hallam University, available from: https://shura.shu.ac.uk/9939/1/Public_works_loan_board_1817-76.pdf, [Accessed 14 December 2021].

Wellings, D., Jefferies, D., Macguire, D., Appleby, J., Hemmings, N., Morris, J. and Schlepper, L. (2022) 'Public satisfaction with the NHS and social care in 2021: Results from the British Social Attitudes Survey', *King's Fund*, available from: https://www.kingsfund.org.uk/sites/default/files/2022–03/BSA%20Survey%20Report%202nd%20pp_0.pdf [Accessed 30 March 2022].

Welsh Government (2022) 'Basic income for care leavers in Wales, pilot announced', available from: https://gov.wales/basic-income-care-leavers-wales-pilot-announced [Accessed 15 February 2022].

Wernesjö, U. (2020) 'Across the threshold: Negotiations of deservingness among unaccompanied young refugees in Sweden', *Journal of Ethnic and Migration Studies*, 46(2): 389–404.

Westall, A. (ed) (2010) *Revisiting Associative Democracy: How to Get More Co-operation, Co-ordination and Collaboration into Our Economy, Our Democracy, Our Public Services, and Our Lives*, London: Lawrence & Wishart.

Wharton, A.S. (2012) *The Sociology of Gender: An Introduction to Theory and Research*, Chichester: John Wiley and Sons.

Wheater, K. (2017) *An Analysis of Claude Lévi-Strauss's Structural Anthropology*, London: Macat.

Whitehead, M., Barr, B. and Taylor-Robonson, D. (2020) 'Covid-19: We are not "all in it together"—less privileged in society are suffering the brunt of the damage', *BMJ Opinion*, available from: https://blogs.bmj.com/bmj/2020/05/22/covid-19-we-are-not-all-in-it-together-less-privileged-in-society-are-suffering-the-brunt-of-the-damage/ [Accessed 3 January 2022].

Whittington, C. (2003) *Collaboration in Social Work Practice*, London: Jessica Kingsley.

Wilkinson, R. and Pickett, K. (2011) *The Spirit Level: Why Equality is Better for Everyone*, London: Bloomsbury.

Wilkinson, R. and Pickett, K. (2019) *The Inner Level: How More Equal Societies Reduce Stress, Restore Sanity and Improve Everyone's Well-being*, London: Penguin.

Williams, S. (2013) 'Unmarried mothers and the new poor law in Hertfordshire', *Local Population Studies*, 91(1): 27–43.

Wilson, E. (1977) *Women and the Welfare State*, London: Routledge.

Wilson, I. (2019) 'Direct payment of Housing Benefit: Responsibilisation at what cost to landlords?', *International Journal of Housing Policy*, 19(4): 566–587.

Wistow, J. (2020) 'Coronavirus: An opportunity to reassess the social contract', *Transforming Society*, 30 March, available from: http://www.transformingsociety.co.uk/2020/03/30/coronavirus-an-opportunity-to-reassess-the-social-contract/ [Accessed 21 November 2020].

Winchester, N. (2021) 'Universal Credit: An end to the uplift', *House of Lords Library*, available from: https://lordslibrary.parliament.uk/universal-credit-an-end-to-the-uplift/ [Accessed 4 February 2022].

Wollstonecraft, M. (1796) *Vindication of the Rights of Woman with Strictures on Political and Moral Subjects* (3rd edn), London: J. Johnson, available from: https://www.google.co.uk/books/edition/A_Vindication_of_the_Rights_of_Woman/qhcFAAAAQAAJ?hl=en&gbpv=1&printsec=frontcover [Accessed 13 March 2016].

Women's Aid (2020) *A Perfect Storm: The Impact of the Covid-19 Pandemic on Domestic Abuse Survivors and the Services Supporting Them*, Bristol: Women's Aid.

Women's Budget Group (2020) 'Crises collide: Women and Covid-19. Examining gender and other equality issues during the Coronavirus outbreak', available from: https://wbg.org.uk/analysis/uk-policy-briefings/crises-collide-women-and-covid-19/ [Accessed 9 April 2020].

Women's Budget Group (2021) 'Autumn Budget 2021: Women and employment in the recovery from Covid-19', available from: https://wbg.org.uk/analysis/autumn-budget-2021-women-and-employment-in-the-recovery-from-covid-19/ [Accessed 28 July 2022].

Wood, A.W. (ed) (1991) *Hegel: Elements of the Philosophy of Right*, Cambridge: Cambridge University Press.

Woodroofe, K. (1962) *From Charity to Social Work*, London: Routledge and Kegan Paul.

Wordsworth, D. (2020) *The Life of Richard Cadbury: Socialist, Philanthropist and Chocolatier*, Barnsley: Pen and Sword.

World Health Organization (WHO) (2022) 'Gender: Definitions', available from: https://www.euro.who.int/en/health-topics/health-determinants/gender/gender-defintions [Accessed 2 February 2022].

Worrell, M. (2013) *Terror: Social, Political and Economic Perspectives*, New York: Routledge.

Wright, S., Dwyer, P., McNeill, J. and Stewart, A. (2016) *First Wave Universal Credit Findings*, Swindon: The Economic and Research Council, available from: http://www.welfareconditionality.ac.uk/publications/first-wave-research-findings [Accessed 15 September 2019].

Wright, S., Fletcher, D.R. and Stewart, A.B.R. (2020) 'Punitive benefit sanctions, welfare conditionality, and the abuse of unemployed people in Britain: Transforming claimants into offenders?', *Social Policy and Administration*, 54(2): 278–294.

Younghusband, E.L. (1947) *Social Work in Britain: A Supplementary Report of the Employment and Training of Social Workers*, Dunfermline: Carnegie United Kingdom Trust.

Zedner, L. (1995) 'Wayward sisters: The prison for women', in N. Morris and D.J. Rothman (eds), *The Oxford History of the Prison: The Practice of Punishment in Western Society*, Oxford: Oxford University Press, pp 329–363.

Zwart, F. de (2015) 'Unintended but not unanticipated consequences', *Theory and Society*, 44(2): 283–297.

Index